T0320111

The EU and the Global Financial Crisis

NEW HORIZONS IN EUROPEAN POLITICS

Series Editor: Julie Smith, *Robinson College, Cambridge, UK*

The New Horizons in European Politics series is an invaluable forum for original research across the spectrum of European politics, promoting innovative cross-disciplinary analysis of contemporary issues and debates. Covering a diverse range of topics, the series examines issues such as: the impacts of the severe challenges brought about by the financial crisis; economic issues, including integration and monetary union; the politics of the EU and other governmental and nongovernmental institutions; environmental politics and the ongoing struggle to mitigate climate change; and the politics of trade, energy and security in Europe. Both international and comparative in its approach, this exciting series encompasses theoretical and empirical work from both well-established researchers and the next generation of scholars.

Titles in the series include:

Building the Knowledge Economy in Europe
New Constellations in European Research and Higher Education Governance
Edited by Meng-Hsuan Chou and Åse Gornitzka

The EU and the Global Financial Crisis
New Varieties of Capitalism
Christian Schweiger

The EU and the Global Financial Crisis

New Varieties of Capitalism

Christian Schweiger

School of Government and International Affairs, Durham University, UK

NEW HORIZONS IN EUROPEAN POLITICS

Edward Elgar

Cheltenham, UK • Northampton, MA, USA

Published by
Edward Elgar Publishing Limited
The Lypiatts
15 Lansdown Road
Cheltenham
Glos GL50 2JA
UK

Edward Elgar Publishing, Inc.
William Pratt House
9 Dewey Court
Northampton
Massachusetts 01060
USA

A catalogue record for this book
is available from the British Library

Library of Congress Control Number: 2013957771

This book is available electronically in the ElgarOnline.com
Social and Political Science Subject Collection, E-ISBN 978 1 78100 389 3

ISBN 978 1 78100 388 6

Typeset by Servis Filmsetting Ltd, Stockport, Cheshire
Printed and bound in Great Britain by T.J. International Ltd, Padstow

To Csilla

Contents

Preface

This book is the result of my long-standing interest in the political economy of Europe which has gradually evolved over the past decade. The publication of this book comes at a critical juncture for the European Union (EU). In the wake of the events of the global financial crisis, which started to emerge in 2007 and peaked in 2008–2009, the EU found itself embroiled in a sovereign debt crisis of previously unseen proportions. Since then the EU has been in crisis mode and looked predominantly inwards with the aim of extinguishing the wildfire of recession, budgetary crises and spiralling unemployment that has taken hold in many countries across the continent. Meanwhile questions about the future direction of the EU and the possibility of the breakup of the eurozone are being raised. The citizens of the EU are puzzled by events and urgently demand answers from political elites on where the journey of the European train will lead them. The rest of the world watches the EU with an equal degree of amazement and concern. The crucial question will be if Europeans have the strength and vision to pull the project of European integration back from the brink.

The purpose of the book is to make some sense of the changes that national Varieties of Capitalism (VoC) have experienced in recent years and to provide a glimpse of the emerging post-crisis set-up of the EU with all its risks and insecurities. I sincerely hope that political leaders in Europe will have the wisdom to lead the EU out of the crisis and towards a new period of stability, unity and prosperity for all its citizens.

My research has taken me to many countries across the continent in recent years and I never cease to be amazed by the rich diversity of our cultures in Europe.

I would like to thank my colleagues in the UACES Collaborative Research Network *The Single Market in the Global Economy*, for their inspiration and support with my research. I would like to thank Lothar Funk in the Department of Business Studies at the University of Applied Sciences in Düsseldorf, Maciej Duszczyk at the Institute of Social Policy at the University of Warsaw, Bela Galgoczi at the European Trade Union Institute in Brussels and Anna Visvizi at the Warsaw School of Economics for the fruitful collaboration over the years. I am also particularly grateful to my friends and colleagues in the Slovak Republic for having given me valuable insights into the perception of the crisis in the Central and Eastern European region. My special thanks goes to Andrej Matisak at *Pravda* daily newspaper, Luboš Blaha who represents SMER in the Slovak national parliament and the colleagues in the *Central European Policy Institute* at the Slovak Atlantic Commission in Bratislava for hosting me as a Visiting Fellow and for offering me important insights into the current debates in the region.

Christian Schweiger
Durham University
September 2013

PART I

The EU policy framework under stress

1. Varieties of Capitalism and the crisis

In spite of having originated more than a decade ago, the Varieties of Capitalism (VoC) paradigm, which Hall and Soskice had introduced in their seminal work published in 2001, remains influential in the analysis of the global political economy. Since its original publication the VoC approach has been referred to by many scholars as a useful framework to categorise economic divergences. The VoC approach nevertheless also received much critical attention. The more critical accounts concentrated on the fact that the VoC approach essentially differentiates between *liberal* and *coordinated* economies on the basis of the variations in the corporate governance and the production model of firms in these economies. The critics have rightly pointed their finger at the weaknesses of Hall and Soskice's core argument, which is their relatively narrow emphasis on a corporate-based analysis. It considers companies as central actors in contemporary economies because of their role as 'key agents of adjustment in the face of technological change or international competition' (Hall and Soskice 2001: 6). Although the approach strongly emphasises the importance of the institutional background on which firms operate, it essentially neglects cultural aspects which are outside the 'competitive advantage' framework. The viability of companies is considered to be the main focus of economic policy-making. Policy-makers are hence reduced to the role of catalysts who have to find effective solutions on how to channel the pressures of globalisation in the right direction. Economic policy-making becomes a means to improve the economic performance of firms by ensuring that domestic institutions support the smooth interaction between economic actors. This follows a logic which assumes that facilitating business transactions and creating a peaceful industrial relations environment should be the principal aim of successful economic policy (Ibid.: 45).

The main contribution of the VoC approach to the globalisation debate at the beginning of the twenty-first century was to offer a new and broader perspective than the one that neoclassical economists put forward. The latter essentially considered it to be a force which inevitably leads to the radical liberalisation of national economies in response to pressure from market forces, such as capital flows. The neoliberal political paradigm of the 1980s and 1990s hence considered globalisation as a process in which economies are orientated towards lowering transaction costs (Keohane 1984). From this perspective a best practice economic convergence model would emerge, whose competitive advantage lies in liberalisation and the openness towards foreign direct investment (FDI), labour market deregulation and the privatisation of public assets (Lane 2005; Sinn 2004a). Hans-Werner Sinn, the prominent German economist and President of the Munich based Institute for Economic Research (*Institut für Wirtschaftsforschung, IFO*) prominently introduced this notion into the public debate in Germany when he warned German policy-makers in 2004 that it was inevitable for the German economy to move towards the model of liberal market economies like the UK and Ireland. In this respect Sinn argued for a fully liberalised economic model with complete flexibility on prices, wages and ultimately also labour markets. From his perspective this would be 'the condition for a successful reaction to globalisation' (Sinn 2004b: 89)

Gill (1995) and others called this a process of 'market civilisation' where market forces manage to impose their priorities on global institutions and consequently increasingly also on national politics (Amin and Luckin 1996). The contribution of the VoC approach to the debate lies mainly in the rejection of the notion of a globalised convergence model and its emphasis on the importance of the differences in the institutional environment in which firms operate (Hall and Soskice 2001: 58). Hence the differentiation between a liberal and a coordinated institutional set-up.

The VoC approach nevertheless is a relatively cautious attempt to give the debate a new direction. It has not managed to offer a fundamental critique of the post-Cold War neoliberal status quo in the global economy. Neither has it identified the core weaknesses in economic policy-making which have led the global economy into its current crisis. On the contrary, VoC has supported that notion that politics would have to be subordinate to economic interests, albeit to different degrees, depending on the individual institutional framework. Hall and Soskice are quite thorough in outlining the differences in political organisation in liberal and coordinated models, which they mainly see in the different levels of centralisation. While the former tend to centralise power on the executive level, the latter show different levels of decentralisation amongst a variety of actors, such as business groups and trade unions, which are often independent from the state. This explains why policy-makers in these coordinated economies tend to avoid the implementation of policies which would threaten to undermine coordinative arrangements amongst economic actors, whilst liberal market economies tend to favour 'market-incentive' policies (Hall and Soskice 2001: 49). Overall the VoC approach clearly considers policy-makers in different institutional contexts to be adamant to avoid any policy changes which would 'threaten the institutions most crucial to the competitive advantage their firms enjoy' (Ibid.: 52). This strong emphasis on the preservation of the competitive advantage of firms may not reflect the full complexity of the real motives behind economic policy-making. Yet it correctly identifies a predominant feature in setting economic policy priorities under the conditions of the post-war system of the Washington consensus. Political considerations such as working conditions, social equality and environmental sustainability were hence largely subordinate to the priority of reducing the regulatory burden for businesses. The European Union (EU) as an organisation has not been immune towards this trend. Instead of following its official rhetoric and adopting the role of a guardian of national welfare state cultures, it has predominantly taken on the role of an economic liberaliser (Hancké et al. 2007). From the national perspective the EU is hence perceived as a force which encourages institutional change towards market liberalisation and the relaxation of regulatory standards for businesses and financial services. At least up until the global financial crisis of 2008–2009, Brussels also principally opposed Keynesian policies like national subsidies and economic stimulus programmes. In the face of a deepening crisis in the eurozone this has changed to a certain degree. Ironically the EU Commission and the European Central Bank (ECB) are now advocating more interventionist policies than some of the leading member states, predominantly Germany and the UK, would like to see.

The original VoC approach of Hall and Soskice has undergone fundamental scrutiny from academic scholars across different disciplines. Its weaknesses but also its strengths in offering a framework of analysis for the changes in contemporary capitalist economies have been outlined in a number of critical publications (most prominently in Allen 2004; Hancké 2009; Hancké et al. 2007; Morgan et al. 2005; Streeck and Thelen 2005) but also by Hall and Soskice themselves in response to their critics (Hall and Soskice 2003).

Whilst taking into account the discussions which have taken place previously, in this book I want to apply the VoC approach in the light of unprecedented circumstances. In the past five years the foundations of the global economy were shaken to the core by the most fundamental crisis since the Great Depression of the 1930s. The crisis emerged primarily as a result of the instability in global financial markets, first in the US and subsequently as a ripple effect on the European continent. It has uncovered fundamental flaws in the regulatory practices of the banking industries and deepened the structural budgetary problems which had previously existed in many countries. The result is a vicious circle of low growth and rising unemployment in a number of eurozone countries. It is made worse by the need to impose noticeable cuts to public spending in the crisis economies, in particular in Southern Europe.

This unprecedented situation confronts scholars across disciplines with a profound challenge to adapt existing frameworks for the analysis of differences in national political economies. Modern capitalist economies have been in a process of constant development and are becoming ever more complex. This is the result of the increasing transparency of national borders in the era of globalisation and the advance of global communication technology which is especially important for business and financial transactions. Analysts of national political economies have therefore in recent years concentrated on examining if and under which conditions institutional change takes place. From the very influential historical institutionalist perspective, which advocates path-dependency, national elites tend to be socialised by their domestic institutional setting and are therefore reluctant to pursue a radical departure from its rules and procedures. The expectation that the continuation along the established national institutional path will lead to secure permanent successful outcomes ('increasing returns') is at the heart of this concept. If changes occur, they tend to be the result of substantial external pressures or 'exogenous shocks'. These are based on the rational consideration of domestic elites that a continuation along the established path is no longer the best option to pursue (Pierson 2000: 266). This perspective is shared by the VoC approach, which has a strong institutionalist bias. VoC also shares the view of historical institutionalists that, in response to fundamental shocks, domestic actors will try to increase the efficiency of institutions and processes. The purpose of this is to enable them to deal with the challenge rather than to fundamentally alter the existing institutional framework. Radical policy adjustment is therefore more likely than fundamental institutional overhaul (Pierson 2000: 259). Key domestic actors, such as companies, stakeholders and policy-makers are likely to look towards finding new ways of efficient interaction within the existing institutional structures of their domestic economy (Hall and Soskice 2001: 63). This perspective has indeed turned out to be far more accurate than the notion of global economic convergence which many economists considered to be an inevitable result of the increasing interdependence of national economies. Before the recent global financial crisis the discussion on convergence vs continuing variety concentrated predominantly on the German model which VoC classified as the classic example of a coordinated economy (Morgan 2005: 6). The question for many scholars in this respect was if the institutional culture of the German economy with its emphasis on widespread consultation amongst a multiplicity of actors across different levels would be unable to withstand competition with liberal models without abandoning core elements of its established industrial relations system (collective bargaining, industry-wide general wage agreements and the principle of co-decision and solidarity between employers and workers) (Streeck and Yamamura 2003). The substantial reforms of the German employment system introduced in 2003 in response to spiralling levels of unemployment, which are discussed in Chapter 5 in this book, led many to believe that they would be the first phase in an inevitable move towards the further liberalisation of the German economy. The impact of the reforms on the institutional core of Germany's market economy continues to be subject of the German domestic political debate. After the introduction of the reforms public opinion in Germany started to become increasingly uneasy with the notion of imposing further institutional changes and prominently rejected the radical liberalisation programme the Christian Democrats (CDU) had proposed during the 2005 general election campaign. The majority of the mainstream political elite in Germany, with the exception of the neoliberal Free Democratic Party (FDP), has refrained from advocating further institutional change. The fact that the global financial crisis has unveiled the strong dependence of liberal models on financial markets as a substantial weakness and the surprisingly strong German economic performance during the crisis has furthered dampened calls for further institutional reforms in Germany. The core of the German employment model has certainly been liberalised as a result of the Hartz labour market reforms. They instilled the Anglo-Saxon principle of welfare-to-work into the German economy and therefore essentially abandoned the traditional post-war principle of life standard guarantee for the unemployed through high wage replacement rates (Kemmerling and Bruttel 2006). Equally the German economy has witnessed substantial changes in two other areas: first, the traditional link between companies and individual commercial 'house' banks has been weakened in favour of the greater reliance on stock market capitalisation and the introduction of the principle of 'shareholder value'. Most analysts agree however that this change has taken place within the existing coordinative setting and consequently enhanced worker participation by enabling them to buy shares while also not having undermined the general consensual approach of German corporations (Deeg 2005; Hancké and Goyer 2005; Vitols 2003). Second, the increasing flexibilisation and decentralisation of wage-setting in Germany, mainly as a result of the creation of many jobs in the low-wage sector, has altered Germany's formerly rigid system of collective bargaining (Bosch 2008). The cooperative climate in which employers and trade unions have negotiated consensual solutions on wage levels and shorter working hours during times of crisis nevertheless shows that the traditional industrial patterns in Germany continue to prevail (Funk 2007). The particularities of the German economy, which neoliberal sceptics had branded as hurdles towards global competitiveness, have turned out to be Germany's competitive advantage. Its consensus-orientated industrial relations system, the strong focus on high quality manufacturing export goods and a much lesser dependence on the financial markets than its liberal counterparts, have allowed Germany to evolve from the crisis relatively unscathed and ultimately once again as the leading economic force in Europe.

In this book I will concentrate on two aspects which I consider to be the main weaknesses in the traditional VoC approach that were revealed by the recent global financial crisis. First, as was outlined in a number of critical accounts, Hall and Soskice underestimated the role the state plays in sustaining economies during fundamental crisis periods. Second, the VoC approach is too focused on companies and therefore ignores the increasingly crucial and frequently destabilising role of financial markets.

I will now address each of these points individually. The financial crisis has substantially shifted the debate on economic policy-making. In recent years it was both intellectually and practically focused on minimising state intervention and advocating shareholder value as a principle which would eventually lead towards the increasing liberalisation of coordinated economies. Here critical accounts of the VoC approach have rightly emphasised its relatively narrow categorisation and its neglect of the variety of different state traditions. Amable (2003) made an attempt to fine-tune the dual typology of VoC by dividing the coordinated model into further groups. Her approach builds on a more fine-tuned categorisation of capitalist typologies like Esping-Andersen's classic welfare state 'regime clusters', which distinguishes between corporatist and social democratic clusters of welfare regime (Esping-Andersen 1989). Amable's differentiation of the VoC coordinated model into continental European, Mediterranean and social democratic economies takes into account the different traditions of the state in these economies. The level of state intervention in the economy increases with each category. In the continental European model the state predominantly adopts the role of a supervisor of economic activity to ensure that established rules (for example collective bargaining in industrial relations) are adhered to by all actors. In the Mediterranean model the state plays a stronger role when it comes to regulating the labour market and industrial relations but is less involved in the provision of welfare, which was traditionally a dominion of the family and the church. The social democratic model, as it predominantly exists in Scandinavian countries, on the contrary accepts a strong role for the state as the guardian against market forces and the provider of strong quality services, high levels of welfare provision and public sector employment. The challenge for many scholars continues to be how to fit in the countries in Central and Eastern Europe (CEE), which were for some time simply subsumed under a *transition model* category. More detailed studies such as Lane and Myant

(2007) have shown that countries in this region have developed a variety of different economic and welfare cultures. Some have been transformed towards the liberal typology and others towards coordinated varieties.

The importance of the state in determining the future of individual economic models is therefore undisputed. The VoC approach acknowledges the state as one element which makes up the institutional particularities of an economy but it tends to underestimate the importance of the state in stabilising and sustaining economic activity, particularly at times of crisis. The state is therefore more than just one of the actors in the coordinative arrangements of an economy. It has maintained far greater autonomy to determine the parameters of a national economy than followers of the functionalist paradigm (such as the VoC) had wanted to concede. The functionalist notion that 'politics follows economics' (Hancké et al. 2007: 23–24) remains valid to a certain degree when one analyses the recent developments in capitalist economies around the world, particularly in Europe. The perception that the separation between the public and economic interests would become increasingly blurred in the process of economic globalisation has nevertheless turned out to be flawed. It is certainly true that, as a result of the ongoing crisis symptoms in many economies in Europe, economic issues tend to dominate the political agenda to an increasing extent. A comprehensive analysis can however not ignore the fact that globalisation has not pushed different economic models towards a high level of convergence. It is now the established consensus that the globalisation convergence theory which assumed the emergence of a best practice liberal economic model was flawed. Instead many scholars have pointed out that each economic model has responded to the challenges of globalisation in a different way and on the basis of its particular institutional background (Crouch 2005; Hall and Gingerich 2009; Hay 2000). In this respect it is highlighted that even though the principle of 'shareholder value' has started to infiltrate coordinated economies, it has not necessarily lead to a complete shake-up of their institutional foundations. Instead, established corporate actors have managed to integrate the principle into their existing institutional practices. Even the reforms in national employment systems, like in the case of Germany, have not completely changed the coordinative institutional core of these economies (Hall and Thelen 2009). It would also be wrong to assume that has managed to eradicate a political and social agenda which goes beyond facilitating market interaction and enhancing profit-orientated business opportunities for the purpose of stimulating growth. States remain responsible for the overall well-being of their citizens. The elected representatives of the state consequently have to look beyond the pure market interest. It consequently makes sense to consider the 'state and the mode of business coordination as analytically independent properties of any given model of capitalism' (Hancké et al. 2007: 24). Hall and Soskice's original approach fails to differentiate between the market and the wider societal interests. This weakness was highlighted by Bruff who argues that the VoC approach fails to adequately acknowledge the domestic social foundations of the national institutional VoC (Bruff 2008 and 2011). Hall and Soskice also tend to accept the predominant view of neoclassical economics that institutions in the national context are shaped by market interests (Crouch 2005: 80). Institutions which do not follow this logic are consequently supposed to be fundamentally altered or even replaced on the basis of a best practice selection of institutional success. These are usually those institutions which support economic competitiveness on the basis of reducing investment and transaction costs for businesses (Barro and Sala-i-Martin 1992; Parker 1998).

The globalisation convergence advocates however also acknowledging that a powerful external shock like a major economic crisis would most likely stall this process (Lane 2005: 105). This is where the importance of the recent global financial crisis comes in. I argue that the crisis has fundamentally shaken the established perception of the role of the state in modern capitalist economies. The globalisation debate failed to establish a consensus on determining to what extent state actors are able to maintain their independence under the conditions of global market interaction. The emerging trend in the field of political economy before the crisis was that active state intervention in the economy in the form of Keynesian demand management and the imposition of regulatory burdens on businesses and markets would be a thing of the past. Instead new concepts of the state as facilitator in the area of employment, welfare and education started to emerge, most prominently advocated by Giddens (1998) as the 'Third Way' economic philosophy to be positioned between the classic neoliberal and leftist Keynesian approaches. It was subsequently adopted by reformed centre-left parties in the 1990s, which branded themselves as modern Social Democrats, such as Bill Clinton's New Democrats in the US and Tony Blair's New Labour Party in the United Kingdom. The 'Third Way' argued for an economic approach without ideological bias, which could combine economic liberalism and social cohesion by limiting the role of the state to that of a facilitator of economic activity. The emphasis was hence on removing regulatory burdens for businesses and markets and making labour markets more flexible through the introduction of a welfare-to-work approach. The latter gives incentives to take up employment or at least education and training opportunities and penalises individuals who remain economically inactive. The 'Third Way' approach was actively promoted at the EU level, especially by the British New Labour government in the run-up to the 2005 revision of the Lisbon Strategy. The Third Way became the basis for a reformed social model, which was to be grounded in a strategy of decentralisation and diversification. In this respect Giddens differentiated the European social model from the liberal model of the US economy by promoting the development of what he called the 'social investment state' (Giddens 2006: 32). In contrast to the US, the state would remain active but concentrate its activities more towards human capital by transferring risk from the welfare state towards the individual. Crucial for this was the promotion of education and learning and the pursuit of an overall strategy which is predominantly orientated towards stimulating economic growth and job creation. This led to the development of a 'flexicurity' strategy for the reform of labour markets which borrowed heavily from the active labour market policy approach in Scandinavian countries like Sweden. The principle combines labour market flexibility with a new form of security. It is aimed at reducing passive welfare support in favour of introducing targeted activation through education and training programmes for the unemployment with the overall purpose of ensuring that they get back into work and are equipped to find a new job quickly (Funk 2008: 357). 'Flexicurity' was the core principle of the labour market and welfare state reforms which the British New Labour government and the German Social Democrats introduced between 1997 and 2003 (Schweiger 2010). As is outlined in greater detail in Chapter 2 in this book, during the run-up to the revision of the Lisbon Strategy in 2005 the British government was very active in promoting this principle successfully against the background of successive years of record domestic levels of economic growth and employment. The result was the emphasis on economic growth and jobs as the new priorities for the revised Lisbon Strategy. Subsequently and even before the effects of the US financial crisis on European economies could really be felt, the debate in the EU switched towards a more critical approach to the Lisbon Strategy and the flexicurity principle.

This was the result of rising inequality and poverty levels even in countries such as the UK, Ireland and Germany) that had actively implemented the flexicurity principle through welfare cuts and increased pressure on individuals to take up work.

The crisis has created a situation where the centrality of the state for the survival of national economies suddenly resurfaced. Ironically it hit those countries in Europe hardest who had rolled back state influence the most. The emerging dramatic flaws in the British and Irish banking industries led to a previously unimaginable level of state interference in the sector in 2007–2008. The governments in London and Dublin invested record amounts of taxpayers' money to stabilise failing banks and effectively nationalised or part-nationalised substantial sections of their banking industry in an attempt to avoid a complete meltdown of a crucial pillar of their economies. The sudden emergence of the state as a safety net for a failing industry which for many years had provided the backbone for the good performance of the British and Irish economies raises doubts on the sustainability of the liberal model's foundations. An increasing number of critical accounts of the three former liberal role model economies of the US, the UK and Ireland have outlined the shaky foundations upon which their growth and jobs miracle was built in the 1990s and early 2000s (Gamble 2009; Hutton 2011; O'Toole 2010; Ross 2010; Stiglitz 2010). Most of all they highlight how a blind trust in markets and a profound scepticism towards government interference in the economy caused a situation where the financial sector was allowed to get away with reckless and unsubstantiated lending in the form of subprime mortgages. This was strengthened by an EU strategy which essentially amounted to *negative* integration: forcing national governments to gradually remove regulatory barriers to competition in more and more sectors of their economy and in particular encouraging them to look towards the liberalisation of the services and the financial industry. Although the EU Commission led by José Manuel Barroso frequently emphasised the differences between the reformed European social model and US-style capitalism, it is obvious that the Lisbon Strategy initiated developments which made it difficult for countries to maintain what Hutton defines as the essential feature of the distinctive European social model: the role of the state as a guardian of citizens against the excesses of market competition. For Hutton this amounts to the notion 'that all citizens should have an equal right to participate in economic and social life, and that the state is more than a safety net of last resort: it is the fundamental vehicle for the delivery of this equality' (Hutton 2002: 63).

The idea that the state should guarantee *social citizenship* is connected to the notion of the existence of a *public space* which is protected from the realm of market competition. Rather than being pushed to the sidelines the state has a crucial role to play as a provider of public services. In addition the state is called on as an established mediator in industrial relations who ensures the adequate protection of workers through regulations such as co-decision, working time directives, a minimum wage and the provision of benefits in case of unemployment. This amounts to *economic citizenship* (Teague 1999: 12). Through its emphasis on market competition and deregulation the EU strategies therefore encouraged European economies with a pronounced state culture to transform themselves towards the liberal model. Combined with the budgetary restraints which were supposed to be introduced under the Stability and Growth Pact (SGP) for eurozone members, the EU hence was set on course to 'mute into little more than a charter of economic liberalization and marketization' (Hay 2000: 528).

The VoC approach has uncritically accompanied this trend by following a logic which portrays liberal economies as better equipped for the challenges of a globalised economy because of their orientation towards the services sector and their openness towards transnational capital flows. This is because coordinated economies tend to display what Hall and Soskice consider to be an 'adjustment problem' (Hall and Soskice 2001: 65) in failing to respond swiftly to new internal and external challenges. While Hall and Soskice acknowledge that 'markets do not necessarily generate superior outcome' (Ibid.: 65), it is clear that they consider the VoC in more market-orientated liberal models to be advantageous. Crouch goes as far as to argue that Hall and Soskice follow the logic of neoclassical economics which considers any non-market institution as potentially not viable for the long term under the conditions of globalisation (Crouch 2009: 80). I would argue that VoC does not offer a fine-tuned analysis on the differences in state cultures across Europe, which are subsumed under the firm-based liberal-coordinated dichotomy. This is a profound weakness of the approach which fortunately has in the meantime been addressed by a number of scholars. It is especially problematic when one applies the VoC approach to the analysis of the political economy of the EU. In order to understand the internal divisions between member states it is essential to refer back to the differences in national state cultures. Siedentop (2000) outlined this in his seminal work on the foundation of democracy in Europe. He argues that the EU supranational institutional framework was essentially built on the tradition of the French state which favours centralisation with little transparency and check and balances. From Siedentop's perspective this explains why other member states with a more restrained state culture, especially the UK, have been struggling to integrate into what is essentially a French institutionalised design (Siedentop 2000: 105–107). The financial crisis and the subsequent sovereign debt crisis have once again re-emphasised the importance of differences in national state cultures in Europe. The eurozone crisis has opened up an obvious divide between those countries who favour austerity, monetary stability and central bank independence and others who are reluctant to abandon the notion of the role of the state as a generous provider of public employment and welfare benefits. At the same time we are witnessing a divide between member states who call for a move towards deeper political and economic integration and others who are profoundly sceptical of further integration and want to set a clear end point to further integration and are even calling for the renationalisation of powers. The advocates of deeper integration are countries which have experience with the division powers between the centre and periphery in a federal system. Examples for this are Germany, Italy, Austria, Spain and to a certain extent also Luxembourg with its system of consensual multi-party government. On the other side of the divide are countries with more unitary political systems that put great emphasis on preserving their national sovereignty over key strategic policies. In the latter category the United Kingdom and the Czech Republic are currently the most ardent defenders of their national sovereignty. These differences in state tradition are crucial to understand how the global financial crisis has affected the VoC in Europe. They also provide the background to the dynamics between national and supranational policy responses to the crisis. The crisis in the eurozone illustrates once again that it was a mistake for Hall and Soskice to neglect the differences in national state traditions, particularly when it comes to introducing a more fine-tuned differentiation between different state cultures within the coordinated typology. Lallement (2011) emphasises this point in his study which attempts to identify the effects on labour markets in different economies in Europe. He emphasises the need to go beyond Hall and Soskice's positioning of a group of predominantly Southern European economies (France, Italy, Spain, Portugal, Greece and Turkey) somewhere between the liberal and the coordinated dichotomy and argues that they should instead clearly be determined as a Mediterranean model. This model has the following characteristics: a key role is assigned to the state, the level of social protection is substantially higher than in coordinated economies, even than in Scandinavian countries, but is not predominantly provided by the state. Education and training systems are weak, levels of labour market participation low, particularly amongst young people. The banking sector plays a key role as a lender to companies and individuals. Lallement identifies the reinforcement of inequalities as the most characteristic effect of the crisis on these economies (Lallement 2011: 637–638). The crisis has accentuated the differences between the Mediterranean and the coordinated group. This is most prominently represented by the clash over policy solutions between Germany and Greece but to a certain extent also between Germany and France over the introduction of eurobonds and the role of the ECB, especially since the election of the Socialist French President François Hollande in 2012.

This leads us directly to the second essential weakness of the VoC approach. The second and probably most devastating global economic crisis in the history of the advanced modern economy had its origins in the financial sector. As the crisis deepens at the regional level in Europe it becomes obvious that national economies are increasingly at the mercy of market forces. Policy-makers have for decades pursued deregulatory policies towards the financial industry on the national as well as the supranational regional and global level. This was part of a neoliberal 'financialisation' strategy which was aimed at promoting the radical overhaul of economic activity towards financial speculation and large-scale borrowing for businesses and consumers (Gamble 2009: 78). Hall and Soskice concentrate predominantly on the manufacturing industry and consequently underestimate the importance of the financial sector's growing influence in what can be classified as an era of financial deregulation. They see the danger that 'financial deregulation could be the string that unravels coordinated market economies' (Hall and Soskice 2001: 64) but offer no critical perspective on the tendency towards the deregulation of the financial sector in liberal economic models. The financial crisis has made obvious that financial markets have acquired substantial powers in the globalised economy. This turned out to be the root of the problems which led to the 2008–2009 global financial crisis. The crisis illustrated to what extent both companies and governments have become increasingly dependent on financial markets as a source for funding. Financial markets have therefore moved into a position where their rating of a company's or even a whole economy's viability has profound implications for their long-term stability. As a result of a growing number of companies across the globe depending on financial markets, the latter are able to force companies to become more profit and budget-orientated and to pursue a shareholder-value strategy (Amable 2003: 28). In addition, they have also strengthened their position in the domestic process of determining economic policy strategies (Hancké et al. 2007: 28).

Policy-makers in the EU are consequently facing a profound struggle to reimpose political control over a largely market-driven economic agenda. Instead they tend to be trapped in a constant process of attempting to reinstil the trust of financial market operators in the viability of individual economies (currently especially Cyprus, Greece, Italy, Portugal and Spain) and the single European currency in general. The ongoing market speculation against the euro and individual countries on the government bond and the credit default swap markets has not only put the membership of the crisis countries but even the future viability of the whole of the eurozone in jeopardy. This unprecedented situation where 'the financial system was rescued by state intervention, only to turn and bite its rescuer' (Lapavitsas et al. 2011: 58) is to a large extent the result of the hesitation of political leaders to fundamentally shake up the regulatory foundations of the global economy. In spite of the profound flaws which were uncovered by the financial crisis the global economy continues to be based on the twentieth century ideology of market dominance and small government (Stiglitz 2010: 207). Under these conditions a firm-centred approach such as the one promoted by the VoC is no longer sufficient to explain the new complexity of economic policy-making in Europe. The argument that companies are essentially the central actors in modern economies has been made superfluous by the new crisis conditions. The focus of economic policy-making is consequently moving on from the agenda of the 1990s and early 2000s, when its predominant focus had been the creation of a business-friendly environment. The budgetary crisis in many economies and the resulting nervous market reactions, have led to the imposition of profound austerity programmes. Political elites seem to be driven by the fear that without these policies the long-term prospects for economic and particularly fiscal recovery may be severely undermined by adverse market speculation. They are therefore determined to pursue the austerity strategy against fierce domestic opposition and in spite of the risk it poses for the fabric of societies in Europe.

As political elites in the EU and particularly in the eurozone realise that their national competitive advantage is strongly interlinked with the overall success of the Single Market and the eurozone, they are also focusing more on the implementation of effective supranational policy solutions. This is especially obvious when one considers the emerging EU policy mechanisms in response to the crisis. In the third chapter of this book I therefore argue that the new policy mechanisms are the result of a new wave of functionalist *spillover* where the external crisis conditions force governments to transfer more of their national authority in the area of economic policy-making to the supranational level than they would be willing to concede under normal circumstances. The crisis is hence leading to the emergence of new set of multiple layers of policies which go substantially beyond the coordinative mechanisms of the *open method of coordination* (OMC). The OMC had been the EU's preferred mechanism for more than a decade before the crisis. Examples for this are the annual European Semester policy mechanism under the Europe 2020 Strategy, the Euro Summit, the newly established European Stability Mechanism (ESM) and to a certain extent even the European System of Financial Supervision (ESFS). The details of the regulatory response to the crisis are discussed in Chapter 2 in this book. Chapter 3 deals with the political implications of the emergence of an increasingly complex set of functionalist policy initiatives which essentially divide the EU into multiple core groups with different levels of integration. The emerging division of the EU membership is essentially based on the horizontal division between eurozone insiders and outsiders and the deepening of vertical integration in the eurozone core with the potential aim of moving towards a political union. The countries outside the eurozone are hence either semi-detached or only very loosely connected to the euro core through the Europe 2020 annual cycle of policy coordination, which applies to all 28 member states.

In spite of its limitations I use the VoC approach as a basic framework for the analysis of the changes in European economies under unprecedented crisis conditions, which is presented in this book. As outlined earlier, I argue that VoC puts too much emphasis on the role of companies and neglects the political dimension of economies. At the same time it pursues essentially an institutionalist perspective. Hall and Soskice correctly assume that change in response to new challenges is most likely to be dependent on the culture within the established institutional coordinative framework. This allows for more radical innovation in liberal market economies and rather incremental and modest change in coordinated economies (Hall and Soskice 2001: 38–39). The perspective that the national institutional setting of an economy determines its competitive advantage and consequently profoundly shapes the behaviour of domestic actors remains crucial to the understanding of the dynamics of institutional and policy development in the EU. This is even more so the case under the new set of circumstances European governments currently face. The crisis has shown us that even in the face of the most adverse external circumstances institutional particularities of individual economies tend to persist. I therefore follow the basic VoC hypothesis that 'the distinctions central to the varieties of capitalism perspective are likely to be of continuing value' (Hall and Gingerich 2009: 169). Since the emergence of the financial crisis the national and EU level discussions on the reform of policies and institutions have been characterised by a diversity of perspectives. All of these are nevertheless deeply rooted in the national institutional cultures of member states. A more active role for the ECB in supporting economies with budgetary problems, the introduction of a national or an EU-wide financial transaction tax, the reform of the eurozone SGP and more recent proposals from the five largest member states (Germany, France, Italy, Spain and Poland) and others for deeper political integration, including integrated financial, budgetary and economic policies (Future of Europe Group 2012) therefore continue to be hotly debated. It is therefore necessary to adapt the VoC approach to the current crisis conditions. They are likely to substantially change the direction of economic and political integration in the EU and will leave a lasting imprint on the national VoC in Europe.

The scope of this book is to offer an analysis of the emerging post-crisis VoC in Europe. It is certainly problematic to speak of a post-crisis situation when the economic and budgetary situation in a number of countries in the EU continues to be fundamentally grave. Given the volatility of events, it is likely that at this stage it is only possible to offer a snapshot of the full extent of the changes which national economies and the EU Single Market as a whole are still likely to be subjected to. Due to the profound nature of the changes that occur it is nevertheless essential to offer a new perspective on the existing categorisation of national capitalisms in Europe. Here the analysis needs to concentrate on the extent to which national institutional cultures continue to determine the preferences of policy-makers and stakeholders and how these in turn influence the shape of supranational EU policies. The particularities of national institutional infrastructures and economic cultures continue and have not been eradicated by the external pressures of globalisation (Hall and Soskice 2001: 57). Even the severity of the pressures following the financial crisis has not pushed economies towards uniform transformation. Instead we witness a process where domestic elites are adamant to defend what they perceive as their national competitive economic advantage. Even in economies where the crisis has revealed that the existing institutional status quo is detrimental to economic recovery, the domestic resistance against change remains substantial.

On the EU level itself we are witnessing a surprisingly strong resistance towards finding common solutions to the crisis. It is therefore obvious that the EU remains based on a strong intergovernmentalist fundament. In practice this means that beyond the official rhetoric member state governments are adamant to remain in control of strategic policy-making (Pollack et al. 2010: 487) and are especially defensive over policy issues which are contentious with voters (Hix and Hoyland 2011: 335). This clashes with the realisation that the creation of a single European currency demands deeper integration of national economic policies beyond the harmonisation of interest rates. This essentially follows the functionalist logic that economic integration will inevitably be followed by deeper political integration. The persisting differences in national economic cultures make it hard for political elites to agree to the further transfer of national sovereignty towards the EU institutional level without the risk of losing the support of their electorate. To argue that the effective resolution of the crisis demands more and not less European integration is currently not very popular with citizens across Europe. The public debate tends to associate proposals to deepen integration with the creation of a transfer union and the sharing of risk in the eurozone. The latest *Eurobarometer* poll on the effects of the crisis shows that only 22 per cent of citizens across the EU-27 considered the EU to be best placed to 'take effective actions against the effects of the financial and economic crisis' (European Commission 2013: 27). The rest favoured either national governments (21 per cent) or other global organisations such as the G20 (13 per cent), the International Monetary Fund (IMF) (13 per cent) and even the US government (8 per cent). Overall trust in the EU has also fallen sharply recently with only 31 per cent of citizens across the EU-27 expressing the view that they have trust in the EU and its institutions (Ibid.: 27).

Large varieties between citizens in different member states persist when it comes to the level of acceptance of EU institutions and the proposals to deepen integration. It may therefore be inevitable that the EU becomes divided into a core eurozone group of countries who move towards full political and economic union, while a smaller group of countries deliberately decide to stay on the sidelines and may even decide to repatriate core powers to the national level. This current division remains highly volatile and is likely to change in the future. This will not only be the result of further countries joining the eurozone. The opposition against the German plans to push the eurozone towards deeper political integration on the basis of a rigid system of monitoring of national macroeconomic and budgetary policies is already substantial. These concerns are likely to grow further once national governments realise the full impact of the proposals for deeper political union for the autonomy of their national policies. It is hence a realistic possibility that more countries both inside and outside the eurozone will decide to opt out of future treaty changes, which are designed to deepen integration.

The emerging vertical and horizontal divisions in the EU in the aftermath of the global financial crisis support the VoC notion that countries concentrate on developing strategies to defend their national competitive economic advantage and that these strategies are fundamentally shaped by their domestic institutional setting. VoC therefore remains prominent in the debate on the future of political and economic integration. The crisis has however also shown that even against the background of a persistence of national interests in the EU, the neofunctionalist concept which assumes that economic integration inevitably leads towards deeper political integration, essentially remains valid. The initial refusal of member states to accompany monetary integration with deeper political integration to ensure the effective coordination of fiscal and macroeconomic policies has turned out to be the fundamental flaw in the design of the eurozone. The deepening of political integration is now emerging as a bitter but arguably inevitable pill which eurozone countries will have to swallow to ensure that the single currency has a long-term future. This is the background upon which the EU institutional and policy changes under crisis conditions are discussed in the second and third chapters in this book.

REFERENCES

Allen, M. (2004) 'The Varieties of Capitalism Paradigm: Not Enough Variety?', *Socio-Economic Review* 2 (1): 87–108.

Amable, B. (2003) *The Diversity of Modern Capitalism*. Oxford: Oxford University Press.

Amin, S. and D. Luckin (1996) 'The Challenge of Globalization', *Review of International Political Economy* 3 (2): 216–259.

Barro, R.J. and X. Sala-i-Martin (1992) 'Convergence', *Journal of Political Economy* 100 (2): 223–252.

Bosch, G. (2008) 'Auflösung des deutschen Tarifsystems', *Wirtschaftsdienst* 1: 16–20.
Bruff, I. (2008) *Culture and Consensus in European Varieties of Capitalism: A 'Common Sense' Analysis*. Basingstoke: Palgrave Macmillan.
Bruff, I. (2011) 'What about the Elephant in the Room? Varieties of Capitalism, Varieties in Capitalism', *New Political Economy* 16 (4): 481–500.
Crouch, C. (2005) *Capitalist Diversity and Change: Recombinant Governance and Institutional Entrepreneurs*. Oxford: Oxford University Press.
Crouch, C. (2009) 'Typologies of Capitalism', in B. Hancké (ed.) *Debating Varieties of Capitalism*. Oxford: Oxford University Press, pp. 75–94.
Deeg, R. (2005) 'Change from Within: German and Italian Finance in the 1990s', in W. Streeck and K. Thelen (eds) *Beyond Continuity: Institutional Change in Advanced Political Economies*. Oxford: Oxford University Press, pp. 169–202.
Esping-Andersen, G. (1989) *The Three Worlds of Welfare State Capitalism*. Cambridge: Polity Press.
European Commission (2013) 'Standard *Eurobarometer 79* Spring: Public Opinion in the European Union First Results', Brussels. Available at: http://ec.europa.eu/public_opinion/archives/eb/eb79/eb79_first_en.pdf (accessed 20 September 2013).
Funk, L. (2007) 'Convergence in Employment-Related Public Policies? A British-German Comparison', *German Politics* 16 (1): 116–136.
Funk, L. (2008) 'European Flexicurity Policies: A Critical Assessment', *International Journal of Comparative Labour Law and Industrial Relations* 24 (3): 349–384.
Future of Europe Group (2012) 'Final Report of the Foreign Ministers of Austria, Belgium, Denmark, France, Italy, Germany, Luxembourg, the Netherlands, Poland, Portugal and Spain'. Available at: http://www.msz.gov.pl/files/docs/komunikaty/20120918RAPORT/report.p (accessed 20 September 2012).
Gamble, A. (2009) *The Spectre at the Feast: Capitalist Crisis and the Politics of Recession*. Basingstoke: Palgrave Macmillan.
Giddens, A. (1998) *The Third Way: The Renewal of Social Democracy*. Cambridge: Polity Press.
Giddens, A. (2006) 'A Social Model for Europe?', in A. Giddens, P. Diamond and R. Liddle (eds) *Global Europe, Social Europe*. Cambridge: Polity Press, pp. 14–36.
Gill, S. (1995) 'Globalization, Market Civilization and Disciplinary Neoliberalism', *Millennium* 24 (3): 399–423.
Hall, P. and D. Gingerich (2009) 'Varieties of Capitalism and Institutional Complementarities in the Political Economy: An Empirical Analysis', in B. Hancké (ed.) *Debating Varieties of Capitalism: A Reader*. Oxford: OxfordUniversity Press, pp. 135–179.
Hall, P. and K. Thelen (2009) 'Institutional Change in Varieties of Capitalism', in B. Hancké (ed.) *Debating Varieties of Capitalism: A Reader*. Oxford: Oxford University Press, pp. 251–272.
Hall, P.A. and D. Soskice (2001) *Varieties of Capitalism: The Institutional Foundations of Comparative Advantage*. Oxford: Oxford University Press.
Hall, P.A. and D. Soskice (2003) 'Varieties of Capitalism and Institutional Change: A Response to Three Critics', *Comparative European Politics* 1 (2): 241–250.
Hancké, B. (2009) *Debating Varieties of Capitalism: A Reader*. Oxford: Oxford University Press.

Hancké, B. and M. Goyer (2005) 'Degrees of Freedom: Rethinking the Institutional Analysis of Economic Change', in G. Morgan, R. Whitley and E. Moen (eds) *Changing Capitalisms? Internationalization, Institutional Change, and Systems of Economic Organization*. Oxford: Oxford University Press, pp. 53–77.

Hancké, B., M. Rhodes and M. Thatcher (2007) 'Beyond Varieties of Capitalism: Conflict, Contradictions, and Complementaries in the European Economy', in B. Hancké, M. Rhodes, M. Thatcher (eds) *Beyond Varieties of Capitalism: Conflict, Contradictions and Complementaries in the European Economy*. Oxford: Oxford University Press, pp. 3–38.

Hay, C. (2000) 'Contemporary Capitalism, Globalization, Regionalization and the Persistence of National Variation', *Review of International Studies* 26 (1): 509–531.

Hix, S. and B. Hoyland (2011) *The Political System of the European Union*. Basingstoke: Palgrave Macmillan.

Hutton, W. (2002) *The World We're In*. London: Little/Brown (Time Warner Books).

Hutton, W. (2011) *Them and Us: Changing Britain – Why We Need a Fair Society*. London: Abacus.

Kemmerling, A. and O. Bruttel (2006) '"New Politics" in German Labour Market Policy? The Implications of the Recent Hartz Reforms for the German Welfare State', *West European Politics* 29 (1): 90–112.

Keohane, R.O. (1984) *After Hegemony: Cooperation and Discord in the World Political Economy*. Princeton, NJ: Princeton University Press.

Lallement, M. (2011) 'Europe and the Economic Crisis: Forms of Labour Market Adjustment and Varieties of Capitalism', *Work, Employment and Society* 25 (4): 627–641.

Lane, C. (2005) 'Institutional Transformation and System Change: Changes in Corporate Governance of German Corporations', in G. Morgan, R. Whitley and E. Moen (eds) (2005) *Changing Capitalisms? Internationalization, Institutional Change, and Systems of Economic Organization*. Oxford: Oxford University Press, pp. 78–109.

Lane, D. and M.R. Myant (2007) *Varieties of Capitalism in Post-Communist Countries*. Basingstoke: Palgrave Macmillan.

Lapavitsas, C., A. Kaltenbrunner, G. Labrinidis, D. Lindo, J. Meadway, J. Mitchell, J.P. Painceira, E. Pires, J. Powell, A. Stenfors, N. Teles and L. Vatikiotis (2011) *Crisis in the Eurozone*. London and New York: Verso.

Morgan, G. (2005) 'Introduction: Changing Capitalisms? Internationalization, Institutional Change, and Systems of Economic Organization', in G. Morgan, R. Whitley and E. Moen (eds) (2005) *Changing Capitalisms? Internationalization, Institutional Change, and Systems of Economic Organization*. Oxford: Oxford University Press, pp. 1–20.

Morgan, G., R. Whitley and E. Moen (eds) (2005) *Changing Capitalisms? Internationalization, Institutional Change, and Systems of Economic Organization*. Oxford: Oxford University Press.

O'Toole, F. (2010) *Ship of Fools: How Stupidity and Corruption Sank the Celtic Tiger*. London: Faber and Faber.

Parker, B. (1998) *Globalization and Business Practice: Managing Across Boundaries*. London: Sage.

Pollack, M.A., H. Wallace and A.R. Young (2010) 'EU Policy-Making in Challenging Times: Adversity, Adaptability and Resilience', in H. Wallace,

M.A. Pollack and A.R. Young (eds) *Policy-Making in the European Union*. Oxford: Oxford University Press, pp. 481–502.

Pierson, P. (2000) 'Increasing Returns, Path Dependence and the Study of Politics', *The American Political Science Review* 94 (2): 251–267.

Ross, S. (2010) *The Bankers: How the Banks Brought Ireland to its Knees*. London: Penguin.

Schweiger, C. (2010) 'Towards Convergence? New Labour's Third Way and the SPD's Agenda 2010 in Comparative Perspective', *German Review of Social Policy/Sozialer Fortschritt* 59 (9): 244–253.

Siedentop, L. (2000) *Democracy in Europe*. London: Allen Lane.

Sinn, H.W. (2004a) 'The Dilemma of Globalisation: A German Perspective', *Economie Internationale* 100: 111–120.

Sinn, H.W. (2004b) *Ist Deutschland noch zu retten?* Munich: Ullstein.

Streeck, W. and K. Yamamura (2003) 'Introduction: Convergence or Diversity? Stability and Change in German Japanese Capitalism', in K. Yamamura and W. Streeck (eds) *The End of Diversity? Prospects for German and Japanese Capitalism*. Ithaca and London: Cornell University Press, pp. 1–50.

Streeck, W. and K. Thelen (2005) *Beyond Continuity: Institutional Change in Advanced Political Economies*. Oxford: Oxford University Press.

Stiglitz, J. (2010) *Freefall: Free Markets and the Sinking of the Global Economy*. London: Penguin.

Teague, P. (1999) *Economic Citizenship in the European Union: Employment Relations in Europe*. London: Routledge.

Vitols, S. (2003) 'From Banks to Markets: The Political Economy of Liberalization of the German and Japanese Financial Systems', in K. Yamamura and W. Streeck (eds) *The End of Diversity? Prospects for German and Japanese Capitalism*. Cornell: Cornell University Press, pp. 240–260.

2. From deregulation towards 'smart' regulation

2.1 TOWARDS THE SINGLE MARKET: THE LIBERAL PATH OF POST-WAR ECONOMIC INTEGRATION

The ambition to create an integrated economic area has always been at the heart of the European integration. Ever since the process of the institutionalised pooling of national sovereignty began in Europe, economic integration has been paramount and political integration followed slowly and with great hesitation. The move from the pooling of sovereignty in individual economic sectors, coal and steel in 1951, towards the establishment of a Common Market in the Treaty of Rome in 1957 was initially considered to be part of a functionalist process of 'spillover' from the economic into the political field. Neofunctionalist theories assumed that in order to successfully introduce the deregulatory regime of the Common Market with the aim of the free movement of goods, people, capital and services, member states would inevitably have to agree to give increasing control to Brussels over their domestic policies (Haas 1958: 313). This was supported by the principles which the Treaty of Rome determined for the Common Market. They went clearly beyond creating a free trade area and emphasised the need for 'progressively approximating the economic policies of the member states' (European Economic Community 1957, article 2). This ambitious goal may have seemed realistic at the time of the signing of the Treaty, when participating member states seemed to be convinced that they could create an 'ever closer union'. In the aftermath of the Treaty of Rome it however became obvious that the integration process was stalling as a result of an emerging gap between what member states had agreed to in the intergovernmental negotiations and the concrete implementation of these principles in the process of actual domestic policy-making. In practice member states were unwilling to give up sovereignty over major policy areas and resisted the harmonisation of standards. Hence the Common Market essentially remained focused on the lowest common denominator of trying to create a level playing field for open competition between the member states. This 'negative' form of integration essentially developed a policy regime in which the Commission became a supervisor of market deregulation at the domestic level on the basis of binding directives which have to be implemented by member states (Scharpf 1999). Even in the area of economic liberalisation member states were far from being wholeheartedly committed to the process. While the progress in the removal of customs for the trade of goods had been substantial in the aftermath of the Treaty of Rome, the liberalisation of national economies in the areas which were covered by the other three principles of free movement (workers, capital and services) faced substantial obstacles in the form of member state protectionism. National governments refused to abandon distinctive features of national regulation in the areas of corporate and financial sector governance, public services and welfare state provision as these were perceived as essential to maintain the competitive advantage of their economies. The balance sheet more than two decades after the creation of the Common Market was therefore disappointing. The spirit of unity which the Treaty of Rome had tried to inspire 'had been overwhelmed by the national protectionist impulses of the member states' (McCann 2010: 26), who were more concerned about their national economic problems than about the completion of the Common Market.

The persistence of national interests and the resulting gap between commitment and implementation of supranational policies has been a persistent feature of the European Union (EU). It explains why progress in the integration process has been slow and characterised by many unsuccessful policy initiatives. Even in the area of market integration member states have over time moved much slower than expected. This is the result of a tendency to either delay the implementation of directives at the national level or to simply not implement them correctly (Young 2005: 108). More than half a century since the integration process began the EU still has not managed to achieve a fully integrated internal market in which the four freedoms that were set out in the Treaty of Rome and then re-emphasised in the 1987 Single European Act (SEA) have become a reality. Since the late 1970s member states have repeatedly relaunched their internal market strategy. The new push towards market integration in the mid-1980s resulted from the fact that most member states were troubled by increasing levels of unemployment in the wake of two oil crises in the early and late 1970s, which had shaken European economies. In spite of substantial differences in their domestic policy agendas and their overall vision of the Common Market, the leaders of the three largest member states France, Britain and Germany decided to cooperate with the Delors Commission in creating a new agenda for rapid market liberalisation. The result was the introduction of the SEA and the decision to set the timeline of December 1992 for the establishment of an internal market based on the four freedoms of the Treaty of Rome (goods, services, people and capital). This showed that François Mitterrand, Margaret Thatcher and Helmut Kohl were all supporting swift market liberalisation as a means to combat unemployment in their respective countries (Moravcsik 1991: 48–53). The intergovernmental debates that followed the SEA illustrated once again that there was little consensus to move beyond market liberalisation. The British Prime Minister Margaret Thatcher famously categorically rejected proposals of the Delors Commission to accompany the internal market with an integrated social package. The renewed impetus towards internal market integration was therefore accompanied by only very limited political integration on the basis of the lowest possible common denominator. The provision in the SEA to use qualified majority voting (QMV) on all matters relating to the internal and the inclusion of a Social Protocol, which mainly set basic common standards for employment across the Common Market, in the annex of the 1993 Maastricht Treaty showed that member states were willing to make some progress to support market liberalisation. Still this was far from the approximation of national economic policies which the Treaty of Rome had envisaged. Subsequently any attempt to make progress in this area failed. During the post-Maastricht negotiations the member states of the organisation that now called itself the EU clearly lacked the political will to move towards a more unified approach in major policy areas such as employment and welfare reform. Attempts by the French Socialist government, led by Prime Minister Lionel Jospin, to gain support for the introduction of a harmonised European employment policy at the EU Summit in Amsterdam in May 1997 did not come to fruition.

Following on from the SEA and Maastricht the EU had developed a dual-track policy regime which tried to reconcile the acceleration of internal market liberalisation with the desire of member states to essentially preserve the sovereignty over their national economic and social policy agenda. The introduction of the Internal Market Strategy (IMS) in 1999, aimed at speeding up the deregulation of national economies to achieve full and open competition in a Single European Market (SEM), was therefore accompanied by a new open method of coordination (OMC) mechanism for politically sensitive areas such as employment and education. The IMS gave the Commission a renewed mandate to drive forward market liberalisation by holding member states to account for the timely and correct implementation of internal market directives on the basis of performance scoreboards. This *hard* liberalisation strategy stands in stark contrast to the *soft* approach of the OMC. Member state governments risk infringement proceedings against them at the European Court of Justice if they ignore the Commission's timeline and guidelines on the implementation of directives. This can result in substantial financial penalties. In contrast the OMC essentially boils down to a *soft* coordinative approach which encourages policy learning between member states on the basis of best practice performance monitoring. The OMC is clearly an attempt to obtain some level of policy coordination against the background of the widespread member state resistance towards the transfer of policy competencies at the EU level. It became the substantial mechanism to push member states towards the economic growth levels and the external competitiveness of the SEM. Member states had set themselves the ambitious target-driven goals of the Lisbon Strategy in 2000 to develop the SEM into the 'most competitive and dynamic knowledge-based economy in the world' (European Council 2000, paragraph 5). The EU was now clearly operating on the basis of the so-called Washington consensus. It had been originally advocated by the economist John Williamson in the early 1990s as a remedy for economic development in Latin America. Based on Williamson the Washington consensus advocates fiscal austerity, targeted public spending in education and health, trade liberalisation, openness towards foreign direct investment (FDI), privatisation of state-owned assets and the move towards generally deregulated economies (Williamson 1990). The free market values of the Washington consensus became part of the EU's self-defining characteristics reflected in the 2003 Copenhagen membership criteria, which explain the preparatory framework for accession candidates. For the eight membership candidates from Central and Eastern Europe (CEE), who aspired to join in 2004, it therefore became obligatory to show that they were making progress in preparing their economic systems for entry into the free market competitive system of the SEM. Swift transition from an economic system of state-run industries and central planning intervention towards open market competition and privatisation had to be a priority for the CEE-8 candidates if they wanted to be sure that they would be allowed to join the EU.

After the first wave of accession of CEE countries in May 2004 the EU made a further push towards the implementation of the Washington consensus. Since the appointment of the Barroso Commission in 2004, the EU had developed an increasingly deregulatory approach, which took the US economy as a role model for the internal flexibility and external competitiveness it wanted to achieve for the Single Market (McCann 2010: 39). The Barroso Commission had the strong backing of the British Prime Minister Tony Blair and the Irish Prime Minister Bertie Ahern in overhauling the Single Market agenda. Barroso commissioned a High Level Group of Experts, led by the former Dutch Prime Minister Wim Kok, to evaluate the progress member states had made with the Lisbon goals. The Group's report, which was published in November 2004, criticised member states for their lack of commitment to the Lisbon targets. The

Kok report explicitly pointed out that national governments had failed to introduce substantial reforms to support economic growth and job creation. The Group called on governments to 'accelerate employment and productivity growth via a wide range of reform policies as well as a wider macroeconomic framework as supportive as possible of growth, demand and employment' (European Commission 2004: 6). The Kok report set the tone for the Barroso Commission's approach on the future of the Single Market. Just like the two most economically successful member states at the time, the UK and the Irish Republic, Barroso considered the US economy as a role model for the reform of national economies in the EU, particularly in relation to greater flexibility and less regulation for businesses and financial services. The Kok report claimed that Lisbon would be far from simply being a 'copy-cat of the US' (Ibid.: 12) and also quoted the rising economies in Asia as main challengers (China, India). In reality the detailed proposals of the High Level Group were nonetheless modelled along what they perceived as the success of the US economy in stimulating growth by creating confidence amongst businesses and the financial industries: 'Europe has no option but radically to improve its knowledge economy and underlying economic performance if it is to respond to the challenges of Asia and the US' (Ibid.: 12).

This was also shown by the fact that in the annex of the Kok report the performance statistics of the member states on the Lisbon goals (GDP growth, prices, levels of employment, education and research and development levels, environmental sustainability) were compared only with US data and not with any data from any of the Asian economies. With the hindsight of the successive events it is almost ironic that the Kok report called for the deregulation of business and financial services activity to allow them to take greater risks. In the report the High Level Group was unequivocal in its belief that existing lending practices to businesses and private consumers in the EU were to cautious when compared with the practices in the US. The report consequently called for the enhancement of the Commission's Financial Services Action Plan towards ensuring 'more access to credit on more competitive terms' for businesses and consumers. The flexible housing market in the US which allowed consumers to gain even larger mortgages for house purchases swiftly was taken as a prime example for stimulating economic growth:

> In particular, reducing restrictions on refinancing mortgage debt and offering improved possibilities to finance a larger proportion of the purchase price of property via more generous and cheaper mortgage loans could extend home-ownership and also boost consumption . . .
>
> More flexible housing markets would encourage labour mobility and the development and efficiency of the financial services sector, empower home-buyers and support more consumer spending (Ibid.: 26–27).

In the subsequent revision of the Lisbon Strategy in early 2005 the Barroso Commission strongly advocated adopting the laissez-faire approach towards regulation which successive US governments had maintained since the 1980s. Backed up by expert advice the Commission argued that growth in many European economies was hampered by a culture of red tape and unnecessary government interference: 'The cumulated burden of regulation, difficult market access and insufficient competitive pressure can hold back innovation in sectors that have a high growth potential' (European Commission 2005: 20). The sector which the Commission considered to have high growth potential was services, especially financial services. Under the Commission's Financial Services Action Plan, which was adopted in 1999, a number of expert groups were commissioned to make recommendations on how to speed up the integration of the financial services sector. One of them was the committee led by Alexander Lamfalussy, an economic adviser and the former President of the European Monetary Institute. The Lamfalussy Committee issued its recommendations for the revision of the regulation of European security markets in November 2000 and they were subsequently adopted for the EU Commission's Financial Services Action Plan in March 2001. The report of the Lamfalussy Committee recommended adopting an approach that eliminated any obstacle which 'in practice impede cross-border securities transactions' (European Commission 2000: 29–30). The report generally favoured self-regulation for financial markets but acknowledged that it would be unlikely to find a political consensus amongst member states to support such an approach. It therefore recommended to orientate EU legislation in this area towards facilitating market operations, 'so as to meet the expectations of dealers and brokers, issuers and investors who wish to be able to deal with one another throughout the EU in an effective, entirely secure and informed manner' (Ibid.).

The laissez-faire approach which the Barroso Commission promoted essentially led to a situation where the highly integrated banking industry was predominantly supervised at the national level rather than by an effective pan-European regulatory framework. In response to the Lamfalussy proposals the EU created a number of supranational bodies which were supposed to support the coordination of national supervisory practices in the financial sector on the basis of information exchange. These bodies (the Banking Supervision Committee within the European Central Bank (ECB) and EU committees to supervise the banking, securities, and insurance and pensions sectors) were essentially operating under the OMC, which meant that they had no binding powers to force member state regulators into compliance. Like in other sectors the weakness of the OMC became obvious in the fact that the voluntary soft coordinative approach allowed the continuing existence of stark differences in regulatory practices between member states, in spite of a substantial increase in cross-border financial services activities. In its assessment of the crisis in the European banking sector, the Organisation for Economic Co-operation and Development (OECD) economics department came to the conclusion that the EU had failed to implement an effective supervisory mechanism: 'The decentralised European supervisory architecture was not sufficiently effective in supervising large cross-border institutions. When the financial crisis hit, the coordination of cross-border rescues proved problematic and complicated efficient resolution' (OECD 2010: 2).

The crisis had shown that this loose regulatory framework which allowed the persistence of substantial differences in national regulatory practises was completely overburdened. It hence failed to avoid a situation where national regulators in a number of countries, most prominently Iceland, Ireland and Southern Europe, had failed to disclose the true state of their national banking systems. The core flaw in the system was that it allowed both national regulators and supranational supervisors to adopt an approach where the application of the established rules by individual banks and financial institutions were deemed to be sufficient. The evolvement of risky lending practices in the sector as a whole were largely ignored, which allowed financial institutions to shift risk around rather than to eliminate it. The basis for this was the adoption of the principle of self-regulation for the sector as a whole which the Lamfalussy Group had advocated. It led to a situation where 'the importance of aggregate risks and overall stability were not attributed the attention they deserved' (Verhelst 2011: 11). This opened the path for the establishment of an US-style regulatory system for the financial industry in the EU and reckless lending practices in some countries. As Posner and Véron point out, the EU simply adopted what was considered to be best practice on regulatory standards but which essentially boiled down to the laissez-faire regulatory practises which were adopted in liberal market economies such as the US and the UK (Posner and Véron 2010: 404).

The adoption of the OMC in core policy areas, where member states resisted the transfer of national sovereignty at the EU level, at first seemed like a practical solution to achieve a gradual convergence of standards and policy outcomes. By adopting an approach where member states essentially are left fully in charge of developing their own national policy solutions but at the same time encouraged to adopt elements of best practice from others, it was hoped that a higher level of policy coordination in relation to outcomes could be achieved. The rather technical target-based approach of the OMC was an attempt to deepen the unity of the Single Market whilst allowing member states to maintain the diversity of their national policy approaches. This was particularly important for policy areas which were considered to affect the core characteristics of national social models, such as employment, welfare, education and training. In practice the OMC was even adopted in areas which should clearly have been governed by binding regulation, such as the supervision of the financial industry and the eurozone Stability and Growth Pact (SGP). Particularly the latter failed in its purpose to become a binding pact for fiscal prudence and instead clearly turned out to be more of a soft gentleman's agreement where individual member state governments could negotiate exceptions and delays directly with the Commission.

It is debatable whether the OMC was the only viable approach the EU could have adopted under circumstances in which member states insisted on maintaining the subsidiary principle in the area of social policy (Borrás and Jacobsson 2004: 190). Since the implementation of the Maastricht Treaty in 1993 member states have definitely shown little enthusiasm for further integrative steps. After the long and controversial ratification of the Maastricht Treaty in many member states there was little desire to create new common policies or institutions, especially not in social policy areas. This became obvious during the negotiations at the intergovernmental summit in Amsterdam in May 1997. Here the French Socialist government under Prime Minister Lionel Jospin attempted to enhance the planned SGP for the eurozone with an integrated and jointly funded EU employment policy. This was not only rejected by the newly elected British Labour Prime Minister Tony Blair but also brushed aside by German Chancellor Helmut Kohl. Kohl, who usually supported French proposals for the deepening of political integration, publicly rejected the Jospin proposals at a press conference which followed a Franco-German summit consultation on 13 June 1997. The Amsterdam summit consequently marked the surfacing of increasing disagreements between French and German elites on the future of the EU. Moreover, with the launch of the European Employment Strategy (EES) the summit also set the path for the OMC, a policy mechanism which represented a lowest common denominator compromise between the leading member states France, Germany and the UK. The EES initiated a new form of governance in the EU which noticeably differed from the classic Community method of pooling sovereignty. The EES allows member state governments to develop their own tailored national policy solutions but aspires to commit them to a policy learning cycle based on the need to develop national reform programmes which explain how member states are expected to meet the targets which are set out under the general employment guidelines. Following the introduction of the EES in 1997, member states decided to implement its core principles in the Lisbon Reform Strategy which was adopted for the Single Market in 2000. The original Lisbon Strategy consisted of a mix of policy targets for member states. The main emphasis was put on stimulating growth through simpler national regulatory frameworks for businesses, services and the financial industries. The strategy also highlighted the need to reform national labour markets by introducing the concept of a 'knowledge economy', based on active labour market policies, investment in education and training as well as lifelong learning strategies with the aim of reducing poverty and social exclusion. Some argue that the original Lisbon Strategy differed from its revised successors in that it still reflected a compromise between centre-left political governments, whose ambitions were to strengthen public investment in education and training, and those on the centre-right who above all favoured the flexibilisation of labour markets (Hix and Hoyland 2011: 202). While it is certainly legitimate to make such a distinction I would argue that the political divide in the EU at the time of the March 2000 Lisbon Summit was too unbalanced to have warranted a genuine balance between reformists and traditionalists. Amongst the five largest member states of the EU-15 (UK, France, Germany, Italy and Spain) only the French Socialist government under Lionel Jospin favoured a more traditional leftist activist social policy. The other four large EU countries were all represented by reformist governments, three of them centre-left (the UK, Germany and Italy) and one centre-right (Spain). They were all united in advocating substantial welfare reforms in European economies on the basis of the introduction of welfare-to-work strategies. This was reflected by the ideas of the British Prime Minister Tony Blair and the German Chancellor Gerhard Schröder that were put forward in their joint position paper published in June 1999. Blair and Schröder suggested a way forward for Europe's Social Democratic Parties by advocating a 'Third Way' middle-of-the-road economic policy philosophy between the neoliberal laissez-faire and traditional leftist Keynesian interventionist approaches. A central demand of the paper was the need to reform welfare systems in Europe to favour personal responsibility, entrepreneurial spirit and a sense of community which, as it was claimed, had in the past been neglected by the desire to ensure universal security for citizens (Blair and Schröder 1999).

In the run-up to the Lisbon summit these ideas were highlighted once again in a joint paper by Blair and the Italian Prime Minister Massimo D'Alema, a former Communist and converted reformist Social Democrat. Both Blair and D'Alema called for greater incentives for the unemployed to take up work by reducing passive welfare benefits. The French Prime Minister Jospin therefore faced a front of reformist governments who favoured labour market flexibilisation and welfare state reform with the aim of instilling greater individual responsibility. This explains why Lisbon made no mention of the need to establish common social standards but rather calls for the fundamental modernisation of the European social model. Jospin cast a lonely figure in the EU when he emphasised these weaknesses of the Lisbon Strategy in a subsequent speech, in which he outlined his vision for the future of an enlarged Europe. Jospin once again called for the development of a 'European societal program' (Jospin 2001), the purpose of which should be the defence of the European social model against the forces of globalisation:

> Economic cohesion must serve social solidarity . . . Europe cannot be merely a free trade zone . . . A genuine body of European social law, establishing ambitious common standards, must be put in place and there must be a special focus on the provision of information to employees and their involvement in the life of companies, as well as on layoffs, the struggle against job insecurity and wage policies. We must aim for a European social treaty (Ibid.).

The 2000 Lisbon Strategy was fundamentally shaped by the spirit of 'Third Way' economics. The intellectual background to this approach came from prominent sociologist and Blair confidant Antony Giddens. In his seminal work *The Third Way* (1998), Giddens advocated the promotion of personal responsibility and flexibility as the basis for a successful economy in the era of globalisation. His notion of a society of 'responsible risk takers' (Giddens 1998: 100) essentially boiled down to a recalibration of the traditional welfare state, which should no longer support passivity but provide individuals with the means to be actively in control of their lives: 'In the positive welfare society, the contract between individual and government shifts, since autonomy and the development of self – the medium of expanding individual responsibility – become the prime focus' (Giddens 1998: 128).

Lisbon incorporated these ideas by emphasising the need for member states to reform their social security systems from passive towards active and targeted support for people across all age groups. The main goal of the welfare reform was the creation of employment, based on the priority target of a total 70 per cent employment rate for all member states (60 per cent for women). For this purpose the EU suggested to combine the acceleration of market liberalisation, particularly in the areas of services and financial markets, with the transformation of social security and education systems in order for them to reflect the 'knowledge economy' concept. Lisbon established improvements in the accessibility and the quality of education and training as the priority for national social policy. Closely linked to this was the necessity for member states to deregulate their labour markets with the aim of making them more accessible for social groups which tend to show greater levels of inactivity, especially women and older people. The mechanism to achieve this was the implementation of the new policy mechanism which strongly built on the design of the EES. The OMC operates on the basis of setting overall policy performance targets which all EU member states are expected to work towards.

The openness in the method stems from the fact that the OMC does not prescribe uniform policies but encourages member states to develop their own national approaches. The role of the Commission in the OMC lies in monitoring national practices and subsequently promoting best practice policy solutions to member states. The OMC restricts the role of the Commission to that of a supervisor and a promoter of policy learning between member states. In contrast to the area of internal market liberalisation, where the Commission has the mandate to enforce supranational policies at the national level timely and correctly, under the OMC it can only name and shame underperforming member states. It was widely hoped that this soft approach would in the long run become an efficient mechanism to push member states towards achieving the goals they had jointly agreed to pursue in the Lisbon agenda. The OMC seemed to be a practical mechanism for the practical implementation of the subsidiary principle on the basis of the realisation that national welfare state cultures in the EU are characterised by profound differences. The variety of these differences was about to increase with the prospect of the imminent accession of a new group of member states in Southern, Central and Eastern Europe. A more sophisticated approach than simply resorting to the classic community method of deepening integration was therefore needed (Hantrais 2007: 22). The logic of the OMC, as set out in the Lisbon Strategy, was to establish a system where member states would develop their national policies in a process of 'periodic monitoring, evaluation and peer review' (European Council 2000, paragraph 37) with the Commission and other member states. The aim was to establish enough peer pressure to ensure the establishment of a permanent 'mutual learning process' between member states (Ibid.), based on what essentially boils down to a two-level game of policy-making. Büchs (2008) has developed the latter notion in relation to Putnam's concept of two-level politics in international relations (Putnam 1988). She argues that the OMC allows member state governments in the first instance to determine the OMC targets in a particular policy area in a bargaining process with one another and with the Commission (Level 1). This is followed by the implementation stage of the OMC targets on the domestic level (Level 2) which takes place in the context of national political strategy determination between the national governments and organised interests. Member state governments are hence very interested in uploading their policy preferences at the OMC level as this increases the chance that their policy strategies gains domestic support, even if they are initially unpopular (Büchs 2008: 29). This leaves the question if the OMC has managed to establish a genuine openness towards policy learning amongst member states and a commitment to the common targets in individual policy areas.

The widespread consensus seems to be that while the OMC may have encouraged some progress in individual cases, the overall picture shows that it failed to create a genuine spirit of ownership of the targets on the national level. This may partly boil down to the fact that frequently a multiplicity of relatively ambitious targets, like those under the Lisbon 2000 and the current Europe 2020 Strategy, are pursued simultaneously. Most of all however the fact remains that without a mechanism of binding policy implementation, the emergence of a gap between the original commitment of national governments to the targets of and the subsequent tendency to either ignore the targets or implement them selectively at the domestic level, was inevitable. The failure of the EU to ensure the involvement of national stakeholders and institutional veto players in the initial development stage of the policy targets has without doubt contributed to a lack of ownership (Dierx and Ilzkovitz 2006: 41). A number of studies on the individual policy areas operated under the OMC have emphasised the lack of engagement of non-government agents in the process of deliberating targets and also a failure to subject the OMC to a broader public discourse (Benz 2007; Büchs 2007; De la Porte and Nanz 2004; Rhodes 2010). Benz probably summarises the weakness of the OMC in this respect best when he points out that in practice the strategy has shown a tendency to operate as a an elitist mode of governance. It is hence dominated by government elites and small circles of experts without a genuine consideration for national parliaments and the wider interests of civil society (Benz 2007: 507). In her very detailed analysis of the OMC Büchs has shown that its acceptance in the domestic context has been mixed, depending on the circumstances in each national case.

By comparing the cases of the UK and Germany under Blair and Schröder, Büchs emphasises that the OMC targets did not play a significant part in the domestic policy discussions. At the same time the Blair's New Labour government tended to emphasise the influence it had on shaping the OMC targets on the basis of its good record in stimulating growth and creating jobs at home. This focus on the ability to upload national preferences stood in stark contrast to the Schröder government's approach in Germany. While the OMC played only a minor role in the domestic discussion on the reform of its labour market and welfare state in the early 2000s, the red–green coalition under Schröder used the OMC targets under Lisbon predominantly to advocate the downloading of policy principles (Büchs 2007: 90). The OMC was therefore to some degree supportive in the overall ambition to achieve domestic consensus in Germany on the implementation of New Labour's welfare-to-work principle (Funk 2007: 132), which was advocated as a necessary process of policy learning from best practice in another member state.

However the overall progress in achieving the targets that had been set out in the Lisbon 2000 Strategy varied greatly between member states and both Lisbon and the OMC seemed to have played only a minor role in determining the shape of national policy reforms. This was highlighted by the evaluation of the strategy in the 2004 Kok report which essentially blamed an overburdening of targets in the original Lisbon Strategy on the lack of progress. According to Kok and his group of experts the major flaw of the strategy lay in the perception amongst member states that it lacked a clear focus on what should be achieved and who would be responsible for the implementation. This was clearly a subtle criticism of the OMC mechanism, where 'everybody is responsible and thus no one' (European Commission 2004: 16). In this respect the report openly criticised the Commission for failing to implement an effective 'naming and shaming' regime against member states who failed to achieve the Lisbon targets (Ibid.: 17). It also pointed the finger at the widespread gap between commitment and implementation where member state governments essentially failed to implement the Single Market policies they had agreed on in Council meetings. The Kok report emphasised that this applied both to binding Single Market directives and to the coordinative targets which were determined under the OMC (Ibid.: 24).The report set the tone for the changes which would be implemented following the spring 2005 EU Summit under the guidance of the new Commission President Barroso. Kok and his group of experts had already recommended that the Commission should work towards a streamlining of the overall Lisbon targets in order to ensure that member state governments would finally engage in the process of mutual performance benchmarking. The High Level Group also called for the implementation of an effective peer pressure mechanism to ensure national compliance with policy targets. For this purpose the group recommended greater engagement with national parliaments and the general public in member states (Ibid.: 43).

The newly appointed Commission President Barroso followed up the recommendations of the Kok report by recalibrating the Lisbon Strategy towards a new emphasis on stimulating GDP growth and job creation in the member states. The revision of the Lisbon Strategy, which he initiated in February 2005, was consequently branded as 'putting jobs and growth centre stage' (European Commission 2005: 12). The revised strategy also drew conclusions from the apparent failure of the OMC to cause national governments to work towards the Lisbon targets. It hence introduced a

Lisbon Action Plan with the need for member states to develop their own national action plans. These would be based on integrated guidelines for member states on macroeconomic, employment and structural reform policies and were supposed to emerge in a dialogue between policy-makers, stakeholders and citizens on the domestic level.

The rather narrow refocusing of the Lisbon Strategy towards growth and job creation emerged on the background of the appointment of the Commission President Barroso who had appeared as reformist candidate for the post. He was strongly backed by Tony Blair and Bertie Ahern, the Prime Ministers of the UK and Ireland, against the wishes of the French and the German governments. Paris and Berlin would have preferred the Belgian Guy Verhofstadt to take up the job of president. Blair's chief of staff Jonathan Powell in retrospect explains the appointment of Barroso as the result of the Blair administration's relative influence and ability to form alliances with other member states against Franco-German interests (*The Guardian* 2013). Consequently two senior members of the British and Irish governments secured high profile positions in Barroso's first Commission. Barroso appointed Tony Blair's former senior spin doctor Peter Mandelson as Commissioner for Trade and Charlie McCreevy, the former Finance Minister in Bertie Ahern's government, as Commissioner for the Internal Market and Services. Like Barroso's appointment itself, his decision to give these two key portfolios to two senior figures of the British and the Irish governments showed the level of influence both countries had acquired since the late 1990s on the basis of their record levels of growth and job creation. Peter Mandelson went as far as to claim that the relaunch of the Lisbon Strategy was 'a programme that we would describe as New Labour' (*The Guardian* 2005). This was an unusual intervention to make for a newly appointed member of the Commission, a role in which he was supposed to promote a collective rather than national point of view. The appointment of Barroso as Commission President and the composition of his first college of Commissioners reflected the changed political reality which had occurred since the original Lisbon Strategy had been adopted in 2000. Since the replacement of the Socialist Lionel Jospin with the centre-right UMP politician Jean-Pierre Raffarin as Prime Minister in France in 2002, all of the five largest EU member states were governed by reformist leaders. The Lisbon relaunch favoured by Barroso was hence backed by a reformist alliance between Blair in the UK, Schröder in Germany, Jean-Pierre Raffarin in France, Silvio Berlusconi in Italy and José María Aznar in Spain. All these leaders were in favour of the EU promoting a strategy of active labour market policies, based on targeted investment in education and training, and replacing welfare dependency with greater individual responsibility. This paved the way for the EU's adoption of the 'flexicurity' strategy in 2007. The concept aspires to combine greater labour market flexibility with enhanced levels of individual responsibility. The approach emerged on the basis of the successes in Scandinavian economies with job creation through a combination of labour market flexibility, active labour market policy and reduction of out-of-work income replacement rates. In economies such as Denmark and Sweden, the security for employees is also further enhanced by wage replacement rates which are above the EU average (Funk 2009: 558) and generous welfare support for those who are in work through widespread access to public childcare and opportunities for further education and training. The latter was emphasised by the EU Commission in its 2007 outline of the principles of the 'flexicurity' concept as part of the need for national governments to pursue 'comprehensive lifelong learning strategies' with the purpose of equipping employees for a rapidly changing labour market in the era of globalisation. The Commission documents argued that access to continuous education and training opportunities for workers throughout their whole employment lifecycle would benefit particularly those groups which tend to be at least temporarily excluded from the labour market (the low-skilled, temporary staff, older workers and the self-employed). It would also be an effective means to increase active labour market participation and reduce long-term unemployment benefit dependency (European Commission 2007a: 12–13). With the adoption of the 'flexicurity' principle as part of the EES the Commission started to move beyond the narrow approach it had adopted under the 2005 Lisbon Strategy, where it essentially favoured job creation without a major consideration for the level of renumeration or the quality of the work that is offered. At the time Barroso had spoken of Lisbon as a means to 'climb the productivity ladder and guarantee that overall our productivity grows quickly' (European Commission 2005: 13). This was fully in line with the strategy's overall ideology which favoured growth and job creation as an effective means against poverty and social exclusion.

The new emphasis on the quality of work emerged from the results of a widespread public consultation on the Lisbon Strategy, which the Commission had initiated in 2006. During the consultation the Commission assembled opinions on the Single Market agenda in hearings with the general public and stakeholders. The outcome of the public review of the Single Market agenda led the Commission to emphasise the need to acknowledge the social and environmental impact of the market liberalisation agenda to a greater extent (European Commission 2007b: 3). The resulting new 'Social Agenda' which the Commission introduced in the midst of the financial crisis and the emerging crisis in the eurozone addressed the issue which particularly many trade unions had urged it to consider: the extent to which work can be a remedy against social exclusion and for lifting people out of poverty. In the 2008 Social Agenda the Commission accepted that 'even employment is not a guarantee against poverty' and acknowledged that the number of people who were registered as employed but nevertheless classified being at the risk of poverty had increased across member states. The Commission therefore vowed to take a closer look at developing measures to 'making work pay' (European Commission 2008: 12). This was in essence an acknowledgement of the imbalance in the 'flexicurity' approach when it came to combining labour market deregulation with effective measures to ensure good working conditions and living wages for workers across the EU (Büchs 2007: 93).

The Social Agenda was nevertheless still strongly centred around the core principles of 'flexicurity' and the OMC policy mechanism. The Commission did not refrain from praising the OMC as an effective mechanism to implement policy change in the member states. At the same time it now started to recognise the need to develop a 'smarter mix' of policy tools which should especially address the weaknesses in the coordination of economic and budgetary policies (Ibid.: 15).

Member states had shown limited commitment to the Lisbon targets before the crisis, something which was partially acknowledged by the Social Agenda. The Commission hence announced that a revised strategy after 2010 could introduce more ambitious targets than previously to ensure that member states would speed up their reform efforts (Ibid.: 16). This stood in stark contrast to the conclusions Barroso seemed to have drawn from the failures of the original Lisbon Strategy to convince member states to work towards its targets. On the occasion of the 2005 relaunch of the Strategy, Barroso criticised the Strategy for having represented an 'overburdened list of policy objectives' (European Commission 2005: 7). The Barroso Commission subsequently has been wavering between attempts to simplify the Lisbon Strategy by refocusing it on stimulating growth and job creation, as it did during the 2005 relaunch, and more recent attempts to commit member states to an ever more ambitious set of policy targets under Europe 2020.

2.2 'BETTER REGULATION': LESSONS DRAWN FROM THE GLOBAL FINANCIAL CRISIS

The 2008–2009 global financial crisis caught the EU by surprise and came at a time when it was hoping to consolidate the progress that had been made since the 2005 revision of the Lisbon Strategy. The crisis forced the Commission to reassess its regulatory approach and to overhaul the Lisbon Strategy once again. In its 2010 reassessment of the Lisbon

Strategy the Commission acknowledged that the Single Market policy framework was not sufficiently focused on identifying and preventing crisis symptoms in national economies. The core elements of the Washington consensus, which had been considered as supportive in accelerating economic growth and job creation in the member states was now identified as the Single Market's main weakness:

> With the benefit of hindsight, it is clear that the strategy should have been organised better to focus more on critical elements which played a key role in origin of the crisis, such as robust supervision and systemic risk in financial markets, speculative bubbles (e.g. in housing markets), and credit-driven consumerism which in some member states, combined with wage increases outpacing productivity gains, fuelled high current account deficits (European Commission 2010a: 4).

The Commission refused calls for the introduction of more regulation across the board. Instead it concentrated on the implementation of what it calls a 'smart regulation agenda' (European Commission 2010b: 19). The aim was to introduce a greater degree of flexibility and diversity in the EU regulatory framework by for example moving away from the tendency to steer internal market liberalisation predominantly through policy directives. The gravity of the 2008–2009 global financial crisis warranted expectations that governments across the EU would be inclined to give up more of their sovereignty for the purpose of introducing a more effective collective regulatory framework for the financial industry. The actual political lessons drawn from the global crisis however turned out to be quite different from these expectations.

Even under severe economic crisis conditions in many member states the governments failed to reach a wide-ranging consensus on creating binding regulatory measures for the banking and financial services sectors on the EU level. Therefore they were unsuccessful in drawing the adequate lessons from the flaws of the regulatory practices, which had turned out to be too ineffective to prevent the spillover of the subprime loan crisis from the US banking sector towards Europe.

In its 2010 assessment of the reasons for the crisis in the European banking system the OECD came to a damning verdict on the widespread practices of laissez-faire banking regulation in many countries in the EU. The OECD report points out that the pre-crisis regulatory environment in the EU was designed to encourage the expansion of bank credits for both private citizens and businesses on the premise that these would be fundamental for stimulating GDP growth (OECD 2010). Figure 2.1 shows that both the levels of consumer credit and lending for house purchases declined after 2000 but then started to rise sharply again from mid-2003 onwards. By mid-2005 the growth in the lending levels for house purchases had almost returned to the 12 per cent levels of the late 1990s.

The ECB played a major role in this by keeping interest rates in the eurozone low to make borrowing more affordable. It also failed to spot the mismatch between the increasing lending activity and the declining assets of banks in Europe (Barnes et al. 2010: 6). Even when the crisis in the US housing market was already in full force and the risk of a spillover towards Europe should have been obvious, the ECB was still largely in denial about the potential risk. In its December 2007 *Financial Stability Review* the ECB acknowledged that it had contributed to a situation where: 'the relentless rise in household indebtedness witnessed over recent years has left households concerned more vulnerable to income and interest rate shocks, while the concomitant shift in the composition of household wealth towards illiquid housing wealth has left them more vulnerable to house price shocks' (ECB 2007: 76).

At the same time the ECB remained optimistic that 'the strengthening of the net wealth position of households' (Ibid.) could act as a buffer against external shocks emerging from the US and elsewhere. This was illusionary given the lack of proper monitoring of the stability of the financial liquidity of the banking system in many member states.

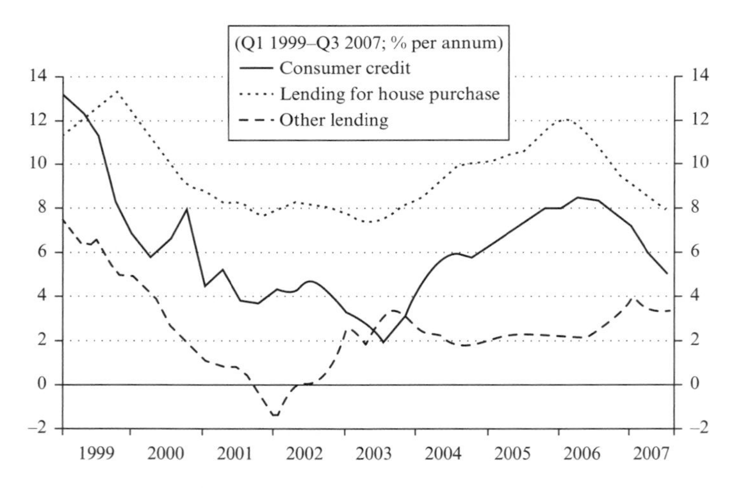

Note: Data are based on financial transactions of MFIs' loans.

Source: ECB (2007).

Figure 2.1 Annual growth in monetary financial institution loans to households in the euro area

The substantial increase of transnational bank lending activities and mergers in the EU in the decade before the crisis took place on the background of a culture where the principle of self-regulation was deemed to be most suitable to enable the swift integration of the financial sector. In the absence of an effective system of macro-level supervision with binding regulatory standards essentially remained at the national level. Substantial discrepancies between national practices and very limited information exchange resulted in a situation where 'in most instances, national supervisors were unable to agree on swift common action or on how to share the burden between the Member States' (Verhelst 2011: 15–16). The failure to accompany the increase in transnational banking activities with proper risk assessment had catastrophic consequences for many banks in the EU, especially within the eurozone. Banks in the eurozone intensified their cross-border lending and merger activities in the period between 2000 and 2006. This period saw the number of mergers doubling and a significant increase in the share of mergers between banks within the eurozone and externally, including with other EU member states (see Figure 2.2).

Banks based in eurozone member states are deemed to have increased their bilateral holdings by around 40 per cent in comparison to those situated

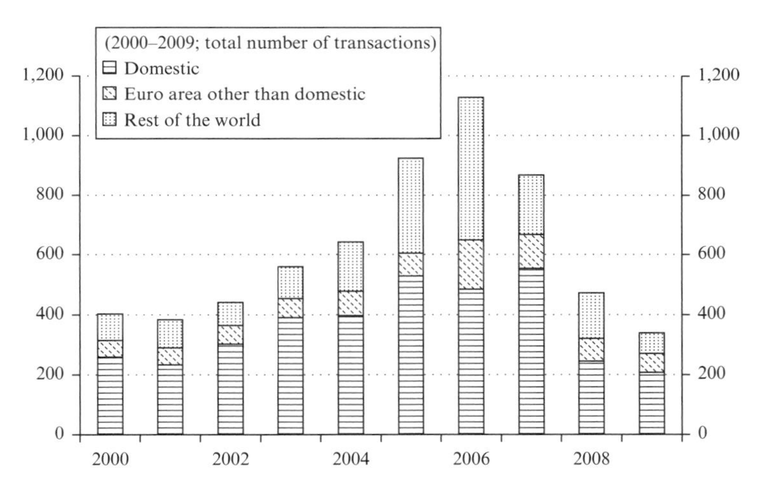

Note: All completed mergers and acquisitions (including international buyouts, joint ventures, management buyout/ins, demergers, minority stakes and share buybacks) where a bank is the acquirer.

Source: ECB (2010a).

Figure 2.2 Number of mergers and acquisitions by euro area banks 2000–2009

outside the Single Currency (Kalemli-Oczan et al. 2010). The Commission's Financial Services Action Plan, which was adopted in 1999, encouraged the focus of banks on cross-border activities. This was part of the ambition to accompany the forthcoming introduction of the single European currency with the development of a Single Financial Market. The action plan categorised the creation of a single wholesale market in the EU as a top priority with the purpose to 'allow investment service providers to offer their services on a cross-border basis without encountering unnecessary hindrances of administrative or legal barriers' (European Commission 1999: 22).

This led to a situation where in selected member states, particularly in those within the eurozone-17, the bulk of public debt was held by non-residential financial institutions, including those from other eurozone/EU countries. Figure 2.3 shows that Portugal, Belgium, Austria, Italy, Ireland and France were particularly vulnerable to external financial instability, with 40 to 60 per cent of their government held by non-residential financial institutions (2009 figures).

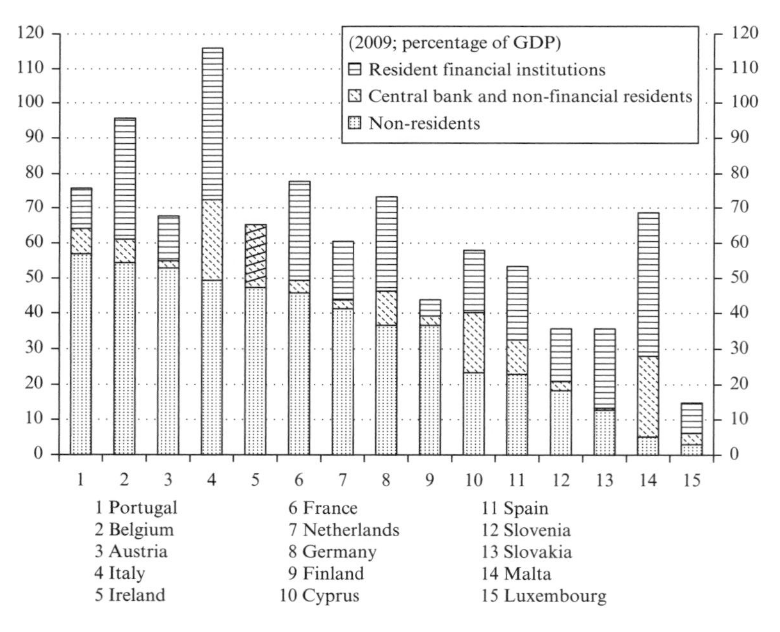

Note: In the case of Greece, data were not available at the cut-off date of this FSR. In the case of Ireland, only the breakdown of the debt by resident and non-resident was available.

Source: ECB (2010b).

Figure 2.3 Government debt in euro area countries by holder

In the case of Ireland, Italy and Portugal this vulnerability had manifested itself in a significant decline of their budgetary position during the financial crisis as a result of a sudden contraction in cross-border capital flows for banks.

The OECD criticised the EU's pre-crisis regulatory framework for having (a) permitted a weak system of corporate governance, (b) tolerated shady banking practices with an overreliance on unsubstantiated funds such as hedge and private equity and (c) allowed banks to rely on predominantly broker-dealer networks (OECD 2010: 16). The overall result was the increase in the risk banks took in their lending operations with the gap between their lending activities and their capital becoming ever wider. In the eurozone this manifested itself in a peak of the funding gap between lending to private consumers and the deposits the lending institution has acquired. Between 2005 and 2008 the funding gap more than doubled from around 6 per cent to 13 per cent which resulted in an increasing dependence of banks on the financial markets or other credit institutions (Figure 2.4).

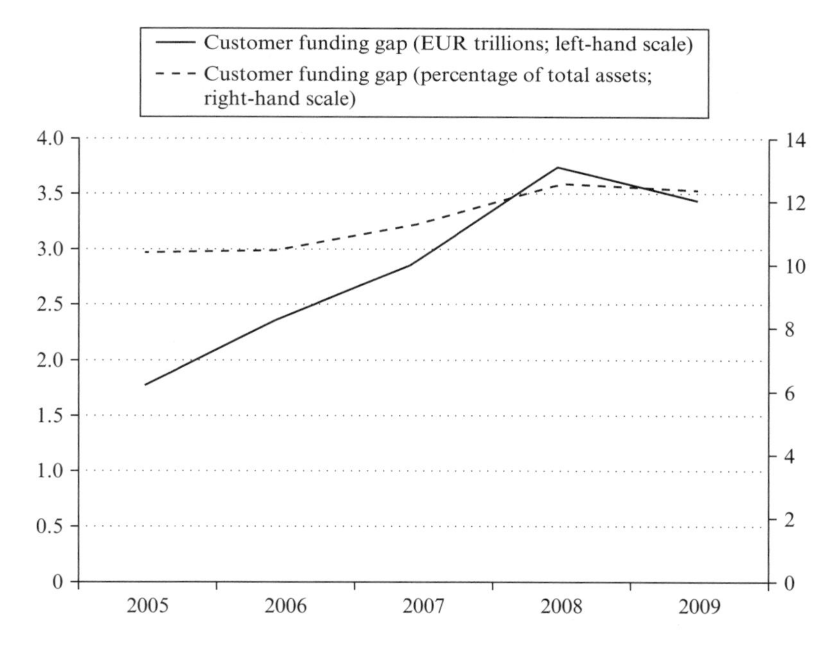

Note: Sample of euro area banks that participated in the EU-wide stress-test exercise.

Source: ECB (2010a).

Figure 2.4 Evolution of euro area banks' customer funding gaps

Before the crisis the EU had much faith in the way financial services were organised in the US. Backed by the proposals of the Lamfalussy Group of experts in 2000, the EU therefore promoted the model for an integrated EU Single Financial Market, which was modelled along the lines of the regulatory practices which existed in the US. The lack of coordination of national supervisory practices in the EU permitted a situation where banks could get away with having relatively little liquidity buffers and instead relied predominantly on external capital flows. When these started to dry up and the shortfall could not be met due to a lack of their own funds, banks across Europe started to face severe liquidity problems. Without government intervention to recapitalise banks with sudden severe liquidity problems substantial parts of the banking industry in countries such as Ireland, the UK, Portugal, Spain and Greece would have faced almost certain collapse with severe ripple effects for the finances of individuals, companies and national economies. British Prime Minister Gordon Brown was the first EU leader to realise the severity of the situation in 2008 and therefore advocated a concerted effort of European leaders to recapitalise their banking systems with public money: 'We were facing a situation that risked to become worse than 1929 . . . People were panicking, asking which would be the next bank to collapse. The financial system was looking over an abyss' (Brown 2010: 59).

The UK was in a relatively robust budgetary position before its banking industry was hit by the fallout of the subprime loan crisis in the US. The Brown government was therefore able to recapitalise British banks with liquidity problems from public funds without external support, even though this subsequently significantly worsened the UK's budgetary position. Other countries in the EU were dependent on external help and received joint loans provided by the International Monetary Fund (IMF) and the EU.

For this purpose in October 2010 the eurozone government leaders founded the European Financial Stability Facility (EFSF). The EFSF was supposed to be a temporary loan facility which would support countries that had been affected by a sovereign debt crisis, particularly those countries whose finances were stretched as a result of the efforts to recapitalise their banking system. The EFSF came about against the resistance of a hesitant Germany under the leadership of Angela Merkel. Merkel initially reacted cautiously to French plans to respond to the emerging crisis in the eurozone with the institutionalisation of financial support (Dyson 2012: 194).

When the budgetary situation in Greece and Ireland reached crisis point in the course of 2010, Merkel was finally pushed by Sarkozy to offer the two countries concerted loans. The initial Greek Loan Facility in May

2010 of €80 billion was operated on a bilateral basis and jointly executed with the IMF, which offered an additional €30 billion. Ireland was actually the first country to receive loans under the EFSF from January 2011 (€85 billion loan facility in total), followed by Portugal in April 2011 (€78 billion) and Greece in February 2012 (€172 billion). The Irish loan was based on a €17.7 billion contribution from the EFSF, including an additional €22.5 billion of collective EU support under the European Financial Stabilisation Mechanism (EFSM) and €4.8 billion in bilateral loans from Denmark, Sweden and the UK, with an overall interest rate of 5.9 per cent. In the case of Portugal, the EFSF contributions amounted to €26 billion with an additional €26 from the EFSM and an interest rate of 6.08 per cent. Greece received a second programme of support under the EFSF which was agreed in February 2012. Greece now had a total of €172.6 billion allocated until February 2013, with €109 billion of support coming from the EFSF, based on an interest rate of a maximum of 5.5 per cent. As for Ireland and Portugal, the Greek Loan Facility is paid out in instalments. Each of the instalments depends on the satisfactory implementation of the reform conditions the EU has imposed on the receiving member state.

The programme is supported by the IMF and the EU has largely adopted the IMF focus on budgetary austerity. For all three EFSF receiving countries the loan programme therefore came with the demand to impose a rigid structural austerity programme, with both the EU and IMF rigorously monitoring the domestic reform processes. The programmes for Ireland and Portugal asked for the correction of the excessive deficit by 2015 and 2013 respectively. In the Irish case the immediate purpose of the loan package was to ensure the stabilisation of the Irish banking system through a strategy of recapitalisation and restructuring. For all three countries the loan facilities were linked to demands to fundamentally reform domestic labour markets and welfare systems, combined with the obligation to implement a drastic austerity programme in the public sector.

The overall guaranteed commitments from participating member states of the EFSF were set at €780 billion with an actual lending capacity of €440 billion. The EFSF uses the capital to issue bonds on the security markets with the purpose of raising the funds which are necessary to provide loans to member states with budgetary problems. The largest share in contributions comes from Germany (29 per cent), France (21 per cent) and surprisingly also from Italy (19 per cent) and Spain (12 per cent), in spite of the fact the latter two countries are themselves in severe budgetary difficulties.

This shows that the purpose of the EFSF was to install a spirit of fiscal solidarity amongst eurozone countries. Although particularly Germany refuses accept the notion of a transfer union in the eurozone, the fact remains that the EFSF has provided loans to countries which are unlikely to be able to meet the conditions for fiscal adjustment and repayment in the long run. This applies particularly to Greece which is sinking ever deeper into a vicious cycle of negative growth, rising unemployment and deepening budgetary woes.

Although the EFSF was conceived as a temporary facility it will only close down once all the outstanding loans it has issued have been repaid by the debtor countries (EFSF 2013: 4). Its successor, the European Stability Mechanism (ESM), was established in July 2011 with the intention of replacing the temporary EFSF by 2013. As eurozone governments realised that more countries would require financial assistance, the ESM came into force earlier than anticipated. After a round of ratifications the ESM has been operational since October 2012 and has already issued €1.8 billion to Spain, which was the next country with an emerging crisis in its banking sector. The overall lending capacity of the ESM is currently set at €500 billion with ongoing discussions between member states about the need to increase this further. The current joint lending capacity of the EFSF and ESM is €700 billion but it is clear that this is unlikely to be sufficient to meet the expected capital needs in the eurozone. With Ireland, Greece and Cyprus likely to require further financial support in the near future and possible upcoming requests from Italy and Slovenia, a number of member states have asked for an increase of the ESM lending capacity. This has so far been blocked by the German government who argues that the countries in question need to make more efforts to cut spending and to increase their tax revenues. The German Finance Minister Wolfgang Schäuble was supported by his Dutch and Finnish colleagues in demanding that financial support for troubled banks in individual member states should be strictly linked to stronger concerted efforts to introduce a mechanism of banking supervision (Kanter 2012). This resulted in the decision of the EU Summit in Brussels in December 2012 to create a banking union for the eurozone by early 2014. The banking union will be based on granting the ECB direct supervisory powers over banks in the eurozone. Meanwhile the political wrangling over the details of the new supervisory framework has intensified. Germany and some of the Northern European economies refuse to agree to the creation of a common resolution fund, which would take away the responsibility to administer failed banks from national governments and effectively communalise the problem (O'Donnel and Kuehnen 2013).

The ESM itself has already started to issue its first funding programmes, with a total of €5.6 billion allocated to Ireland, €4.5 billion to Portugal and €16.5 billion to Greece for 2013 (EFSF/ESM 2012: 2). The ESM has also started to distribute money to the Spanish government for the purpose of assisting it in the recapitalisation of its banks. Under the EFSF and the ESM a total of €100 billion was committed to Spain in support of its banking sector but the country has only received €41.3 billion and exited the programme in December 2013. This has been paid in instalments since December 2012, with the latest two issued by the ESM (€39.4 billion in December 2012 and €1.865 billion in February 2013).

The ESM establishes a much more institutionalised mechanism for assisting countries in financial difficulties. Due to its reliance on national contributions, the ESM is classified as an 'intergovernmental organisation' which the EU envisages as a permanent crisis resolution body for the eurozone within its institutional setting (ESM 2013a). The ESM has a Board of Governors which consists of the eurozone country finance ministers, which decide by unanimity on the extent and the conditions for loans which are given to eurozone countries (including a provision for an emergency loan procedure which is decided by QMV). The ESM is generally limited to eurozone countries but remains open to new members. This however has to be approved by a qualified majority of the Governors. The Board of Governors is also supported by a Board of Directors from each of the participating countries and a Managing Director who is responsible for the day-to-day operation of the organisation. The capital subscription of participating in the ESM is based on the individual size of member states and overall GDP capacity, which explains why Germany (€190 billion) and France (€142 billion) are the largest shareholders in the ESM, surprisingly followed by crisis country Italy (€125 billion). The ESM is supposed to represent a new framework for reinforced economic surveillance and for this purpose a close coordination with the supervision of national budgetary and macroeconomic policies under the European Semester and the EU Fiscal Compact is intended. The ESM generally is more fine-tuned when it comes to addressing the root of the problem of a country which is seeking financial assistance. It differentiates between the purpose of the loans provided for a country and categorises the ESM support instruments into the following sections: bank recapitalisations, precautionary financial assistance, primary market and secondary market support facility. Each of the support instruments are subject to different conditions. Funds for the recapitalisation of national banks are mainly dependent on the proof of national governments that they are unable to finance the recapitalisation from other domestic sources. Moreover, a crucial condition is that 'the financial institution(s) concerned should be of systemic relevance or pose a serious threat to the financial stability of the euro area as a whole or of its member states' (ESM 2013a: 13). If the plans for the Eurozone Banking Union are finalised as intended it is likely that the ESM will be able to provide financial assistance directly to banks which are in crisis rather than to the government in the member state where they are situated. The ESM also offers help to countries which are not in immediate need for financial support but are implementing macroeconomic policy reforms which are aimed at preventing the emergence of a crisis. The precautionary financial assistance instrument offers eurozone countries financial support for the purpose of achieving one of the main goals of the Europe 2020 strategy: to maintain sustainable economic growth and avoid situations of boom and bust. The precautionary financial assistance falls into two categories: the precautionary conditioned credit line (PCCL) for countries without any major economic or budgetary problems who can also show evidence that this is the case and the enhanced conditions credit line (ECCL) for those who are not able to provide evidence of stability in all areas of their economy. Finally, the ESM is also able to support countries with their purchases of bonds in the primary security market and the stabilisation of their position in the secondary security markets. The primary and secondary market support facilities are hence mainly orientated towards stabilising the position of eurozone countries on the security markets and to avoid a situation where consolidation measures of member states are undermined further by the downgrading of a country's position by a credit rating agency.

As a long-term institutionalised loan facility for the eurozone, the ESM is essentially aimed at ensuring that the reform targets for crisis economies are not exclusively determined by the IMF but predominantly collectively amongst eurozone members. Loan facilities issued by the ESM are nevertheless strictly conditional and linked to the implementation of rigid budgetary and macroeconomic reforms in the receiving countries. Most importantly, in all cases ESM loans are subject to the receiving country demonstrating the ability to be able to pay it back eventually, even if the agreed timeframe for reimbursement may change. In this respect the ESM takes a much more rigid approach than the EFSF and foresees the possibility to change the conditions of a loan if a country is unable to meet the terms of the initial agreement. This can either be by increasing the rate of interest for the loan or by revising the attached reform programme (European Council 2012, Article 25, paragraph 2: 40).

In order to avoid such problems the ESM insists that countries that are offered a loan are able to show a 'sound fiscal and macroeconomic policy record' (ESM 2013a: 13). It is at this point where the new mechanisms of macroeconomic and budgetary surveillance under the Europe 2020 and the Fiscal Compact, which are outlined in detail in Chapter 3 of this book, become crucial for the functioning of the ESM. The ESM is hence a piece in the wider jigsaw of the emerging deeper political and economic cooperation in the eurozone and goes beyond simply acting as a permanent institutionalised loan facility.

Especially the German government insisted on linking the ESM loan mechanisms with detailed rules for domestic consolidation efforts of economies. German Finance Minister Schäuble emphasised the conditionality of financial support under the ESM in his speech to parliament on the occasion of the introduction of the 2013 German federal budget:

> In any case it is crucial that without fundamental reforms, negotiated with the three institutions, the International Monetary Fund, the European Central Bank and the EU Commission, and rigidly monitored by them, what we call 'Troika', nothing will happen in the member states. This is called conditionality. This conditionality is an indispensable precondition for each European support programme (Schäuble 2013).

Schäuble himself was on the one hand keen to establish the ESM in order to avoid a situation where eurozone countries would have to rely exclusively on financial support from the IMF. On the other hand the ESM treaty emphasises that the institution will work in close cooperation with the IMF, not just in terms of seeking financial support but also with regard to the determination of national reform conditions. Applicant countries are also expected to make a separate application to the IMF for additional support when submitting a bid to the ESM (European Council 2012: 5).

Cyprus, who only joined the eurozone in 2008, is the latest member state with a sovereign debt crisis which was allocated a maximum of €9 billion in financial support from the ESM, with an additional €1 billion from the IMF. The conditions for the loan are a fundamental restructuring of the banking sector in Cyprus and also an unprecedented restriction on the movement of capital to prevent the massive withdrawal of funds which are held by foreign investors from the country (ESM 2013b: 4). The ESM agreement with Cyprus also contains the controversial decision to make citizens living in the country partly liable by imposing a punitive levy on individual savings. Originally Germany had intended to introduce a levy of 6.75 per cent on all savings in Cyprus of up to €100,000. This was subsequently vetoed by the Cypriot parliament and the subsequent compromise deal makes savings under €100,000 exempt from any levy. Instead any savings above this limit are subject to the payment of a 37.5 per cent tax (*SPIEGEL* online 2013). The Cyprus example illustrates to what extent the regulatory influence of EU institutions has been strengthened inside the eurozone. The ESM argues that the temporary restriction of the free movement of capital, which limited the withdrawal of cash for bank customers to €100, was essential in order to ensure the stability of the banking sector and the financial markets in Cyprus. It also emphasises that imposition of limits to the free movement of capital, which are permitted under EU law, should generally only be applied 'in exceptional circumstances and under strict conditions on the grounds of public policy or public security' (ESM 2013b: 4). In practice eurozone countries with sovereign debt problems, who seek financial assistance from the ESM and the IMF, are nevertheless de facto subjected to an external financial regulation regime, which is jointly exercised by the ESM, the ECB and the European Commission. This can go as far as in the case of Greece and Italy, where the external political pressure for the instalment of unelected technocratic governments became a precondition for the consideration of financial support.

The regulatory framework for the financial industry in the wider Single Market remains weak even after the changes that were introduced in response to the sovereign debt crisis. In 2009 the European Commission developed a new financial supervisory framework for the EU in response to the obvious weaknesses in the existing supervisory architecture. The Financial Supervision Package which came into effect in January 2011, after it was approved by the European Parliament and the European Council, essentially leaves the bulk of the supervisory responsibility with national regulators. At the same time the new framework tries to ensure that coordination and information exchange between national supervisors is improved and that common rules and standards are properly implemented. For this purpose the EU has created a European Systemic Risk Board (ESRB) which works closely with the ECB Council and the Commission in identifying macroeconomic risks and vulnerabilities. The ESRB is supposed to work closely with the three European supervisory authorities in the areas of banking (European Banking Authority based in London), insurances and pension authority (European Insurance and Occupational Pensions Authority in Frankfurt) and also securities markets (European Securities Markets Authority (ESMA) in Paris). Amongst the three only the ESMA has direct supervisory powers over credit agencies, the other two are limited to monitoring and developing guidelines for national supervisors and to act as an arbitrator in settling disputes between national regulations in order to ensure that EU regulations are properly implemented. The overall approach of the new financial supervisory framework remains strongly focused on keeping the supervision of financial institutions on the national level. This is the result of the persistent resistance of member states to concede sovereignty in regulating the financial industry. The Commission therefore emphasises that 'supervision is best done at national level' and that the European supervisory authorities will only become active in 'areas where there is clear added value' (European Commission 2010c: 6). The new framework essentially maintains an OMC approach. The result is that 'successive coordinating layers have been established that do what they can to fill in the gaps' (Donnelly 2011: 391). The aim is to achieve greater regulatory efficiency in the financial sector by strengthening macro- and micro-level monitoring, information exchange on potential risks and establish a single rulebook on the basis of which all national supervisors operate. Given the gravity of the regulatory failures which were exposed by the crisis the initial expectations that the EU would move towards strengthening macro-level regulatory powers substantially were disappointed. The regulatory weaknesses which the financial crisis exposed were not enough to overcome the deep-seated member state hostility towards conceding sovereignty in the area of financial regulation. The new financial supervision framework still has to be considered as a starting point for potential further integration in this area. If the creation of a banking union with direct supervisory powers for the ECB in the eurozone becomes a reality, it would mark a decisive step towards the establishment of an integrated macro-level regulatory framework. It would also be a major step towards the implementation of the regulatory standards and minimum capital requirements which are set out in the Basel III Agreement on Banking Supervisory Reforms. The EU has the clear goal to implement these in response to the crisis (Buti and Carnot 2012: 908; Council of the European Union 2013). Progress on the implementation of Basel III progress in the EU still remains patchy and there are noticeable differences in the extent to which individual member states would like to push these further (Visvizi 2012: 21).

REFERENCES

Barnes, S., P.R. Lane and A.R. Radziwill (2010) *Minimising Risks from Imbalances in European Banking*. OECD Economics Department Working Paper No. 828. Paris: OECD.

Benz, A. (2007) 'Accountable Multilevel Governance by the Open Method of Coordination?', *European Law Journal* 13 (4): 505–522.

Blair, T. and G. Schröder (1999) 'The Way Forward for Europe's Social Democrats', Joint Position Paper, 8 June. Available at: http://web.archive.org/web/19990819090124/http://www.labour.org.uk/views/items/00000053.html (accessed 13 March 2013).

Borrás, S. and K. Jacobsson (2004) 'The Open Method of Co-ordination and New Governance Patterns in the EU', *Journal of European Public Policy* 11 (2): 185–208.

Brown, G. (2010) *Beyond the Crash: Overcoming the First Crisis of Globalisation*. London: Simon and Schuster.

Büchs, M. (2007) *New Governance in European Social Policy*. Basingstoke: Palgrave Macmillan.

Büchs, M. (2008) 'The Open Method of Coordination as a "Two-Level Game"', *Policy and Politics* 36 (1): 21–37.

Buti, M. and N. Carnot (2012) 'The EMU Debt Crisis: Early Lessons and Reforms', *Journal of Common Market Studies* 50 (6): 899–911.

Council of the European Union (2013) 'Bank Capital Rules: Council Endorses Agreement with EP'. Press Release 7088/13, 5 March. Brussels: EU.
De la Porte, C. and P. Nanz (2004) 'The OMC – a Deliberative-Democratic Mode of Governance? The Cases of Employment and Pensions', *Journal of European Public Policy* 11 (2): 267–288.
Dierx, A. and F. Ilzkovitz (2006) 'Economic Growth in Europe: Pursuing the Lisbon Strategy', in S. Mundschenk, M.H. Stierle, U. Stierle-von Schutz and I. Traistaru (eds) *Competitiveness and Growth in Europe: Lessons and Policy Implications for the Lisbon Strategy*. Cheltenham, UK and Northampton, MA, USA: Edward Elgar, pp. 15–46.
Donnelly, S. (2011) 'The Public Interest and the Economy in Europe in the Wake of the Financial Crisis', *European Political Science* 10 (3): 384–392.
Dyson, K. (2012) 'Economic and Monetary Disunion?', in J. Hayward and R. Wurzel (eds) *European Disunion: Between Sovereignty and Solidarity*. Basingstoke: Palgrave Macmillan, pp. 181–199.
European Central Bank (ECB) (2007) *Financial Stability Review December*. Frankfurt: ECB. Available at: http://www.ecb.europa.eu/pub/pdf/other/financialstabilityreview200712en.pdf?353b0c4283d432a6c751d74fb7d1963d (accessed 13 March 2013).
European Central Bank (ECB) (2010a) *Financial Stability Review December, based on Bureau van Dijk data*. Frankfurt: ECB. Available at: http://www.ecb.europa.eu/pub/pdf/other/financialstabilityreview201012en.pdf?cd3d821010bce731ce2d7cdb7875d411 (accessed 13 March 2013).
European Central Bank (ECB) (2010b) *Financial Stability Review December, based on ESCB and Eurostat data*. Frankfurt: ECB. Available at: http://www.ecb.europa.eu/pub/pdf/other/financialstabilityreview201012en.pdf?cd3d821010bce731ce2d7cdb7875d411 (accessed 13 March 2013).
European Commission (1999) *Financial Services: Implementing the Framework for Financial Markets: Action Plan*. COM (1999) 232, 11 May.
European Commission (2000) *Initial Report of the Committee of Wise Men on the Regulation of European Securities Markets*, 9 November. Brussels: EU.
European Commission (2004) *Facing the Challenge: The Lisbon Strategy for Growth and Employment*. Report from the High Level Group chaired by Wim Kok, November. Brussels: EU.
European Commission (2005) *Working Together for Growth and Jobs: A New Start for the Lisbon Strategy*. Communication to the Spring European Council, COM (2005) 24, 2 February. Brussels: EU.
European Commission (2007a) *Towards Common Principles of Flexicurity: More and Better Jobs Through Flexibility and Security*. Brussels: EU.
European Commission (2007b) *Communication from the Commission to the European Parliament, the Council, the European Economic and Social Committee and the Committee of the Regions: A Single Market for 21st Century Europe*. COM (2007) 724 final, 20 November. Brussels: EU.
European Commission (2008) *Communication from the Commission to the European Parliament, the Council, the European Economic and Social Committee and the Committee of the Regions: Renewed Social Agenda: Opportunities, Access and Solidarity in 21st century Europe*. COM (2008) 412 final, 2 July. Brussels: EU.
European Commission (2010a) *Lisbon Strategy Evaluation Document*. Brussels: EU.
European Commission (2010b) *Europe 2020: A Strategy for Smart, Sustainable and Inclusive Growth*. COM (2010) 2020, 3 March. Brussels: EU.

European Commission (2010c) *Financial Supervision Package – Frequently Asked Questions*. MEMO/10/434, 22 September.
European Council (2000) '*Lisbon European Council* Presidency Conclusions'. Available at: http://www.consilium.europa.eu/uedocs/cms_data/docs/pressdata/en/ec/00100-r1.en0.htm (accessed 15 March 2013).
European Council (2012) *Treaty Establishing the European Stability Mechanism*. Brussels: EU.
European Economic Community (1957) *The Treaty of Rome*. Available at: http://ec.europa.eu/economy_finance/emu_history/documents/treaties/rometreaty2.pdf (accessed 3 March 2013).
European Financial Stability Facility (EFSF) (2013) 'Frequently Asked Questions'. Available at: http://www.efsf.europa.eu/attachments/faq_en.pdf (accessed 3 March 2013).
European Financial Stability Facility/European Stability Mechanism (EFSF/ESM) (2012) 'Newsletter No. 7'. December. Available at: http://www.esm.europa.eu/pdf/EFSF_ESM_NEWSLETTER_DECEMBER_2012.pdf (accessed 15 March 2013).
European Stability Mechanism (ESM) (2013a) 'Frequently Asked Questions'. Luxembourg: ESM. Available at: http://www.esm.europa.eu/pdf/FAQ%20ESM%2016052013.pdf (accessed 15 March 2013).
European Stability Mechanism (ESM) (2013b) 'FAQ – Financial assistance for Cyprus'. Luxembourg: ESM. Available at: http://www.esm.europa.eu/pdf/FAQ%20Cyprus%2016052013.pdf (accessed 15 March 2013).
Funk, L. (2007) 'Convergence in Employment-Related Public Policies? A British-German Comparison', *German Politics* 16 (1): 116–136.
Funk, L. (2009) 'Labour Market Trends and Problems in the EU's Central and Eastern European Member States: Is Flexicurity the Answer?', *Journal of Contemporary European Research* 5 (4): 557–580.
Giddens, A. (1998) *The Third Way: The Renewal of Social Democracy*. Cambridge: Polity Press.
Haas, E.B. (1958) *The Uniting of Europe: Political, Social, and Economic Forces, 1950–1957*. Stanford: Stanford University Press.
Hantrais, L. (2007) *Social Policy in the European Union*. Basingstoke: Palgrave Macmillan, 3rd edn.
Hix, S. and B. Hoyland (2011) *The Political System of the European Union*. Basingstoke, Palgrave Macmillan, 3rd edn.
Jospin, L. (2001) 'The Future of an Enlarged Europe'. Speech at the French Ministry for Foreign Affairs, Paris, 28 May.
Kalemli-Oczan, S., E. Papaioannou and J.L. Peydro (2010) 'What Lies Beneath the Euro's Effect on Financial Integration? Currency Risk, Legal Harmonisation or Trade?', *Journal of International Economics* 81 (1): 75–88.
Kanter, J. (2012) 'Europe tries to Ease Concerns Over Rescue Plan for Banks', *New York Times*, 26 September.
McCann, D. (2010) *The Political Economy of the European Union*. Cambridge: Polity Press.
Moravcsik, A. (1991) 'Negotiating the Single European Act', in R.O. Keohane and S. Hoffmann (eds) *The New European Community: Decision Making and Institutional Change*. Boulder, CO: Westview Press, pp. 41–84.
OECD (2010) *Minimising Risks from Imbalances in European Banking*. Economics Department Working Paper No. 828.

O'Donnel, J. and E. Kuehnen (2013) 'Cracks Appear in European Banking Union Scheme', *Reuters*, 8 February. Available at: http://www.reuters.com/article/2013/02/08/us-eu-ecb-supervisionidUSBRE9170GX20130208 (accessed 15 March 2013).

Posner, E. and N. Véron N. (2010) 'The EU and Financial Regulation: Power Without Purpose?', *Journal of European Public Policy* 17 (3): 400–415.

Putnam, R.D. (1988) 'Diplomacy and Domestic Politics: the Logic of Two-Level Games', *International Organization* 42 (3): 427–460.

Rhodes, M. (2010) 'Employment Policy', in H. Wallace, M.A. Pollack and A.R. Young (eds) *Policy-Making in the European Union*. Oxford: Oxford University Press, 6th edn.

Scharpf, F.W. (1999) *Governing in Europe: Effective and Democratic?* Oxford: Oxford University Press.

SPIEGEL online (2013) 'Hit by the Levy: Cyprus Mulls Citizenship Offer for Russians'. Available at: http://www.spiegel.de/international/europe/cyprus-mulls-giving-russian-investors-citizenship-a-894409.html (accessed 19 May 2013).

Schäuble, W. (2013) Speech to the German Parliament on the Occasion of the Introduction of the German Federal Budget 2013. Available at: http://www.bundesfinanzministerium.de/Content/DE/Reden/2012/2012–09–11-rede-einbringung-bundeshaushalt-2013.html (accessed 17 March 2013).

The Guardian (2005) 'New Labour is Inspiring Europe, says Mandelson', 3 February.

The Guardian (2013) 'Cameron's Fatal Mistake', 26 January.

Verhelst, S. (2011) *Renewed Financial Supervision in Europe – Final or Transitory?* Brussels: Academia Press.

Visvizi, A. (2012) 'The Eurozone Crisis in Perspective: Causes and Implications', in A. Visvizi and T. Stepniewski (eds) *The Eurozone Crisis: Implications for Central and Eastern Europe*. Yearbook of the Institute of East-Central Europe 10 (5), pp. 13–32.

Williamson, J. (1990) 'What Washington Means by Policy Reform', in J. Williams (ed.) *Latin American Adjustment: How Much has Happened*. Washington: Institute for International Economics.

Young, A.R. (2005) 'The Single Market', in H. Wallace, W. Wallace and M.A. Pollack (eds) *Policy-Making in the European Union*. Oxford: Oxford University Press, pp. 93–112, 5th edn.

3. Europe 2020 and the eurozone crisis: a new functionalist era?

3.1 THE RETURN OF 'SPILLOVER' UNDER CRISIS CONDITIONS

For a considerable amount of time the European integration has been determined by processes of interstate bargaining, which made it important to concentrate on the preferences of domestic elites and the underlying differences in the cultures of national political systems, economies and welfare state models. The state-centric paradigm in European integration theory consequently seemed to have won the long-standing debate with the neofunctionalists over defining the drivers of the integration process. Approaches such as Moravcsik's liberal intergovernmentalism in the 1990s, and also more recently social constructivist explanations of the micro-level of interest formation and decision-making processes in the European Union (EU), seemed to reflect the reality of what was actually happening in the EU. The neofunctionalist notion of an increasing spillover of political integration in response to the deepening of economic integration, which would eventually result in a fundamental shift of the loyalties of nation actors towards the supranational institutional level (Haas 1968: 16) seemed to have been overtaken by real events. The first setback for neofunctionalists presented itself in the 1960s and 1970s, when the Treaty of Rome's vision of an ever closer union between the member states of the European Economic Community (EEC) was shattered by the re-emergence of national interests. It culminated in the empty chair crisis of 1965–1966, where France under President Charles de Gaulle essentially withdrew from intergovernmental negotiations in the Council due to disagreements with the other five EEC members on the future path for the Community. The stalling of the integration process gave a boost to the realist intergovernmentalist critics of the neofunctionalist paradigm. Realist intergovernmentalists like Stanley Hoffmann accused the theory of having rashly sounded the death bell for the nation state, an entity which in their view had lost none of its powers as the 'initiator, pace-setter, supervisor, and often destroyer of the larger entity' (Hoffmann 1966: 908).

Neofunctionalism had a brief revival in the wake of the Maastricht

Treaty when it seemed that the creation of the Single European Market (SEM) and the move towards monetary union would set in motion a new wave of political integration, particularly in the areas of social policy and foreign and security policy. Some scholars hence argued at the time that the period since the mid-1980s which led up to the establishment of the Single European Act (SEA) and eventually Maastricht were evidence that 'neo-functionalist pressures – functional, political and cultivated – are at least as much in evidence now as they were in the early years of the EEC' (Tranholm-Mikkelsen 1991: 16). This optimism turned out to be short-lived. Following hard bargaining over the shape of monetary union during the 1997 Intergovernmental Conference in Amsterdam, the emphasis on the divergence of national interests was back on the agenda. Amsterdam had shown that after Maastricht, which had caused a lot of controversy domestically, member state governments were suffering from integration fatigue and were hence not willing to accompany the creation of the Single Market and the euro with the further harmonisation of major policy areas. The open method of coordination (OMC) became the symbol for this renewed focus on intergovernmentalism, which made it impossible to go further than to introduce mechanisms for the coordination of national interests. The failure of Maastricht to initiate a new wave of spillover in the newly created EU gave renewed impetus to the critics of neofunctionalism. One of the most prominent critics is Andrew Moravcsik, whose liberal intergovernmentalist approach seemed to explain the internal post-Maastricht developments in the EU more adequately than his neofunctionalist counterparts. Moravcsik emphasised the continuing importance of national interests and explained the developments in the EU on the basis of a two-level game. In a first step member states develop their national preferences in a process of liberal preference formation between domestic actors with a variety of interests and with different degrees of influence. Once this process is complete national governments enter the second stage of interstate bargaining at the EU level, where their primary goal is to maintain their national interests and to transfer them towards the supranational EU policy level.

Moravcsik himself fundamentally criticised neofunctionalism for what he considered to be its central assumption that unintended spillover would occur beyond the control of national governments. In spite of Moravcsik's fundamental disagreement with the core of the neofunctionalist approach, it is evident that his liberal intergovernmentalist approach is much closer to the idea of 'spillover' than classic intergovernmentalist accounts. This is the result of Moravcsik having based his liberal intergovernmentalist approach firmly on international political economy analysis. Moravcsik accepted the existence of transnational coalitions between interests groups in an environment of increasing economic interdependence, which would in turn also influence the first level of national preference formation (Moravcsik 1993: 481 and 517). This implies that the neofunctionalist logic of a spillover of loyalties and interests beyond the national level can at least in part occur, particularly when it comes to the interests of economic stakeholders who under the conditions of economic globalisation no longer define their interests exclusively on a national basis. It is therefore not unreasonable to argue that the supposed irreconcilable differences between neofunctionalism and intergovernmentalism result from a narrow focus on the initial neofunctionalist approach, which seemed to determine a mechanical advance of spillover towards deeper integration, almost by default. The efforts neofunctionalists have made to adapt their approach to the changing reality of European integration over the years were therefore largely ignored (Rosamond 2006: 243–244) or taken as evidence that the approach had made flawed assumptions about the path of European integration, which had to be frequently corrected (Moravcsik 2005: 354).

The latter criticism was to a certain extent justified as it correctly emphasises that initially neofunctionalist scholars used to be rather rigid in their interpretation of the integration process. The pessimist view of the nation state's future which neofunctionalists put forward has certainly turned out to be profoundly unjustified. The inherent scepticism towards the nation state in neofunctionalism stems from the fact that it adopted David Mitrany's functionalist vision of a gradual shift of power from the national level towards a set of supranational institutions, which would each have its own purpose (Mitrany 1943: 107). At the heart of this functionalist vision was the belief that with the declining importance of the nation state the loyalties of citizens would over time shift from a narrow national perspective towards that of an internationalist political community with shared interests. Mitrany was an ardent sceptic of the nation state which he considered to be an artificial unit that breeds nationalism and ultimately military conflict and therefore called for the development of a 'spreading web of international activities and agencies, in which and through which the interests and life of all nations would be gradually integrated' (Mitrany 1943: 95). Mitrany was even sceptical of the creation of supranational states in the form of federations, which he considered to be a replica of the nation state on a higher level (Mitrany 1965: 141–142). This explains why, in stark contrast to his disciple Ernst B. Haas, he showed little enthusiasm for the process of regional institutionalised integration in Europe (Mitrany 1975: 69–70).

Haas himself followed Mitrany's logic by applying the 'spillover' concept to the process of emerging institutionalised integration in Europe in the 1950s. Haas considered European integration as a process which predominantly occurred on the basis of the necessity of countries in Europe to deepen their economic cooperation following the devastation of the Second World War. The resulting sectoral economic integration in the form of the European Coal and Steel Community (ECSC), Euratom, and eventually the creation of the Common Market under the Treaty of Rome in 1957, caused Haas to develop his concept of the spillover of integration. For Haas these developments illustrated the gradual spillover of economic integration from one sector to another and eventually to an increasing part of the economy. He considers this spillover to be driven by an increasing shift in the loyalties of national elites and stakeholders towards the emerging supranational institutional framework. The result would be more transnational lobbying and ultimately, if interest groups deem supranational integration to be beneficial, support for the further deepening of integration (Haas 1968: 317). According to Haas, 'spillover' of economic integration into an increasing number of sectors of the national economies inevitably has to lead to the deepening of political integration. Economic integration raises an increasing need for political supervision. From the neofunctionalist point of view a parallel process of political institutionalisation is therefore unavoidable. The final outcome is considered to be the establishment of an increasingly dense and complex supranational institutional framework, towards which the nation states have lost large parts of their autonomy and which has become the new focal point for national actors: 'Political integration is the process whereby political actors in several distinct national settings are persuaded to shift their loyalties, expectations and political activities toward a new centre, whose institutions possess or demand jurisdiction over the pre-existing national states' (Haas 1968: 16).

Haas considered the evolvement of the integration process from the limited level of political integration under the ECSC in 1951 towards the complex supranational institutional setting of the EEC in 1957 as practical evidence for the validity of his spillover concept. As a result in his early accounts of the integration process in the 1950s Haas put forward a vision of the quasi inevitability of the emergence of a political federal union as the end result of the integration process in Europe: 'All other things being equal, it is as inconceivable that this form of co-operation should not result in new patterns of profound interdependence as it is unlikely that the General Common Market can avoid a species of political federalism in order to function as an economic organ' (Haas 1968: 317).

Haas drew this early conclusions about the future of European integration on the basis of the expectation that the initial 'short-range, limited and "tactical"' shifting of loyalties by national actors would in the long run most likely converse into a deeper European identity with permanent loyalties, provided that the new supranational entity would meet the expectations of national elites and stakeholders (Haas 1968: 293). Unlike Haas the other major early neofunctionalist scholar, Leon N. Lindberg, was more cautious when it came to the prediction of the future course of European integration. In his study of the European integration process Lindberg differed from Haas in that he did not share the view that the EEC would ultimately end up as a federation. Even if political integration deepens, the ultimate outcome of a political federation is not inevitable: 'It seems to me that it is logically and empirically possible that collective decision-making procedures involving a significant amount of political integration can be achieved without moving toward a "political community" as defined by arts' (Lindberg 1963: 5).

Lindberg was also much more cautious about a shift of national actors' loyalties towards the Community level. It was his belief that actors would change expectations in selected areas which are under increasing Community regulations rather than to permanently shift their loyalties to the supranational level: 'Actors with political power in the national community will restructure their expectations and activities only if the tasks granted to the new institutions are of immediate concern to them, and only if they involve a significant change in the conditions of the actor's environment' (Lindberg 1963: 9).

This shows that even in its early days neofunctionalism was rather varied in its approach. Haas's interpretation was the one which was most vulnerable to justified criticism from realist intergovernmentalists. His rather utopian core assumptions about the shift of national loyalties to a new centre were swiftly overtaken by the harsh reality in which hard-nosed national interests prevented further swift progress towards supranationalisation. Haas swiftly reacted to the criticism and the new reality of stalling integration which characterised the decade of the 1960s. At the beginning of the 1970s he started to shift towards the more cautious approach of his neofunctionalist contemporaries Lindberg and Schmitter who refused to determine a definite final outcome for the integration process. His contemporary neofunctionalist Philippe C. Schmitter argued that supranational integration is unlikely to take a linear course towards a perceived end goal. Instead one would have to expect many twists and turns in the course of integration: 'Plotted over time, the evolution of a national integration policy or regional institution (the negotiated sum of national policies) is quite likely to be erratic and may well demonstrate no cumulative trend at all' (Schmitter 1970: 846).

Schmitter proposed a much broader set of options for national actors in response to the creation of regional supranational integration. He suggested that 'spillover' in the form of an increasing transfer of expectations towards the new institutional level was only one possibility. At the same time it would be possible for national actors to carefully control the nature and the extent of further integration, either in the vertical direction towards deepening or repatriation ('upwards' or 'downwards'), or in the horizontal direction towards expansion to new policy areas ('forward'). The exclusion of formerly integrated policy areas ('backward') was also a possibility (Schmitter 1970: 844–845). Schmitter proposed a number of conceptual approaches for neofunctionalists beyond spillover to reflect the reality of the process of regional integration: (a) either limiting the transfer of further authority but extending it to new policy areas ('spill-around'); (b) increase the authority of supranational institutions without expanding it into further policy area ('build-up'); (c) expand cooperative mechanisms between nations while reducing the authority of the supranational level ('retrench'); (d) or allow greater deliberation of policy issues at the supranational administrative level whilst reducing supranational authority ('muddle-about'). Schmitter also suggested the possibility that national actors could decide to 'spillback' authority towards the national level, even to the point of pushing the level of integration back to its initial exit point. In terms of the reality he however considered it to be most likely that actors would decide to continue adapting the regional integrative framework to external challenges ('encapsulate') (Schmitter 1970: 846).

Haas himself reinterpreted the neofunctionalist approach in the light of the failure of EEC members to accelerate the integration process towards a European federation as he had originally envisaged. In his discussion on the 'joy and the anguish of pretheorizing', Haas acknowledged the differences between neofunctionalist scholars in determining the final outcome of the future of the European Community. He was also a lot more cautious about predicting what would be the end result of European integration: 'Neo-functionalist practitioners have difficulty achieving closure on a given case of regional integration because the terminal condition being observed is uncertain' (Haas 1970: 628).

Having moved away from the prediction of a European federation, Haas now shared Schmitter's more fine-tuned analysis of the reality of European integration and conceded that there is actually the potential for 'self-encapsulation', that is, maintaining the status quo of integration, and also 'spill-around', that is, the creation of new organisations rather than the deepening of European integration (Haas 1970: 615). In contrast to Schmitter, Haas however was a lot more sceptical of the ability of neofunctionalism to be able to explain future developments in European integration. By the beginning of the twenty-first century neofunctionalism seemed to have finally met its nemesis. Over more than a decade since Maastricht member states had failed to reach a far-reaching compromise on how to reform the EU's institutions in order to ensure that new member states could be accommodated without having a detrimental impact on the EU's overall efficiency. The disagreements over the long-term vision of what the EU as an entity should ultimately become resulted in the instalment of a European convention with the purpose of developing a constitution for the EU. The constitutional treaty which emerged from this in 2004 had initially been promoted as the grand compromise by EU leaders. Its rejection in public referenda in France and the Netherlands in 2005 painfully illustrated to what extent citizens in Europe had become sceptical of the European project and consequently of attempts to deepen integration further. Moravcsik's own interpretation of the developments in 2005 was that the EU had reached constitutional maturity and that its '*status quo* appears stable and normatively attractive' (Moravcsik 2005: 351). At the same time he rejected the notion that this constitutional status quo could lead to further major steps in integration towards a full federal union which would weaken the national sovereignty of the member states: 'Beyond incremental changes in policy, it is difficult to imagine functional pressures, institutional pressures, or normative concerns upsetting the stability of the basic constitutional equilibrium in Europe today' (Ibid.: 351).

This belief was relatively widespread following the failure to ratify the constitutional treaty in the EU. Its rescue in the form of the rather conventional Lisbon Treaty under the German EU Presidency in 2006 seemed to set an endpoint to further integration. The relatively limited advance of vertical (deeper) integration under Lisbon in the form of the creation of an EU Council President and a High Representative for Defence and Security Policy who was also Vice-President of the Commission showed the extent of integration fatigue which had beset member states.

Haas was nevertheless right to point out in his final writings that in spite of its shortcomings neofunctionalist thought could play a role in explaining future developments in the EU. Nobody could foresee the gravity of the more recent events which have completely shaken up the kaleidoscope of European integration. The changed environment following the 2008–2009 global financial crisis warrant a return to the spillover concept as they cannot adequately be explained through a purely intergovernmentalist lens. The external pressures which have descended on the EU since the financial crisis can be classified as functionalist spillover pressures in the way they were foreseen in more recent revised neofunctionalist writings, which pointed to spillover to occur in situations where 'internationally induced incentives drive or reinforce the rationale for seeking supranational solutions' (Niemann and Schmitter 2009: 59). The neofunctionalist approach which Haas, Lindberg and Schmitter have developed since the 1960s is much broader than Haas's original concept. Therefore it can be very usefully applied to explain the more recent developments in the integration process with one crucial exception: the assumption of the spillover of loyalties from the national towards the supranational level. Almost six decades since the Treaty of Rome it is clear that the nation state will continue to play a central role as a point of reference for citizens, policy-makers and stakeholders. The initial expectation Haas had in the 1950s that national loyalties would shift towards an increasingly powerful body of European institutions has turned out to be illusionary. To his credit Haas modified this claim soon after. In his seminal work *Beyond the Nation-State* published in 1964, Haas emphasised that the question if 'people "learn" to think in non-national terms merely because of a pattern of technical cooperation' was the big question mark which functionalists could not yet definitely answer (Haas 1964: 34). Haas subsequently offered a more fine-tuned analysis of the potential spillover of loyalties when he accepted that the integration process was not proceeding in a linear fashion but showed a rather mixed picture of integration in different policy areas. Haas therefore concluded that as vertical integration in the European Community would be 'distributed asymmetrically among several centers' (Haas 1970: 635), there would also be markedly different levels of legitimacy for supranational Community institutions: 'The ensemble would enjoy legitimacy in the eyes of its citizens though it would be difficult to pinpoint the focus of the legitimacy in a single authority center; rather, the image of infinitely tiered multiple loyalties might be the appropriate one' (Ibid.).

Before the financial crisis spillover had predominantly been occurring in the area of Single Market integration, which represents the core of the EU. Here the Commission obtained a mandate from the member states to monitor national compliance with Single Market directives and to initiate infringement proceedings against governments in case of the failure to implement directives in a correct and timely fashion. Particularly in the area of competition policy the Commission has turned into a quasi-independent regulator of economic activity in the member states (Buonanno and Nugent 2013: 43). This policy mode has been characterised as the EU regulatory mode, where the Commission takes an active role in shaping and implementing the agenda (Wallace 2010: 95). At the same time the deepening of market integration in the EU has also caused the emergence of an increasingly dense horizontal network of cooperation between national agents in the form of policy-makers, businesses and other stakeholders (Pollack et al. 2010: 487). It is in the latter area where national actors are inevitably forced to focus their attention beyond the national level and where consequently transnational socialisation processes occur. This has however not caused any noticeable shift in positive loyalties towards the EU level. The *Eurobarometer* poll conducted in the autumn of

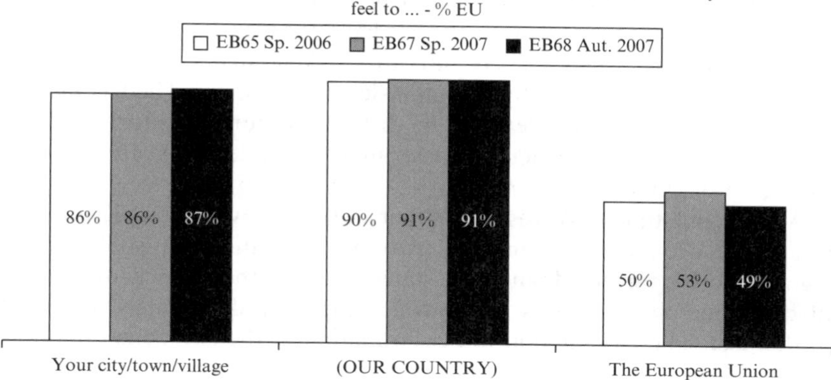

Source: European Commission (2008): 68.

Figure 3.1 Feeling of attachment amongst citizens in the EU-27

2007, just before the global financial crisis showed its full effects in Europe, asked citizens across Europe about which level they feel particularly attached to (regional, national or European). The results in Figure 3.1 show a much lower level of attachment to the EU as an organisation than to the region and the nation people are affiliated with.

In terms of the overall level of trust into the EU and its institutions the crisis continues to have a detrimental effect. The latest *Eurobarometer* results show a sharp decline in trust in the EU across member states. General trust in the EU has declined from 57 per cent in 2007 to a historic low of 31 per cent in the autumn of 2013 (European Commission 2013: 5). The last time the Commission presented a more detailed analysis on the public view of individual EU institutions in 2011, it also illustrated that trust in the EU's core institutions has declined from already modest levels before the crisis (between 43 and 52 per cent) towards new lows under the crisis conditions. Only the European parliament still maintains a 41 per cent level of trust while the Commission is now only trusted by 36 per cent (European Commission 2011: 21).

These results are a clear rebuttal of the neofunctionalist assumption that the spillover from economic towards political integration comes with the transfer of national loyalties towards the Community level. The reasons why loyalties of national actors have not shifted towards the EU institutional level are twofold. Most importantly, it is obvious that the satisfaction with the problem-solving capacities of the EU institutions is limited.

The EU has therefore never managed to instil an overarching confidence amongst citizens across Europe that major challenges are better dealt with at the EU level. At the same time the EU lacks the transparency for citizens and even national policy-makers and other stakeholders to grasp what has become a very complex system of multi-level governance. The EU institutional level is hence considered to be distant and for individuals without expert knowledge it is difficult to determine which decisions are made on the EU level (Risse 2005).

At the same time the crisis shows that spillover towards deeper political integration occurs even against the resistance of member states. The sovereign debt crisis forced EU member states to revisit the political dimension of economic and monetary union which they had deliberately neglected in the past. The lack of political coordination in the eurozone undoubtedly proved to be the major weakness of the single currency. The lack of political control over national budgets and macroeconomic policy targets allowed a situation to occur where the uniform interest rate for the whole of the eurozone was utilised by some governments to encourage excessive private borrowing. Moreover, in the absence of a binding mechanism of policy coordination other than the loose OMC which had no consequences for member states other than 'naming and shaming', a mixed pattern of performance on the Lisbon targets for domestic policy reform emerged in the eurozone. The consequence was the evolvement of a eurozone which consisted of 'leaders' and 'laggards' when it came to levels of GDP growth, employment, budgetary stability as well as social and environmental cohesion (Dyson 2012: 189). Southern European countries maintained wage levels which were substantially above their national productivity levels, while in Germany trade unions supported wage restraint in order to maintain jobs and support the competitiveness of the country's export economy (Lapavitsas et al. 2012: 28–29). At the same time it has to be acknowledged that as part of the eurozone framework, where the competence for monetary policy rests with the European Central Bank (ECB) in Frankfurt, governments in Southern Europe were unable to use currency devaluation as a means to counter the increasing inflationary pressures in their economies. These resulted predominantly from the demand-orientated economic policies pursued by countries like Greece, Spain, Portugal, Italy and also Ireland (Hall 2012: 359).

The design of the eurozone was hence in stark contrast to the original ambition of particularly the French socialists (Mitterrand, Delors and later Jospin) to combine the creation of a single currency with economic union, which would have implied a stronger coordination or even harmonisation of fiscal, employment, welfare and education policies. The resulting deepening of political integration towards a political union, which particularly

French President Mitterrand had envisaged when he negotiated plans for monetary union with his German counterpart Helmut Kohl (Paterson 2012: 237), would have been straight out of the rulebook of neofunctionalists. If EU member states had decided to accompany the creation of the single currency with the institutionalised harmonisation of core policies areas, by for example establishing a European labour ministry, it would have been conceivable that expectations and loyalties could have shifted to these new institutions over time. The deepening of economic integration which the Maastricht Treaty determined by initiating the Single Market and accompanying monetary union was however not followed by a wave of political spillover. On the contrary, after Maastricht divergent national interests started to dominate the agenda and the deepening of political integration was therefore abandoned in favour of the cautious coordination of national policies under the OMC. With the expansion of qualified majority voting (QMV) and the introduction of an opt-out clause the emphasis after Maastricht was hence on the flexibilisation rather than on the harmonisation of the integration process. Moreover, Maastricht had introduced the subsidiary principle which in essence demanded that any further supranationalisation in areas which are under member state control would have to be justified by an obvious need to take collective action.

The crisis has pushed the EU towards a new dimension in the integration process, which nobody would have expected under the general set-up which had prevailed before 2008. While the long-term political consequences of the more recent developments cannot yet be determined with certainty, it is obvious that under crisis conditions political spillover occurs in areas where member states were originally determined not to concede further autonomy. Although political elites present the new set of policy mechanisms as a desirable step forward towards achieving the ambition of political union in the eurozone, it is obvious that these developments are driven by external forces. The negative reaction of bond markets to the deterioration of the budgetary situation in individual countries forced policy-makers to repeatedly develop new additional coordinative and supervisory mechanisms with the aim of restoring market confidence. The political spillover therefore emerged predominantly from external factors: a global financial crisis with a subsequent banking crisis in Europe which pushed many eurozone countries into severe sovereign debt problems. In response markets became nervous and also started downgrading the credit rating of individual countries. This makes it harder for those particular countries to obtain financial capital on the bond markets and ultimately to resolve their sovereign debt problems. According to the neofunctionalist logic the spillover process we have been witnessing in the EU since the advent of the crisis is clearly one caused by what Schmitter called 'exceptional (unpredictable) or exogenous conditions not present in the original convergence' (Schmitter 1970: 847).

Political decision-makers had to put measures in place which restored market confidence. This could only be done by providing external financial support to countries with sovereign debt problems to ensure that they remain solvent and could, if necessary, introduce measures to stabilise their banking system. This explains why first the European Financial Stability Facility (EFSF) as a temporary lending facility was established. When it became clear that the crisis in the eurozone was more structural than originally anticipated and could affect more countries in the future, EU leaders then moved on to establish the European Stability Mechanism (ESM) as a permanent lending facility. As the financial support for structurally weak economies in the eurozone was widely portrayed as the emergence of a transfer union in the media, particularly Germany was adamant to ensure that EFSF and ESM loans would operate in a similar fashion as the International Monetary Fund (IMF) lending system. This meant that loans would be strictly conditional and linked to the implementation of profound domestic reforms which needed to be permanently monitored. Germany, with the reluctant support of France, therefore pushed towards the development of a new mechanism of binding policy coordination for the eurozone which went beyond the relatively loose mechanisms of the OMC. These new multiple layers of policy coordination emerged gradually and in a functionalist manner. The German Chancellor Angela Merkel was initially very reluctant to support any collective action at the EU level (Hübner 2012: 163). In the course of 2010 it became clear that the sovereign debt problems would not be limited to Greece and Ireland. Moreover, in October 2009 the rating agency Standard & Poor had lowered Greece's credit rating which set in motion a rollercoaster where political decision-makers essentially were driven by market reactions and struggled to set the agenda.

The speed and gravity with which the crisis took hold of Europe in the course of 2010–2011 changed Merkel's perspective. The revived Franco-German leadership duo Merkel and Sarkozy subsequently were driven from one policy initiative to another by increasingly jittery bond markets that seemed to have lost confidence in the viability of the eurozone. In March 2011 the European Semester was therefore accompanied by the Euro Plus Pact (EPP), which obliged the eurozone countries and participating outsiders to commit themselves to a more detailed policy reform agenda and enhance the policy coordination between them. When in 2011 Portugal also fell into a sovereign debt crisis and asked for financial support from the EFSF and rating agencies threatened to downgrade a number of eurozone economies, including Germany, Merkel and Sarkozy went further and started to negotiate changes to the EU treaty structure.

The aim was to commit not just the eurozone countries but all 27 EU member states to the introduction of a debt limit into their national legal framework. Merkel herself characterised this as an important step towards the long-term goal of achieving political union in the eurozone. Her rationale was that the implementation of a debt limit in the national constitutions of each of the 27 member states in the EU would initiate a process of self-limitation of national budgetary policies amongst the eurozone-17 and prospective members:

> In the face of the non-existing budgetary competence of the European Commission the inherent link of the debt rule with national law is best suited to make it compulsory for all of us . . . I therefore believe that it is the biggest sanction to be condemned in your own country (Merkel and Sarkozy 2011).

President Sarkozy promoted this as the first step towards the creation of an 'economic government' for the eurozone and Merkel spoke of the need for eurozone members to 'closely interlink their fiscal and economic policies' with the aim of gradually rebuilding confidence in the convergence and the competitiveness of eurozone economies (Ibid.). Merkel's aim to include the pact into the EU's treaty structure was vetoed by British Prime Minister David Cameron at the December 2011 EU Summit in Brussels. Britain's veto left Merkel and Sarkozy little option but to introduce the pact as an intergovernmental treaty (Traynor et al. 2011)

The spillover process which had started to occur under crisis conditions essentially followed the neofunctionalist logic which assumes that economic integration will inevitably have to result in the deepening of political integration (Boerzel 2005: 225). The inevitability comes from the need to ensure that political supervision of the rules and procedures of economic integration is guaranteed. Just as it was necessary to equip the Commission with powers to ensure the compliance of member states in the area of market integration the crisis has shown that monetary integration has little perspective to be successful without adequate political control. This requires member states to (albeit reluctantly) accept the loss of their autonomy in core policy areas, in this case fiscal, macroeconomic policy. The new policy mechanisms in the eurozone are clearly designed with the intention to achieve further integrative steps, such as the supranationalisation of banking supervision under the plans for a eurozone banking union and eventually the creation of a common corporate tax base, an explicit ambition which is set out in the EPP (European Council 2011: 20). As was mentioned earlier, the acceptance of the possibility that spillover could be followed by 'spill-around' in the form of a creation of rival organisations or even 'spillback' towards the national level was accepted by Haas himself and stated in his 1970 revision of neofunctionalism. He considered this possibility to occur if the supranational institutional setting, which had evolved as a result of spillover, should favour certain groups of actors over others. Haas considered this particularly to be the case in the area of market integration: 'Actors will evaluate interdependence as negative if they feel their regional partners profit more than they; negative evaluations can be predicted in common markets and free trade areas of less developed countries' (Haas 1970: 614–615).

This inherent flexibility of neofunctionalism (particularly in its more recent variations), which has also been described as 'dynamic' (Rosamond 2006: 238), makes it a useful theoretical approach to analyse the developments in the eurozone and the whole of the EU in response to the crisis. There is a realistic possibility that future progress in the EU will not be linear in the form of a uniform progression of spillover from the Single Market towards full political union. A far more likely scenario is one where the new policy mechanisms in the EU and the eurozone are developed further or are even discarded again. Once the full implications on the national sovereignty of member states and especially the sovereign decision-making powers of national parliaments have become obvious and lead to growing domestic opposition, it is not inconceivable that individual countries will call for the renegotiation of the mechanism. If this turns out not be possible countries could ultimately decide to withdraw from them. This includes France and Germany, the two countries who were the driving forces behind the new mechanisms, could have second thoughts. The new French President Hollande has publicly expressed his discontent with the European Commission's more active role in issuing guidelines on structural reforms to member states. In May 2013 President Hollande angrily reacted to the Commission's call on the French government to implement profound reforms of its employment and pension system to counter the country's deepening economic malaise. Hollande surprisingly re-emphasised the national prerogative to make sovereign decisions in these policy areas:

> The Commission cannot dictate us what we have to do. It can simply say that France must balance its public accounts. As far as structural reforms are concerned, especially pension reforms, it is up to us, and us alone, to say which is the best path to attain this objective (Waterfield 2013).

This in essence contradicts the provisions of the new policy framework where member states are required to take notice of European Commission recommendations when they develop their National Stability and Convergence Plans under the European Semester and to discuss further details under the EPP provisions. In Germany the Federal Constitutional Court, which tends to act as the guardian of German national sovereignty, emphasised in its evaluation of the provision of the Lisbon Treaty back in 2009 that further moves towards the harmonisation of key policy areas political union would not be in line with the German basic law in its current form. In this respect the Court stressed that 'European unification on the basis of a treaty union of sovereign countries must not be realised in a way which leaves member states no sufficient scope for the political design of the economic, cultural and social living conditions' (Bundesverfassungsgericht 2009).

The Court made it clear that the development of the EU towards a full federal political union with Germany as a member could only occur on the basis of a new German constitution, which would have to be decided on the basis of a public referendum. This Court has consequently set a substantial hurdle for German policy-makers when it comes to further integration. This is something which is currently hardly discussed in the German domestic political context. However, it is likely to resurface if and when further plans to move towards full political union in the eurozone emerge. What Haas had assumed about the lack of strategic direction of political decision-makers therefore turns out to be more valid than ever. He emphasised that particularly the changes in the economic conditions or the political circumstances cause actors to re-evaluate a chosen direction (Haas 1970: 617). Overall, he was certain that: 'most political actors are incapable of long-range purposive behaviour because they stumble from one set of decision into the next as a result of not having been able to foresee many of the implications and consequences of earlier decisions' (Haas 1970: 627).

The sovereign debt crisis in the eurozone provides us with factual evidence that this is the case. The crucial question in this respect is who actually determines the future shape of European integration: politicians or market forces? As things currently stand it seems that political elites have lost the control over the agenda to rating agencies and bond markets and are hence driven by events rather than to be able to control them.

3.2 A NEW VARIETY OF MULTI-LEVEL GOVERNANCE

Under the leadership of Germany governments in the EU responded to the eurozone sovereign debt crisis with the creation of a set of overlapping policy initiatives. After attempts to stabilise the fiscal position of crisis economies through the loan mechanisms of the EFSF (and now the ESM), the EU concentrated on strengthening policy coordination in the Single

Market and especially in the eurozone. With its accompanying European Semester annual cycle of policy coordination, the new Europe 2020 Strategy has noticeably moved on from the OMC. The OMC was based on the aspiration to achieve progress on national policy reforms by introducing a naming and shaming comparative peer review process of best and worst performers with regard to the overall targets set under the Lisbon Strategy. However in practice the peer pressure proved to be too weak to encourage governments to move beyond the policy preferences they had set themselves. Progress tended to occur predominantly in areas in which governments had already prioritised in their domestic agenda, like in the case of the profound labour market reforms initiated by the Schröder government in Germany in 2003, which coincided with the overall welfare-to-work ideology of Lisbon. The failure of external peer pressure under Lisbon to make a significant impact on the domestic agenda explains why Lisbon's ambition to achieve greater policy coherence between member states remained largely unfulfilled. The High Level Expert Group report chaired by the former Dutch Prime Minister Wim Kok emphasised this in their report on the Lisbon Strategy in 2004: 'Individual member states have made progress in one or more of these policy priority areas but none has succeeded consistently across a broad front. If Europe is to achieve its targets, it needs to step up its efforts considerably' (European Commission 2004: 7). In 2005 the newly appointed Barroso Commission had recalibrated the Lisbon Strategy on the priorities of growth and jobs, based on the expectation that clear progress could be made in the acceleration of market liberalisation in the area of services and more specifically the financial services sector. In spite of having narrowed down what the Kok report had considered to be an overburdened policy agenda, five years later the Commission again had to concede that overall reform progress in many member states remained disappointing. In its 2010 reassessment of the Lisbon Strategy the Commission came to the conclusion that 'the delivery gap between commitments and actions has not been closed' (European Commission 2010: 4).

The Lisbon successor, the Europe 2020 Strategy, is even more ambitious than the original Lisbon Strategy and presents member states with a large set of detailed policy targets in the areas of employment, education and training, research and development, and environmental sustainability. This is an astonishingly bold approach, given the fact that most member states currently have very little financial leeway to invest in these policy initiatives. In practice the main focus of the European Semester annual policy cycle under Europe 2020 lies in ensuring budgetary and macroeconomic stability, particularly in the eurozone. All member states are required to develop annual national fiscal and macroeconomic reform plans with targets which are agreed in cooperation with the Commission. Non-compliance with the targets set out in the reform plans however only has consequences for the eurozone-17 countries in the form of financial penalties. This is the result of the provisions of the intergovernmental Treaty on Stability, Coordination and Governance in the Economic and Monetary Union ('Fiscal Compact') which was signed in March 2012 and which entered into force in January 2013. The Fiscal Compact was signed by the eurozone-17 plus eight other EU member states, excluding the Czech Republic and the United Kingdom. The veto by British Prime Minister David Cameron was responsible for the treaty ending up as an intergovernmental agreement rather than an amendment to the EU's existing treaty structure. The latter would have been preferred by Germany's Chancellor Angela Merkel. All signatories to the treaty are expected to determine the 'golden' fiscal rule in their constitutional set-up, which limits the structural level of debt to 0.5 per cent of the national GDP at market prices. The Fiscal Compact also enhances the supervisory role of the Commission in that it can initiate an Excessive Deficit Procedure (EDP) against a eurozone country without prior consultation of the other member states in the Council. Only if a qualified majority of member states in the Council object to the initiation of an EDP against a member state will it not be initiated ('reverse QMV').

The fact that under the provisions of monetary union the ECB has been in charge of setting one-size-fits-all interest rates for the whole of the eurozone has opened it up to criticisms. The latter centre on the accusation that the interest rates were generally set too low. This encouraged the Southern European eurozone member states to exercise a predominantly demand-orientated growth strategy which was largely based on the expansion of consumer credit. In this respect, it has to be acknowledged that it has always been an nearly impossible task to determine the right interest rate for all economies of the eurozone. The ECB was faced with the stark reality of a variety of economic models with profound differences in their competitive advantages and a lack of coordination of national fiscal policies. Setting a higher interest rate may have deterred the demand-orientated economies in the South from expanding their credit-driven strategies. However at the same time it would have undermined the export-driven economies of Northern Europe, most of all Germany, which would consequently have risked dampening the sluggish growth levels in the EU further (Hall 2012: 360).

Nevertheless the biggest weakness in the project of monetary integration lies in the failure of eurozone member states to stick to the rules they had jointly determined for the project of monetary union. The Stability and Growth Pact (SGP), which the German government had insisted on as a condition for allowing Greece to join the emerging single currency, subsequently essentially turned into a gentleman's agreement. Under this system member states could argue that they had to exceed the annual level of borrowing by more than 3 per cent in relation to their GDP if the economy had been affected by a severe downturn or any other unusual event. The Commission also had to consider not implementing an EDP if there was a risk that this would undermine the growth potential of a country in the medium term and impact on its ability to pursue the Lisbon goals. This explains why both France and Germany were able to get away with breaking the annual deficit criteria of the SGP soon after the euro had come into operation. In the French case it was for two years (2002–2004) and three consecutive years (2002–2005) in the German case. Both countries negotiated successfully with the European Commission to avoid the initiation of an EDP by arguing that the effects of the economic downturn following 9/11 and structural problems such as the ongoing effects of reunification in Germany had to be taken into account. They found a cooperative partner in the Commission which was then headed by the former Italian Prime Minister Romano Prodi. The latter had publicly expressed his scepticism about the SGP, which he called 'rigid' and 'stupid' (Osborn 2002).

The second criteria which limited the level of government gross debt to 60 per cent of a country's GDP was largely ignored, mainly based on the expectation that eurozone members with a large structural deficit would be able to reduce their deficit during periods of economic growth. Greece was therefore allowed to join the economic and monetary union (EMU) in 2001 although its annual borrowing level stood at 4.5 per cent of its GDP and its structural deficit at 103.7 per cent (Eurostat 2013). The budgetary situation of Italy was even worse. In spite of the fact that its structural deficit had fluctuated between 105 and 120 per cent throughout the late 1990s and early 2000s, the country was included in the eurozone's founding group in 1999.

The governance light approach in the eurozone was part of the EU's embrace of the wider globalisation agenda, which favoured minimising red tape for businesses and the financial industry. Ironically under the loose OMC a more detailed target-driven regulatory framework, which was supposed to increase the level of policy coordination between governments activities, was developed without ensuring that it would be strictly implemented in practice. Both the economic and social reform targets under the Lisbon Strategy and the operation of the eurozone SGP were in practice operated under the OMC (Borrás and Jacobsson 2004). The result was a predictable high level of vulnerability towards external shocks such as the global financial crisis (Underhill 2011: 368).

3.3 TOWARDS MULTIPLE CORES OF DIFFERENTIATED INTEGRATION

The political response to the crisis in the EU has created a new complex policy framework with multiple layers of responsibility which essentially divides its membership base into three cores with noticeable differences in the level of integration and influence: a gradual political union in an ever more deeply integrated eurozone core, a Euro Plus Group of countries who voluntarily adhere to the eurozone SGP criteria and a fringe group of countries that prefer to limit themselves to the OMC under the European Semester.

The political architecture which emerges from the crisis has divided the EU both in horizontal and in vertical terms. Officially the aim of the various initiatives is to maintain the coherence of the Single Market. The vertical division of the EU membership base however already started with the Europe 2020 Strategy.

The agreed targets in the national stability and convergence programmes under the European Semester are only binding for the euro-17 countries. Equally the intergovernmental Fiscal Compact, which has 25 signatories, only foresees consequences for a breach of the 'golden' fiscal rule for the euro-17 countries. The level of horizontal integration is therefore strongest in the euro-17 core, where the role of the European Commission has been transformed into that of an executive regulatory body with binding direct supervisory powers over national fiscal and macroeconomic policies. Whatever shape the political dimension of the eurozone will take in the future, it is likely to equip the Commission with substantially more supervisory powers over national policies. Eventually the Commission could move into a position which is equivalent to that of a national executive. German Finance Minister Wolfgang Schäuble called for the creation of a directly elected European President who would lead the Commission which would also get stronger regulatory powers. Schäuble's vision is to develop the Commission into a fully-fledged European executive (Schäuble 2013). Attempts to deepen political union in the eurozone are also evident in the latest Commission proposals for enhanced economic and fiscal policy integration. The Commission envisages the 'possibility to require a revision of national budgets in line with European commitments' (European Commission 2012: 25) as a realistic goal which should be achieved within the next five years. Its practical implementation will have a profound impact on the ability of national governments and parliaments to decide budgetary and economic policy priorities independently. Once the practical implications of the compact become evident it is not unrealistic to assume that other eurozone outsiders such as Denmark, Sweden or Hungary could reconsider their position as signatories to the compact. This leads us back to the neofunctionalist notion that the 'spillback' of powers is possible if certain groups of actors consider it to be necessary.

The EPP of 2011 is an attempt to limit the vertical division between the now eurozone-18 and the ten outsiders, some of which are aspiring members, by creating a deeper policy coordination between euro insiders and outsiders beyond the Europe 2020 targets. The aim of the EPP is to encourage the eurozone-18 countries and the participating outsiders Bulgaria, Denmark, Latvia, Lithuania, Poland and Romania to implement policies which enhance economic competitiveness, speed up the reform of their labour markets and welfare systems, stabilise their financial sector and implement budgetary austerity. Member state governments initially set their own targets. These are subsequently monitored by all EPP members on the basis of annual Commission progress reports (*Pact for the Euro* 2011).

The multiple layers of policy coordination and supervision, which are linked with a variety of targets, however risk once again to overburden member states in a similar fashion as was the case with the original Lisbon Strategy. The eurozone outsiders who are signatories to the EPP and the Fiscal Compact have little incentive to do more than just to meet the SGP criteria, which will eventually secure them entry into the eurozone. The Commission is keen to stress that the various policy initiatives and mechanisms are closely interlinked. It also wants the deepening of political integration to occur within the existing treaty structure of the EU and to avoid further intergovernmental agreements which would exclude individual member states or groups of countries. It is more than doubtful that this can be achieved in practice. The EPP may contribute to reducing the distance in terms of vertical integration between the eurozone and the rest of the EU-27. Horizontally the EPP has nevertheless caused a further division of the membership base into not just two but now four cores with descending levels of vertical integration in the following order:

1. The euro-18 group (which now includes the first member of the EPP with Latvia having joined in January 2014);
2. The closely connected Euro Plus Group;
3. The semi-detached group of countries who are only signatories to the Fiscal Compact (Hungary and Sweden);
4. The periphery group of countries positioned on the fringe of Single Market cooperation (the UK and the Czech Republic).

Figure 3.2 illustrates this vertical and horizontal division which should be considered as an interim development. In the foreseeable future the eurozone core could grow further, if the sovereign debt crisis is resolved

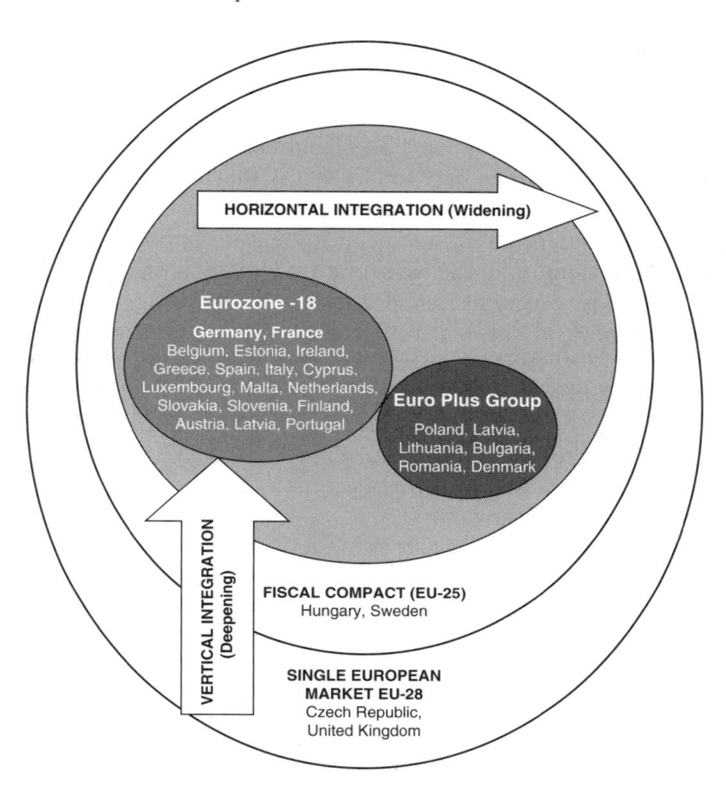

Source: The author.

Figure 3.2 The EU's emerging multiple cores

and the euro is stabilised as a global currency. Alternatively it could shrink if the crisis deepens further and (a) either no new members are allowed to enter in the short to medium term or (b) the structurally weak members are either forced out or decide to leave voluntarily. In the case of (b) it is likely that the EPP would become superfluent and a starker vertical division between insiders and outsiders would be re-established. Even the internal division of the eurozone into two groupings (for example a Northern and Southern group) remains a possibility under deepening crisis conditions.

The short-term political effects of the Franco-German drive towards political union can be seen in the further alienation of sceptical member states, such as the UK and the Czech Republic. A major factor in the decision of British Prime Minister David Cameron to promise a public referendum on EU membership in 2017 is the British scepticism towards the emerging plans for the deepening of political integration in the EU. A similar sentiment can be found across the political spectrum in the Czech Republic. There is a realistic and to date unprecedented prospect that the UK, one of the leading member states, could leave the EU within the next five years. Other countries may follow suit if they feel that staying in the EU severely undermines the autonomy to determine key domestic policy preferences. Eurosceptic sentiments and domestic opposition against the plans for political union in the eurozone are already growing substantially. Even in Germany economists and business leaders who are opposed to a further pooling of national sovereignty and the participation of the country in the EFSF/ESM loan mechanisms have organised themselves in a new Anti-Euro Party. The Alternative for Germany (ADF), which will stand at the 2013 German general election, wants to abolish the eurozone and calls for the return to national currencies in the EU. Similar groupings, some of them with a fascist inclination, have appeared in the UK, Italy, Greece, Belgium and Hungary.

The multiple layers of policy coordination amongst the eurozone-18 and aspiring members may manage to restore market confidence in the single currency. In the end the fundamental question remains how citizens will react to the complexity of these new policy mechanisms, which have the division of responsibilities between the national and EU institutional level further. The danger which lies in this for the future of the EU is that it may result in an even deeper rift between the (albeit reluctant) aspirations of the political elites to deepen political union and the desire of citizens. The latter seem to tend towards supporting the repatriation of powers to the national level in order to be able to address domestic problems (such as spiralling youth unemployment) with specific national solutions without the constraints of the need for binding policy coordination at the EU level. The essential question is therefore how long the spillover pressures towards deeper political integration, which were initiated by external crisis conditions, will continue if the expectations and loyalties of national actors should indeed shift substantially in favour of the spillback of powers towards the domestic level. If Ernst B. Haas could witness these developments today he would most likely speak of exciting times for the neofunctionalist paradigm.

REFERENCES

Boerzel, T.A. (2005) 'Mind the Gap! European Integration Between Level and Scope', *Journal of European Public Policy* 12 (2): 217–236.

Borrás, S. and K. Jacobsson (2004) 'The Open Method of Co-ordination and New Governance Patterns in the EU', *Journal of European Public Policy* 11 (2): 185–208.

Bundesverfassungsgericht (2009) *Leitsätze zum Urteil des Zweiten Senats*. 30 June. Karlsruhe: BVG.

Buonanno, L. and N. Nugent (2013) *Policies and Policy Processes of the European Union*. Basingstoke: Palgrave Macmillan.

Dyson, K. (2012) 'Economic and Monetary Disunion?', in J. Hayward and R. Wurzel (eds) *European Disunion: Between Sovereignty and Solidarity*. Basingstoke: Palgrave Macmillan, pp. 181–199.

European Commission (2004) *Facing the Challenge: The Lisbon Strategy for Growth and Employment*. Report from the High Level Group chaired by Wim Kok, November. Brussels: EU.

European Commission (2008) *Eurobarometer 68: Public Opinion in the European Union*. Brussels: EU.

European Commission (2010) *Lisbon Evaluation Document*. SEC (2010) 114 final. Brussels: EU.

European Commission (2011) *Eurobarometer 76: Public Opinion in the European Union*. Brussels: EU.

European Commission (2012) *A Blueprint for a Deep and Genuine Economic and Monetary Union: Launching a European Debate*. COM (2012) 777 final/2, 30 November.

European Commission (2013) *Standard Eurobarometer 80 Autumn 2013: Public Opinion in the European Union*. Brussels: EU.

European Council (2011) 'Conclusions from the European Council 24/25 March', Brussels: EU. Available at: http://www.consilium.europa.eu/uedocs/cms_data/docs/pressdata/en/ec/120296.pdf (accessed 7 July 2013).

Eurostat (2013) 'Government Deficit/Surplus and General Government deficit/surplus'. Available at: http://epp.eurostat.ec.europa.eu/tgm/table.do?tab=table&init=1&language=en&pcode=tec00127&plugin=1 and http://epp.eurostat.ec.europa.eu/tgm/table.do?tab=table&init=1&language=en&pcode=tec00127&plugin=1 (accessed 13 March 2013).

Haas, E.B. (1964) *Beyond the Nation-State: Functionalism and International Organization*. Stanford: Stanford University Press.

Haas, E.B. (1968) *The Uniting of Europe: Political, Social, and Economic Forces, 1950–57*. Stanford: Standford University Press, 2nd edn.

Haas, E.B. (1970) 'The Study of Regional Integration: Reflections on the Joy and Anguish of Pretheorizing', *International Organization* 24 (4): 606–646.

Hall, P.A. (2012) 'The Economics and Politics of the Euro Crisis', *German Politics* 21 (4): 355–371.

Hoffmann, S. (1966) 'Obstinate or Obsolete? The Fate of the Nation-State and the Case of Western Europe', *Daedalus* 95: 863–911.

Hübner, K. (2012) 'German Crisis Management and Leadership – from Ignorance to Procrastination to Action', *Asia Europe Journal* 9 (2–4): 159–177.

Lapavitsas, C., A. Kaltenbrunner, G. Labrinidis, D. Lindo, J. Meadway, J. Mitchell, J.P. Painceira, E. Pires, J. Powell, A. Stenfors, N. Teles and L. Vatikiotis (2012) *Crisis in the Eurozone*. London and New York: Verso.

Lindberg, L.N. (1963) *The Political Dynamics of European Economic Integration*. Stanford: Stanford University Press.

Merkel, A. and N. Sarkozy (2011) Joint Press Conference, Paris, 16 August.

Mitrany, D. (1943) 'A Working Peace System', reprinted in B.F. Nelsen and A. Stubb (eds) *The European Union: Readings on the Theory and Practice of European Integration*. Basingstoke: Palgrave Macmillan, pp. 93–113.

Mitrany, D. (1965) 'The Prospect of Integration: Federal or Functional?', *Journal of Common Market Studies*, 4: 119–145.
Mitrany, D. (1975) 'The Prospect of Integration: Federal or Functional', in A.J.R. Groom and P. Taylor (eds), *Functionalism: Theory and Practice in International Relations*. London: University of London Press, pp. 68–78.
Moravcsik, A. (1993) 'Preferences and Power in the European Community: A Liberal Intergovernmentalist Approach', *Journal of Common Market Studies* 31: 473–524.
Moravcsik, A. (2005) 'The European Constitutional Compromise and the Neofunctionalist Legacy', *Journal of European Public Policy* 12 (2): 349–386.
Niemann, A. and P. Schmitter (2009) 'Neofunctionalism', in A. Wiener and T. Diez (eds) *European Integration Theory*. Oxford: Oxford University Press, pp. 45–66.
Osborn, A. (2002) 'Prodi Disowns "Stupid" Stability Pact', *The Guardian*, 18 October. Available at: http://www.theguardian.com/business/2002/oct/18/theeuro.europeanunion (accessed 13 March 2013).
Pact for the Euro (2011) 'Conclusions of the Heads of State of Government of the Euro Area', 11 March. Available at: http://www.consilium.europa.eu/uedocs/cms_Data/docs/pressdata/en/ec/119809.pdf (accessed 13 March 2013).
Paterson, W. (2012) 'A Contested Franco-German Duumvirate', in J. Hayward and R. Wurzel (eds) *European Disunion: Between Sovereignty and Solidarity*. Basingstoke: Palgrave Macmillan.
Pollack, M.A., H. Wallace and A.R. Young (2010) 'EU Policy-Making in Challenging Times: Adversity, Adaptability and Resilience', in H. Wallace, M.A. Pollack and A.R. Young (eds) *Policy-Making in the European Union*. Oxford: Oxford University Press, pp. 481–501.
Risse, T. (2005) 'Neofunctionalism, European Identity, and the Puzzles of European Integration', *Journal of European Public Policy* 12 (2): 291–309.
Rosamond, B. (2006) 'The Uniting of Europe and the Foundation of EU Studies: Revisiting the Neofunctionalism of Ernst B. Haas', *Journal of European Public Policy* 12 (2): 237–254.
Schäuble, W. (2013) Speech at the Award Ceremony for the 2012 Charlemagne Prize, Aachen, Germany, 17 May.
Schmitter, P.C. (1970) 'A Revised Theory of Regional Integration', *International Organization* 24 (4): 836–868.
Tranholm-Mikkelsen, J. (1991) 'Neo-Functionalism: Obstinate or Obsolete? A Reappraisal in the Light of the New Dynamism of the EC', *Journal of International Studies* 20 (1): 1–22.
Traynor, I., N. Watt and D. Gow (2011) 'David Cameron Blocks EU Treaty with Veto, Casting Britain Adrift in Europe', *The Guardian*, 9 December.
Underhill, G.R. (2011) 'Paved with Good Intentions: Global Financial Integration and the Eurozone's Response', *European Political Science* 10 (3): 366–374.
Wallace, H. (2010) 'An Institutional Anatomy and Five Policy Modes', in H. Wallace, M.A. Pollack and A.R. Young (eds) *Policy-Making in the European Union*. Oxford: Oxford University Press, pp. 69–106.
Waterfield, B. (2013) 'François Hollande tells European Commission it Can't "Dictate" to France', *Daily Telegraph*, 29 May. Available at: http://www.telegraph.co.uk/finance/financialcrisis/10088005/Francois-Hollande-tells-European-Commission-it-cant-dictate-to-France.html (accessed 13 March 2013).

PART II

National varieties of economic and social models in the EU-27

4. The United Kingdom – still the liberal model?

The British economy has been firmly placed in the liberal paradigm of the Varieties of Capitalism (VoC) approach since Prime Minister Margaret Thatcher had introduced fundamental reforms in the late 1970s. In the decade between 1979 and 1989 the British model underwent a radical transformation from its traditional post-war approach, which was characterised by Keynesian economic policies with high levels of taxation and public spending combined with a significant political influence for the trade unions.

The history of Britain's relationship with the post-war project of institutionalised European integration has been a troubled one right from the start. By the 1960s it became obvious that the British model had fallen substantially behind many of its continental partners (particularly Germany) which were benefiting from the trading opportunities opened by the creation of the Common European Market in 1957. While the continent was booming, Britain moved through repeated cycles of boom and bust and generally struggled with sluggish growth and high levels of unemployment. Britain had pursued an alternative route to membership of the European Economic Community (EEC), which it considered to be far too much of a political club, by creating the European Free Trade Association (EFTA) in 1960 with Austria, Denmark, Norway and Switzerland.

The EFTA failed to produce the benefits for the British economy that political leaders had originally anticipated. Britain's GDP grew at a substantially lower rate than that of its continental European counterparts in the 1950s and 1960s, when its GDP per capita ranking was below all other European countries (Sanders 1990: 117). At the same time trade with countries in the sterling zone and the Commonwealth decreased substantially. By the mid-1960s more than half of British goods were exported to countries in Western Europe and the US. This emphasised the growing importance of the newly created Common European Market for the UK. The British political elite started to shift towards favouring EEC entry but was rejected twice, by French President de Gaulle in 1963 and 1967. De Gaulle vetoed British entry by arguing that it would undermine the future of the European project. De Gaulle essentially considered the UK as a Trojan horse which, once inside the EEC, would try to oppose the further deepening of political integration (George 1998: 35). When Britain finally joined in 1973 the Common Market was fundamentally shaken by the oil crisis which had emerged in the wake of the military confrontation between Israel and Arab countries in 1967. Britain consequently obtained little immediate economic benefit from joining the Common Market. Within a few years the combination of high levels of public spending, slow or even negative growth combined with spiralling inflation had pushed the country to the brink of financial disaster (Hay 2007: 195). In 1976 Labour Chancellor Denis Healey had to submit a humiliating request for financial support to the International Monetary Fund (IMF). Britain subsequently received a £2.3 billion loan from the IMF. The continuing disputes between the Labour government headed by James Callaghan and the trade unions mounted in the infamous winter of discontent in 1978–1979 during which public services in the UK essentially came to a halt. The widespread public perception that the trade unions could put a stranglehold on the country and consequently hold the government to ransom under Labour substantially strengthened the Conservative opposition. In combination with rising levels of unemployment and an obvious decline in the external competitiveness of British manufacturing industry this proved disastrous for the Labour Party's economic record. Conservative leader Margaret Thatcher hence led a successful election campaign in 1979 with the slogan 'Labour isn't working', a pun on the rising levels of unemployment in the country, which resulted in her winning an overwhelming mandate to become Prime Minister.

In addition to joining the EEC at a time of crisis, Britain also entered an organisation which had developed its institution and policies for 16 years under Franco-German leadership. Once inside the EEC British leaders realised that some of the EEC's existing policies, such as the Common Agricultural Policy, were of little benefit to the country which has a much smaller agricultural sector than for example France. At the same time Britain became a substantial net contributor to the Community budget. Any attempts to fundamentally change the established structures and policies of the EEC met the fierce resistance of France, which was usually supported by a compliant West Germany. Only two years after Britain had joined the EEC, Harold Wilson's Labour government decided to put the question of membership to a public vote in a referendum. The outcome of the public referendum in April 1975, in which 67.2 per cent of the British electorate voted to stay inside the EEC, seemed to provide a boost to the pro-European argument in the UK. The referendum itself however failed to settle the deep-seated scepticism about the benefits of Britain's membership of the EEC. Before Margaret Thatcher became leader, the

Conservative Party was the pro-European party in British politics, which considered the removal of trade barriers between the member states of the Common Market as beneficial for the British economy. The Labour Party on the other hand became increasingly sceptical of the European project. Especially the left of the party and the trade unions considered it to be a project aimed at implementing a capitalist free market agenda which risked undermining the scope to determine social policies at home (Heffernan 2000: 384). This culminated in the Labour Party's 1983 general election manifesto in which it advocated withdrawal from the European Community (EC). When Margaret Thatcher as Prime Minister pursued an increasingly radical right-wing agenda at home, the attitude of those on the left of the political spectrum towards the EC started to shift. From the mid-1980s onwards Labour considered the Community no longer as a threat but as an opportunity and a platform against Thatcherist policies at home. This was the result of a perceived shift in the EC's agenda under the Delors Commission, which had the ambition to enhance the creation of the Single European Market (SEM) with a common social policy agenda. At the same time the ambitions of the socialist Commission President Jacques Delors fundamentally changed Mrs Thatcher's view of the Community. Previously she had been a stark defender of Britain's membership and campaigned actively for the country to remain in the Common Market during the 1975 referendum campaign.

It was her expectation that the sole purpose of the EC should be the creation of a free trade area, in her own words a 'treaty for "economic liberty" from which all member states, most of all the UK, would benefit' (Thatcher 2002: 372). When the vision of political union cropped up again in the run-up to the Maastricht Treaty Thatcher turned into an ardent Eurosceptic who openly defended what she perceived as Britain's national interest. At the EC Summit in Fontainebleau in 1984 Thatcher had already negotiated a controversial permanent rebate from the EC budget for UK to compensate for the British contributions to the Community budget which were disproportionate to the country's overall GDP (Gowland and Turner 2000: 167). Thatcher followed this up by uttering the three famous 'no's' against what she perceived as Jacques Delors's plans to create a federal superstate in her address to the House of Commons on October 1990. An essential part of Thatcher's legacy is that she instilled an ardent scepticism about the purpose of the European project into the British psyche which no subsequent government has dared to seriously challenge. She was strongly supported in this by parts of the British media, particularly the newspapers which were under the control of the Australian born media mogul Rupert Murdoch. Like Thatcher he is an ardent Eurosceptic. Ever since Thatcher's departure Murdoch's Eurosceptic tabloids have relentlessly pushed forward the notion that even political cooperation with continental Europe, let alone deeper political integration, would quasi inevitably result in the loss of national sovereignty. Britain's engagement in the EU is therefore presented as a process of weakening national and parliamentary sovereignty and ultimately of undermining the long-standing tradition of Westminster democracy (Young 1998: 508).

To challenge this notion it would have been essential for the political elite to put forward a sustained public argument in favour of Britain's engagement in the EU which especially highlights the benefits of the country's membership of the Single Market. For a while it seemed that this task would be taken over by the first Labour government since 1979. Elected in 1997 it was spearheaded by a young Prime Minister who had promised to redefine his country's relations with the EU. Tony Blair spoke of his ambition to turn Britain into a leader in the EU alongside France and Germany by engaging constructively on European issues (Blair 1995a). He also vowed to take on domestic Euroscepticism head on and to lead a positive debate on Europe, which initially even included the ambition to convince the country of entry into the eurozone, provided that the economic conditions would be right (Blair 2000). Blair abandoned his European vocation after the military intervention in Iraq when he started to concentrate on his moral crusade against what he perceived to be Islamic radicalism. Prominent pro-European voices in the government such as Robin Cook, Mo Mowlam or Peter Mandelson had either resigned or were increasingly sidelined. At the same time the Conservative opposition had adopted a profoundly Thatcherite approach towards the EU under the leadership of successive Tory opposition leaders since 1997. William Hague, Michael Howard, Ian Duncan Smith and the current leader David Cameron are long-standing Eurosceptics. The Liberal Democrats hence remained as the only party represented in parliament which actively made the case for British engagement in Europe. As a smaller party in opposition it could however only have limited impact on the public debate. Since it entered a coalition with the Conservatives in 2010, senior Liberal Democrats have been far less outspoken on Europe and had to reluctantly support the rather uncooperative stance of Conservative Prime Minister David Cameron towards the EU.

The public debate and media coverage of the EU in Britain has therefore remained predominantly negative and in the Thatcherite tradition of warning of the negative implications for the country's national interests and sovereignty. EU institutions and policies are predominantly portrayed as excessively bureaucratic, wasteful and remote from the interests of the citizens. Since the advent of the global financial crisis Conservative ministers and parts of the tabloid media have run a sustained campaign which highlights the negative impact of the freedom of movement for EU citizens on the British labour market and public services. Labour migration from other EU countries is widely portrayed as a burden on public services and as having the effect of driving down working standards and wages for British workers. Tabloid headlines such as 'EU wants migrants to take our jobs' (Hall 2012) and 'True toll of mass migration on UK life: half of Britons suffer under strain placed on schools, police, NHS and housing' (Black 2013) are now commonplace. This explains why the majority of the British public is far less convinced of the benefits of being part of the SEM than citizens in other member states. *Eurobarometer 78* (Autumn 78) recorded that only 37 per cent of British people state that the four freedoms of the Single Market are the most positive result of the EU. This represents a noticeable contrast to the EU-27 average of 52 per cent (European Commission 2012a). Even in the Czech Republic, which is frequently portrayed as a Eurosceptic country, 70 per cent consider the SEM as the most positive achievement of the European integration process (European Commission 2012b).

The deep-seated scepticism towards the EU as an organisation and the process of pooling sovereignty with its European neighbours is an essential part of the UK's cultural heritage. It is hence important to consider it in the analysis of the political economy of contemporary Britain. It helps to explains why the British economic model has been more resistant to fundamental change than other European economies. The case of the British economy illustrates that Hall and Soskice's original VoC approach is too narrow to explain the full complexity of the institutional foundations of comparative advantage. The firm-centred approach of VoC remains rather vague when it comes to the impact the domestic state culture has on the development of a country's political economy. Hall and Soskice acknowledge that 'the character of a political regime may contribute to the development of a particular type of economy' (Hall and Soskice 2001: 49). In this respect they emphasise the differences between the centralised Westminster system of government, which is predominantly found in liberal market economies and the 'consociational' government regime of coordinated market economies, which is characterised by cooperation, consensus and multiple veto points. Their conclusion with respect to the impact of these regime differences on the level of institutional change is however limited. The overall assumption is that governments allow institutional change only to the extent that it does not substantially undermine the competitive advantage of domestic firms (Ibid.: 52).

The British case shows more than any other example in Europe that resistance to institutional change has deeper roots than simply the defence of the national competitive advantage. The British scepticism towards the

EU can certainly at least in part be explained by the concern that conceding greater powers to Brussels may force Britain to abandon its light touch regulatory approach towards the financial industry, which is considered to be a crucial pillar for its economy. British opposition towards the deepening of political integration to a growing extent stems from the desire to defend its national competitive advantage, which is perceived to lie in maintaining the role of the City of London as a global financial hub.

I would argue that the Euroscepticism in the UK has now become so deep-seated that it is most likely that a majority of the British people would reject moves towards the deepening of economic and political integration even if it was in the country's economic interest. A Sky News poll in June 2013 found that 51 per cent of British people would vote to leave the EU in the public referendum which is likely to be held by 2017. The same percentage stated that they would not change their mind about the EU, even if the government managed to substantially renegotiate British membership. Forty nine per cent of British voters would choose to leave the EU if the country was forced to introduce the euro as part of its membership commitments (Sky News 2013). The *Eurobarometer 79* poll conducted in May 2013 shows a similar picture, with 79 per cent of British people categorically rejecting the concept of a single European currency. The latter may be considered to be a temporary anti-euro peak given the current crisis symptoms in the eurozone and the fact that public opinion in other EU countries outside the eurozone has also turned increasingly against the euro (Denmark 66 per cent, Poland 63 per cent, Czech Republic 71 per cent and Sweden 79 per cent) (European Commission 2013: 24). Combined with the British scepticism of even limited economic integration within the Single Market framework it however paints the picture of an inherently Eurosceptic country. Currently 33 per cent of voters consider EU membership as harmful to the British economy and 58 per cent reject the SEM principle of the freedom of movement of people as harmful to British interests (Sky News 2013). The fact that the UK never went through a radical overhaul of its constitutional setting distinguishes the country noticeably from its continental European neighbours who frequently went through internal political revolutions and periods of foreign occupation. The failure to have experienced 'a serious, house-clearing revolution' (Denman 1997: 289) at home explains why the British remain fundamentally attached to their unwritten domestic constitutional setting, which has evolved over centuries. An essential core feature of the British state is parliamentary sovereignty and the representation of the monarchy through acts of parliament. The notion of transferring sovereign powers of decision-making to unelected and unaccountable supranational bodies such as the European Commission fundamentally contradicts the

British state tradition. Moreover, the British political system of centralised decision-making in Whitehall and the first-past-the-post electoral system which usually results in a one party government, make it difficult for the country's political elite to come to terms with the system of multi-level governance of the EU. In spite of the developments over the past decade where regulatory powers were devolved to Scotland and Wales and the first formal government coalition since 1945 was formed, the British political elite and the public continue to consider power-sharing in the EU as an alien concept (Young 2000: 199). Most continental countries who have political cultures where frequent compromise, often on the basis of the lowest common denominator between various actors, is commonplace find it much easier to adapt to the almost permanent process of intergovernmental bargaining and renegotiation in the EU. From the British perspective it is a burdensome and time-consuming process which lacks efficiency and purpose. Margaret Thatcher, the most Eurosceptic post-war Prime Minister characterised it as an 'un-British combination of high-flown rhetoric and pork-barrel politics which passed for European statemanship' (Thatcher 1993: 727). Thatcher's successors all shared the frustration with the way with which the EU is being run beyond their dividing party lines. Tony Blair returned from the difficult intergovernmental EU Summit in Nice in December 2000, where he clashed with his French counterpart Jacques Chirac over proposals for major EU institutional reform, with the conclusion that 'we cannot continue to take decisions as important as this in this way' (*The Times* 2000). His successor Gordon Brown had already struggled with the EU's decision-making processes as Chancellor and did not find them less frustrating as Prime Minister. He was widely perceived as a Eurosceptic who stopped Blair from taking Britain into the eurozone and was far less open towards the further deepening of integration than Blair (Norton 2012: 260).The current Prime Minister David Cameron has made no attempt to conceal his frustration with doing business in the EU. At a recent press conference, which followed very complicated negotiations on the EU budget for 2013, he publicly expressed this: 'It is, and I won't lie, it is immensely frustrating sometimes, the way this organisation works' (Tapsfield 2013).

Britain's deep unease with its membership of the EU is a central element of its political economy and explains its development since the radical transformation it underwent during the Thatcherite revolution. The less than half-hearted commitment to engagement in Europe is also closely linked to the dominant characteristic of Britain's 'new' economy since 1979: the growing and by now fundamental dependence on the financial sector and the neglect of the former industrial core distinctly went hand-in-hand with the perception that Thatcher had tried to instil into the

British psyche. From her perspective Britain's new economy had little in common with those on the continent, who continued to be highly regulated, burdened by an excessive welfare state and the subsidy of the traditional manufacturing sector (Thatcher 2002: 329–331). Instead Britain's new economy was strongly influenced by the liberal model of the US with its unregulated enterprise culture and strong emphasis on financial services and demand-driven growth through the facilitation of universal consumer credit. This came with a cultural shift where the state was perceived as a burdensome intrusion into the personal freedom and the liberalisation from state control as a means to set free individual ambition. The purpose of the latter was unashamedly promoted as one of maximising individual profit rather than the collective good. In the spirit of Thatcher's famous uttering of 'there is no such thing as society' the new principle was that 'greed is good', particularly for those who were engaged in the thriving financial industry in the City of London (Jenkins 2007: 164). Over the past four decades Britain has been firmly in what Will Hutton characterised as the 'American bear hug' (Hutton 2002: 262). The US ideology of deregulation, privatisation and the rejection of an open tax and spend agenda has been relentlessly promoted, implemented and maintained by the British political elite across party lines. This included most importantly a relatively free reign for the financial industry which became the backbone for growth by providing jobs and a constant flow of credit to businesses and consumers with the purpose of fuelling a demand-driven economy which over time increasingly relied on a speculative bubble in the housing market. The British financial system consequently ended up becoming 'an almost exact replica of New York, but within the European time zone' (Hutton 2002: 272).

The defence of this system against any attempt to impose external regulation, particularly from the EU, became the main priority of Eurosceptics in the UK. Prominent Conservative Eurosceptics like Bill Cash and John Redwood and also the increasingly prominent leader of the UK Independence Party, Nigel Farage, do not grow tired of warning the British public that membership of the EU would be a serious hurdle to Britain's economic competiveness. The supposed tendency of the European Commission to impose red tape on British businesses and plans to impose an EU-wide financial transaction tax provide substantial ammunition to the Eurosceptic voices who promote exit from the EU as a viable and desirable alternative path for the British economy. The main argument being put forward in this respect is that outside the EU the British economy could intensify its global trade links, especially the bilateral economic relations with the US (Cash 2011: 26; Redwood 1999: 155).

In Chapter 1 of this book I emphasised that apart from narrowing down the importance of culture to the firm level and its related network of relations, another fundamental weakness of Hall and Soskice's VoC approach is that they consider financial markets almost exclusively in their capacity as a financial source for firms. In liberal economies companies hence have to be more attentive to the price of their shares on equity markets (Hall and Soskice 2001: 44). The approach fails to consider the wider impact the liberal model's strong dependence on financial markets has on the scope for fundamental systemic change and the development of public policy in general. The British economy shows that this impact is quite considerable as it gives policy-makers little room for radical reform of the established status quo. Instead public policy priorities are set within the ultimate parameters of maintaining market confidence.

Since 1979 the changes to the British political economy have been modest and broadly aimed at consolidating the fundaments of the Thatcherite new British economy. Colin Crouch has very adequately characterised this economic policy regime as one of 'privatised Keynesianism', a model which originally emerged from the US but subsequently was also applied in the Republic of Ireland from the late 1980s onwards (see Chapter 6). Crouch rightly emphasises that in the new British economy the political support for traditional Keynesian economics vanished and could never be regained after Thatcher. Private finance gradually took over the traditional role of the state and it therefore became the new provider of wealth for individual citizens: 'The bases of prosperity shifted from the social democratic formula of working classes supported by government intervention to the neo-liberal conservative one of banks, stock exchanges and financial markets' (Crouch 2009: 392).

The precondition for this was to ensure that the markets were not burdened by regulation and could operate under a relatively free regime and were trusted by the government that they would act responsibly. Tony Blair emphasised his belief that 'today, the role of government is not to command but to facilitate, and to do so in partnership with industry in limited but key areas' (Blair 1995c). This became the basic principle of Britain's Thatcherite New Economy which persisted under the reformed Labour Party which replaced the Conservatives in government after 1997. However New Labour was radical when it came to the presentation of its agenda. Catchphrases such as 'New Labour, New Britain', 'education, education, education' or '24 hours to save the NHS' were supposed to reassure traditional Labour supporters that under a New Labour government a radical departure from the Thatcherite agenda would occur in the form of significantly higher levels of public investment. Before the 1997 general election, Blair was therefore not afraid to characterise himself as a reformed socialist who vowed to carry forward the mantle of Clement

Attlee's socialism once he entered government. Blair spoke of the need to heal the divisions which the country had witnessed during the Conservative area and to build 'one nation – tolerant, fair, enterprising, inclusive' based on the belief that 'the good of each depends on the good of all' (Blair 1995b). This essentially was a rebuttal of Thatcher's belief that there would be no such thing as society. At the same time it was clear that the leading figures of New Labour had departed substantially from the traditional Labour perception of what the purpose of the welfare state should be. In its 1997 general election manifesto New Labour had proposed the concept of the 'stakeholder economy', at the core of which lay the belief that each citizen had a responsibility to actively work towards realising his or her own potential rather than to passively rely on state support (Labour Party 1997: 19). Blair himself emphasised responsibility as being the fundamental thing of the stakeholder economy in which no one would be left behind: 'Responsibility is a value shared. If it doesn't apply to everyone it ends up applying to no one' (Blair 1994).

New Labour was elected by a landslide majority in May 1997. Shortly after the election the government introduced a welfare-to-work budget which it branded as the 'New Deal' for the UK. 'Welfare-to-work' essentially made it compulsory for all young people (aged 18–24) who were out of work for more than six months and anyone over 25 who was registered as unemployed for over 18 months to either enter into further education or training or to take up subsidised or even voluntary employment. Work became the core strategy of New Labour's economic policy. Reducing the number of people who remained passive benefit recipients was essential for two reasons.

First it allowed the New Labour government to refrain from introducing openly redistributive measures without risking sliding into fiscal problems. Instead Labour adopted an approach which was based on budgetary frugality during its first term by sticking to the spending limits set by the preceding Conservative administration. Deficit reduction became the golden rule for New Labour Chancellor Gordon Brown; the golden rule was set out in his first budget in July 1997 that public debt would have to be kept at a stable level over each economic cycle (Brown 1997). In addition the government introduced a system of tax credits for people in work and especially for those with families. This essentially amounted to redistribution by stealth. Figure 4.1 compiled by the Institute for Fiscal Studies shows these tax benefits have boosted the income of working households with children who are at the bottom of the income decile group but to a much lesser extent of those households which are childless.

The focus on work became the core of New Labour's 'Third Way' economic philosophy, which claimed to combine economic competitiveness

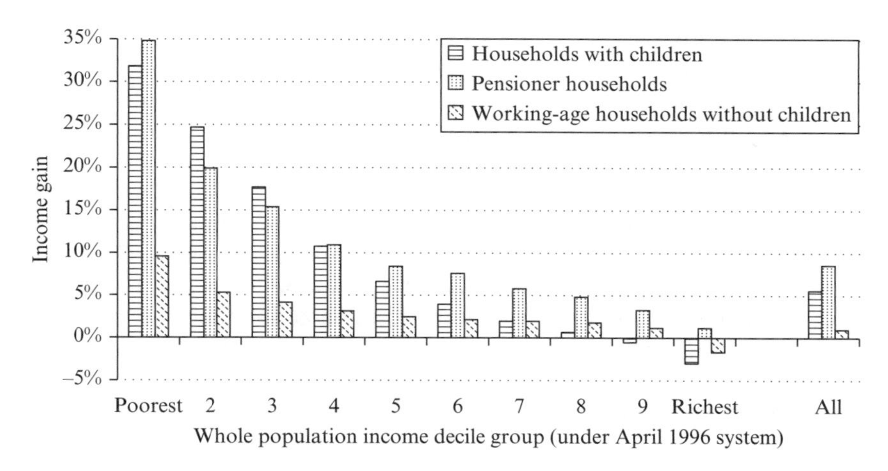

Source: Cribb et al. (2013): 91.

Figure 4.1 Impact of direct tax and benefit reforms introduced between April 1996 and April 2011, by income decile group and household type

with social justice. Work was fundamentally considered as the most effective means against poverty and social exclusion. The stakeholder economy approach was supposed to present equality of opportunity to everyone through targeted government action by investing in education and training. The Labour Party's 1997 election manifesto highlighted this: 'The best way to tackle poverty is to help people into jobs – real jobs' (Labour Party 1997: 19).

The reforms were also profoundly aimed at maintaining the Thatcherite system of privatised Keynesianism. Officially the government was keen to stress that it was its long-term intention to break with the short termism of the past and to create a new foundation for the British economy where growth would be based predominantly on financial bubbles. Gordon Brown emphasised this in his first budget: 'It is essential that consumer spending is underpinned by investment and industrial growth. Britain cannot afford a recurrence of the all too familiar pattern of previous recoveries: accelerating consumer spending, earnings, and money supply are continuing even as industrial production and manufacturing output have been recovering only slowly' (Brown 1997).

In reality the government seemed pretty content with continuing down the path of demand-based growth. Under New Labour the UK witnessed almost a decade of record levels of growth and employment. Britain's annual real GDP per capita growth stood between 2 and 4 per cent during the period from 1997 until 2000. Even when the global economy was hit by the effects of the terrorist attacks on the US on 11 September 2001, the UK continued to grow (2.3 per cent of real GDP growth in 2002). By 2003 it had almost returned to the pre-9/11 growth figures and showed real GDP growth between 2.8 and 3.9 per cent (Eurostat 2013a). The basis for this was however not the revival of Britain's manufacturing industry but a continuation of the demand-led growth which had characterised the previous boom periods under Thatcher and Major in the 1980s and 1990s. The fact that Britain did not fall back into recession at any time between 1997 and 2007 allowed Chancellor Gordon Brown to claim that New Labour's economic approach had put an end to the boom and bust cycles which were characteristic for the UK economy in the past. In this final budget speech as Chancellor of the Exchequer Brown claimed that there would be 'no return to boom and bust' in the British economy (Brown 2006), a claim that was widely ridiculed after Britain was pushed back into recession as a result of the financial crisis.

New Labour continued the light touch regulatory strategy towards the financial sector which Thatcher had originally adopted and turned a blind eye to increasingly risky lending practices, particularly in the mortgage sector. Gordon Brown's final speech as Chancellor at the Mansion House in 2007 was a very honest admission that New Labour's 'Third Way' economic policy approach had to a large extent continued the Thatcherite reliance on the financial sector. Brown spoke of the need for 'enhancing a risk-based regulatory approach' to ensure that the City would continue to thrive and emphasised the importance of the financial services sector for the British economy: 'The financial services sector in Britain and the City of London at the centre of it, is a great example of a highly skilled, high value added, talent driven industry that shows how we can excel in a world of global competition' (Brown 2007).

The sharp rise in mortgage lending in the UK under New Labour was based on the manifestation that success in the 'stakeholder economy' would be measured by the ability of individuals to climb the property ladder by purchasing more than one property in their lifetime. Originating from Margaret Thatcher's original campaign in the 1980s to facilitate the sale of council houses to tenants, New Labour's decade of boom was very much driven by a housing and a consumer credit bubble. Figure 4.2 below shows the sharp rise in mortgage lending for both first-time buyers and remortgaging between 1997 and 2005 which only slowed down when house prices had reached excessive levels in parts of the country, particularly the South-East.

UK mortgage providers adopted similar lending practices as their counterparts in the US. The most prominent example for this was Northern

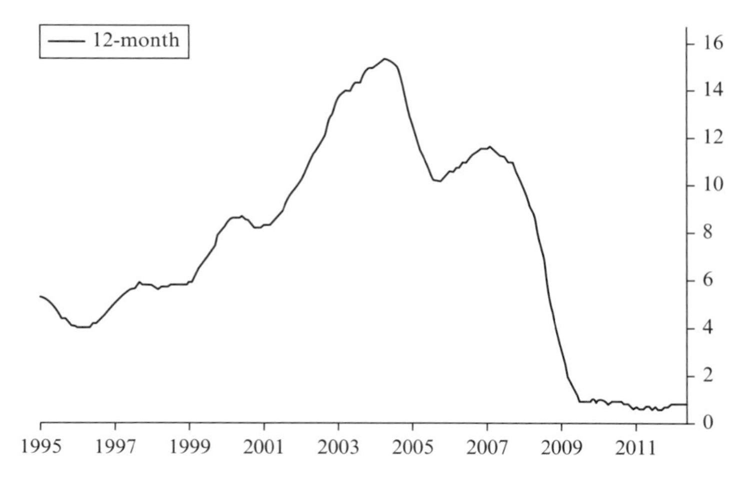

Source: Bank of England (2012).

Figure 4.2 Growth rate of lending secured on dwellings long run (seasonally adjusted)

Rock, a bank which offered individuals risky mortgage deals of 100 per cent or more of the purchasing price, in some cases up to 125 per cent. Like in the US the risk was shifted from the buyer to the financial markets, very much in line with what Gordon Brown had hailed as the risk-based approach. Like its counterparts Freddie Mac, Fannie Mae and Lehman Brothers across the Atlantic, Northern Rock also faced a sudden severe liquidity problem when it was unable to maintain credit supply from the global financial markets (Gamble 2009: 26). The Brown government soon realised that it had to take action in order to stop the collapse of Northern Rock and anticipated ripple effects on the rest of the British banking sector when customers queued to withdraw their assets from the bank in September 2007. The government effectively had to take over Northern Rock and subsequently recapitalised the British banking sector with a rescue package amounting to £500 billion (£50 billion to purchase bank capital and equity, a £250 billion credit guarantee scheme and £200 billion for additional liquidity demand). British taxpayers therefore practically became the owners of Northern Rock and shareholders in other major British banks such as Lloyds TSB and the Royal Bank of Scotland (National Audit Office 2010).

The financial crisis fundamentally damaged the credibility of New Labour's economic policy approach as it not only put an end to Gordon Brown's golden fiscal rule but also proved wrong his claim that New

Labour had ended the boom to bust cycles in the British economy. The financial effort the government had to make in order to prevent the British banking industry from potential collapse substantially weakened the country's budgetary position. The UK hence lost its position as a role model economy which seemed to show that it could combine record levels of public spending on education and health with sound budgetary finances. Following the 2001 budget, which brought the end to the Conservative spending limits which Labour had abided by during its first term in office, the government doubled spending on the NHS which rose to £102 billion by 2008 (HM Treasury 2009). At the same time the UK was in a much better fiscal position than most of the countries in the eurozone, including France and Germany. The UK met the eurozone debt criteria continuously between 1997 and 2002 and only exceeded the annual borrowing limit of 3 per cent slightly in 2003 (3.4 per cent), 2004 (3.5 per cent) and 2005 (3.4 per cent), to return to 2.7 per cent in 2006 and 2.8 per cent in 2007 (Eurostat 2013b). In respect of the second criteria, the gross level of debt, the UK remained a role model at all times, in stark contrast to the rest of the eurozone. Figure 4.3 shows that the UK only broke the horizontal line

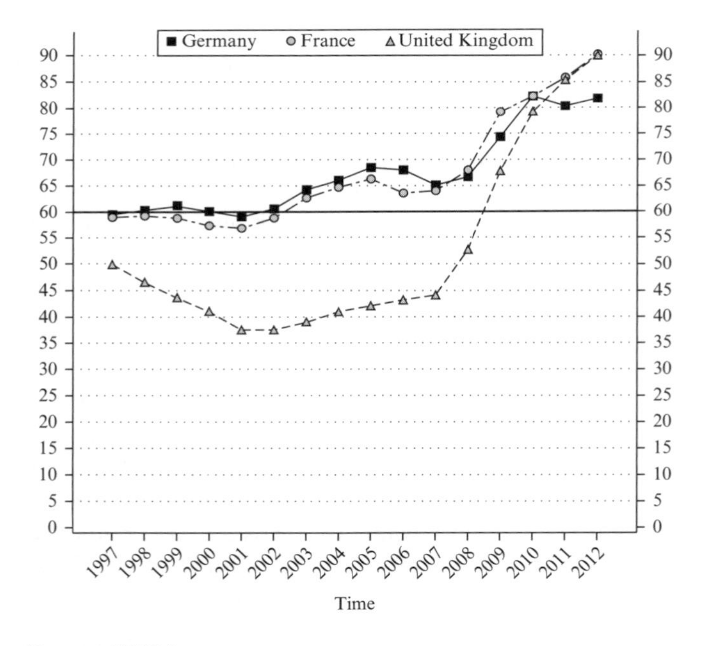

Source: Eurostat (2013c).

Figure 4.3 General government gross debt (percentage of GDP)

of the 60 per cent gross debt limit after 2007, while France and Germany had already done so in 2002 and have never managed to meet the second Maastricht criteria ever since.

After 2007 the UK economy hence slid down the path towards a sovereign debt crisis which faced the prospect of having to implement substantial austerity measures to avoid structural long-term problems. The crisis in effect ended the notion that New Labour had established what Andrew Gamble calls a 'social investment state' (Gamble 2009: 106). This was the core of the 'Third Way' approach which aspired to show that economic liberalism could be combined with greater levels of social cohesion. Gordon Brown's catchphrase in this respect was 'no child left behind' and he spoke of the need for government investment to ensure that each individual could be empowered: 'That a strong civic society needs a good enabling government on peoples side to deliver fairness – and that to enlarge the civic space you do not need to eliminate the rest of the public realm – is a lesson we must learn and relearn in every generation' (Brown 2005).

Even before the financial crisis it was however clear that the notion of the social investment state New Labour had promoted had achieved very limited results when it came to reducing poverty and increasing social cohesion in the whole of Britain. The Gini coefficient, which measures the degree of inequality on the basis of the distribution of family inequality, remained higher in the UK during New Labour's period in office than the EU-15 average. Since 1979 it has risen steadily in the UK, most dramatically under Thatcher/Major governments from 0.25 in 1979 to 0.34 in 1991 (Cribb et al. 2013: 38). The rise in the 1990s continued both under John Major and Tony Blair's New Labour government. Under New Labour it was nevertheless much slower and the Gini coefficient even fell slightly from 0.35 in 2001 to around 0.33 in 2006 and has since remained below 0.35. For the available Eurostat (2013d) date comparison since 2003 (for the EU-15 average) and 2005 (for the EU-27 average) it however remains higher than the European average (see Figure 4.4).

At the same time the Gini coefficient in other larger EU member states such as Germany and France remained below 30. Even after a decade of New Labour's investment in education and training Britain remains one of the most unequal societies in the whole of Europe. The latest OECD data shows that Britain's Gini coefficient is the second highest in the whole of the EU (just behind Portugal) and is the seventh highest in the OECD-34 (OECD 2013b). Incomes amongst the top earners have risen sharply since the 1980s and continued to rise very noticeably under New Labour in the 1990s and the first decade of the 2000s. During the Blair/Brown era the incomes of the lowest income percentiles (5–30 percentile) also rose, albeit rather modestly in comparison to the top percentiles (90–99 per cent) (Cribb

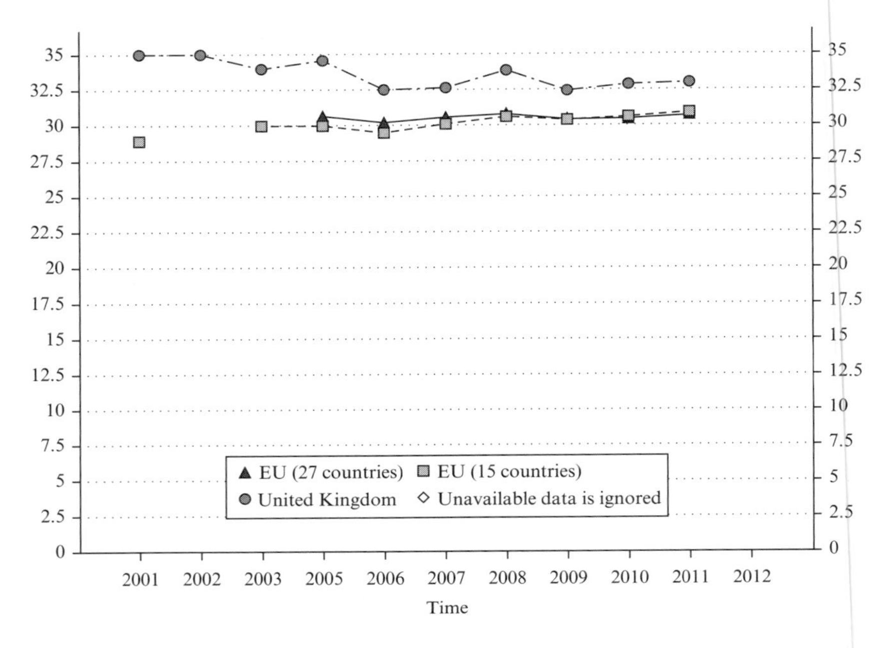

Source: Eurostat (2013d).

Figure 4.4 Gini coefficient of equivalised disposable income (number)

et al. 2013: 37). The gap between middle incomes and top earners also increased noticeably after 1997 which supports the notion that New Labour, in the words of the former spin doctor Peter Mandelson, were 'relaxed about people getting filthy rich as long as they pay their taxes' (Mandelson 1998).

New Labour's claim that employment itself is a remedy against poverty therefore has to be seen with profound scepticism. The job market in Britain is definitely more flexible than in other European countries and the New Labour government managed to reduce the level of youth unemployment between 1997 and 2005, when it fell to around 12 per cent (Eurostat 2013e). At the same time the level of people who are in work but considered to be at the risk of poverty continued to rise in the UK. In 2005 8.3 per cent of people who had a job were considered to be below the risk of poverty threshold, which the EU sets at 60 per cent of the national median equivalised income and the figure has remained between 7–8 per cent ever since, which is about the EU-15 average (Eurostat 2013f). At the same time Britain remains one of the countries which has a noticeable gender pay gap. The difference in the median earnings between men and women in the

UK has fallen from 25 per cent in 2000 to around 18 per cent in 2010 but the country still remains above the OECD average when it comes to gender pay inequality (OECD 2013a: 257).

New Labour was therefore definitely not in a position to present the UK economy as a best practice model for the rest of the EU in how to combine economic growth with greater levels of social cohesion. New Labour was widely accused of using its welfare-to-work strategy predominantly for the purpose of reducing the welfare budget rather than having to seriously pursue a strategy to reduce poverty and social exclusion (Levitas 2005: 157; Hutton 2003: 118). Beyond the mantra of getting people into work and in spite of the fact that they had introduced the minimum wage and supported working people with tax credits, New Labour certainly neglected the quality and level of renumeration of work in the UK. The campaign for a living wage, which was initiated by the Labour Party after it had lost power in 2010 is now supported across party lines, including by the London Mayor Boris Johnson, a very prominent Conservative politician. This shows that the increasing discrepancy between the rising cost of living and stagnating incomes remains a major issue in the UK. The Labour leader Ed Miliband claims that the UK currently has almost 5 million people in work who do not earn enough to ensure that they can have a decent standard of living for themselves and their families (Miliband 2012). London Mayor Johnson introduced the living wage, which asks employers to renumerate their workers voluntarily above the minimum wage, back in 2005 and this has since increased to £8.55 in November 2012. Similarly, the recent debate on effects of a massive expansion of zero-hour contracts in leading British businesses, even in Buckingham Palace, shows that strong emphasis on labour market flexibility under New Labour has lasting and unresolved social effects. The *Financial Times* columnist John McDermott brings this to the point when he states that the spread of zero-hour contracts, which give workers no specified weekly or monthly minimum working hours, are a reflection of the business model in large parts of Britain's services industries:

> For many companies, zero-hours contracts are a logical extension of the business model. Low-cost goods and flexible labour markets are the result. For some, that is enough. But many people on zero-hour contracts do not want flexibility. They want a proper job, with training and progression. And our economy can't give it to them (McDermott 2013).

The vulnerabilities of the British model which were exposed by the 2008–2009 financial crisis had initially opened up the prospect for a systemic shift. The recapitalisation programme for the ailing banking sector introduced by the Brown government, which ultimately amounted to the part-nationalisation strategy of an industry whose independence from government regulation was hailed as the cornerstone of success for Britain's new economy, seemed to indicate that Britain's liberal model would become more coordinated as a result of the crisis. Even if the government shares in major British banks were clearly designed as a temporary measure, there was a widespread view that Britain had gone too far in letting its financial sector off the leash. Andrew Rawnsley in *The Observer* spoke of 'high finance' having been 'dethroned' by the events and predicted a major shift in the British economic model:

> The full extent and shape of this power shift will take time to become clear. This much is already certain. Political leaders will not fawn before money as they once did. The era of uncritical awe for financiers is over. The epoch of blind faith in the market is done with (Rawnsley 2008).

With hindsight the Brown government's recapitalisation programme for the UK's banking sector turned out to be an attempt to consolidate the foundations of Britain's new economy rather than to recalibrate its foundations in the wake of the financial crisis. Brown's immediate aim was to enable banks to return to normal operability and to be able to provide credit supply for consumers and businesses, even under temporarily tighter lending criteria (Watson 2013: 17). Gordon Brown himself acknowledged that the financial markets should have been regulated more efficiently and spoke of 'moral failure' (Brown 2010: 66). Rather than blaming New Labour's domestic aversion towards imposing market regulation he nevertheless pushed the responsibility for the crisis towards the failure to establish adequate regulatory practices on the European and the international institutional level (Brown 2010: 14). That the crisis had only very limited impact on the domestic perception of the failures of Britain's economic model was shown even more by the response of the Conservative opposition who completely rejected calls to give the EU greater regulatory powers over the financial industry in Britain. Instead Conservative leader David Cameron ran his election campaign on the basis of blaming Labour's post-2001 investment in the public sector, which he branded as a 'decade of mismanagement' (Conservative Party 2010: 7). The campaign was hence largely reduced to a discussion on the speed and depth with which the country's deficit should be reduced. This came at the expense of a fundamental debate on the flaws of Britain's post-Thatcher economic model.

A majority of the British electorate hence still predominantly considers the events of 2008–2009 as a budgetary crisis rather than the symptom of a deeper malaise in Britain's financial sector. The scale and the speed with which the government coalition of Conservatives and Liberal Democrats, which defeated Labour in the 2010 general election, implemented budget cuts in the UK continues to be the subject of fierce public controversy. Latest opinion polls nevertheless show that a majority of people in Britain think that the root of the crisis lies in New Labour having been too generous with public finances before 2007 (Boffey 2013). In spite of having criticised New Labour's 'Third Way' economy as the 'age of irresponsibility' (Conservative Party 2010: 3) which encouraged reckless lending and consumer borrowing, the Conservative Chancellor George Osborne is trying to ensure that the housing market in the UK can return to a position where it becomes the backbone for economic growth. For this purpose the Chancellor recently introduced the 'Help to Buy' Scheme, which offers a government loan to first-time buyers and home movers of up to 20 per cent of the property price, provided that the buyer can contribute at least a 5 per cent deposit.

The chief economic commentator of the *Financial Times*, Martin Wolf, has repeatedly criticised the Conservative–Liberal Democrat coalition for being too complacent and relying on austerity as a means to restore the UK economy to its pre-crisis setting. Wolf highlights that without fundamental regulatory reform of Britain's financial industry, the UK model is likely to repeat the mistakes of the past. Wolf warns of the dangers of pursuing a 'business model based on minimal equity and support from taxpayers' (Wolf 2013). In this respect both he and the leading Cambridge economist Ha-Joon Chang are extremely critical of Osborne's 'Help to Buy' Scheme for first-time buyers, which would risk creating 'state-sponsored asset bubbles' and pushing the British economy towards a 'lost decade' (Chang 2013).

Under the Conservative-led coalition the British economy is being recalibrated towards the classic Thatcherite model. Within the coalition Prime Minister David Cameron and Conservative ministers are keen on reducing the modest increase of the role of the state in the economy, which took place between 1997 and 2010. The government has cut back public spending on education and training. Most controversially it drastically cut public funding of higher education teaching which is being made up for by allowing universities to charge undergraduate students annual fees of up to £9,000. The government is also in the process of fundamentally reforming the National Health Service (NHS). The NHS as a fully publicly funded health service is free at the point of use for all citizens and has always been somewhat uncharacteristic for an economy which is overall orientated towards privatisation and open market competition. Under the coalition's NHS reform programme, the role of private sector providers in offering healthcare will be substantially enhanced with the aim of cutting back public spending on healthcare. Junior doctors within the British Medical Association (BMA) are accusing the government of privatising the NHS by stealth (British Medical Association News 2013).The gradual weakening of the public sector monopoly in the NHS was to a certain extent initiated under the Blair government, which introduced public–private partnerships in the NHS for the purpose of building hospitals and raising the quality of service. The abolition of NHS trusts and the transformation of GP's towards independent budget holders represent a much deeper overhaul of the NHS, which will undoubtedly change its character in the long term. In effect it is also likely to reduce the role of the state in the British welfare model further.

The only major institutional change which seems to prevail from the New Labour era is therefore the independence of the Bank of England. When then Chancellor Gordon Brown introduced this major change straight after the 1997 election victory, it was initially considered as a move to prepare the entry of the British economy into the eurozone by establishing an independent central bank model which replicates the German *Bundesbank*. In fact it was actually more of a move towards enhancing the economic policy credibility of the newly elected Labour government by giving the control over interest rates to an independent body (Clift and Thomlinson 2006: 62). After some initial hesitation the Conservative Party embraced this change and is now fully in favour of central bank independence. Apart from this David Cameron's coalition pursues a strategy where it dresses up an essentially Thatcherite political agenda with a compassionate Conservative rhetoric. Slogans such as 'we are all in this together' (Cameron 2010) or 'I love the NHS' (Mason 2013) are window dressing for quite radical public policy reforms that are being implemented by the coalition. They are also supposed to distract the attention from the negative effects of the drastic austerity measures that the government has imposed since it came to power in May 2010. The emphasis on austerity as the prime objective of the government's economic agenda raises substantial doubts about its ambition to rebalance the British economy from a predominantly demand-driven model towards a more export-orientated one. The government still has to show that the jobs which are disappearing in the public sector, can be rebuilt in the private sector, particularly the manufacturing industry. In the absence of large-scale public investment, Britain's ailing manufacturing industries are in urgent need of a substantial boost of capital from the private sector. With the cost of raising capital remaining high after the financial crisis, a significant boost in private investment is unlikely in the foreseeable future. Therefore as things currently stand it seems that the coalition's solution to the crisis amounts to little more than to attempt to return to the privatised Keynesianism which had prevailed before the financial crisis. As Colin Hay rightly highlights the approach since the 2010 general election towards mending the British economy has been 'paradigm-reinforcing rather than paradigm-threatening' (Hay 2013: 23).

In the very useful comparative classification of institutional governance models in Europe, which McCann developed on the basis of various data before the financial crisis, Britain is presented as the most liberal model in Europe, closely followed by the Irish Republic (McCann 2010: 15). McCann uses the following categories to back up this classification: the coordination index provided by Hall and Gingerich (2004), the level of product market regulation, state control, employment protection and employee co-determination based on data provided by Höpner (2007). I would suggest that the most significant data in this set for the classification of economic models under the current crisis conditions are category 1 (the level of coordination and here particularly the size of the stock market) and category 3 (the level of state control). In both cases the data presented give some indication of the cultural inclination of an economic model but the quantitative data on its own (stock market size in category 1; public ownership and state involvement in business) is not sufficient to determine the model's full complexity. What is missing here are other crucial cultural determinants which shape the political economy of a country, such as the socialisation of its political elite in terms of domestic policy preferences and attitudes towards cooperation at the supranational level. The case of the new British economy after 1979 shows that the full extent of its political economy can only be grasped when one considers aspects of political culture which go beyond a rational competitive advantage perspective. In the British case this is the particular state culture, which emphasises sovereign national decision-making and the reluctance to transfer powers to external bodies, combined with a decisively strong reliance on financial markets as the foundation for growth.

The former explains why political elites in the UK are likely to continue to resist supranational solutions to the financial crisis, even if these would be likely to support the country's economic recovery. A prime example for this is the Fiscal Compact, which asks participating countries to introduce a constitutional debt limit. Although this would support the current government's ambition to set Britain on a firm path of budget consolidation, David Cameron vetoed the treaty and made clear that he would under no circumstances sign up to it. The persistently strong dependence on the financial sector in the UK on the other hand explains why the UK is resisting attempts to impose higher levels of external regulation on its financial sector. Britain under David Cameron is the fiercest opponent amongst the group of larger EU states against the introduction of an EU-wide financial transaction tax (Chu 2012). The strong influence British finance has on domestic policy-making is well documented by Will Hutton in his recent book on the financial crisis. Hutton points out that the British political elite refrains from embarking on a root and branch reform of the financial regulatory system because of the perception that, even after the crisis the financial industry remains the 'goose that lays the golden egg' (Hutton 2011: 184).

Given these cultural parameters in the British economy it is justified to return to Hutton's assumption from a decade ago where he argued that Britain would be firmly in the American 'bear hug'. Developments since then, and particularly after the financial crisis, illustrate that the UK is content to remain in this position for the foreseeable future. I would go even further and argue that by firmly maintaining the pre-crisis status quo of its economy, Britain is in the process of separating itself from the rest of Europe. On the European continent the scepticism towards market-based growth has grown substantially and one can detect, a greater willingness to adopt common solutions towards tackling the profound economic challenges the crisis has presented. The growing Eurosceptic sentiment in the UK, which links the country's disappointing economic performance since the crisis with the supposed regulatory constraints EU membership imposes on British business (Whyte 2013: 5), makes it likely that a majority of voters could opt to exit the EU in a forthcoming referendum. This would risk turning the British economy into an isolated and unbalanced growth model whose economic success relies fundamentally more on global financial markets than most of its continental European counterparts. In the case of Britain, the liberal classification is here to stay for the foreseeable future. Britain could soon become the liberal model in a dual sense, combining economic liberalism with a return to purely national regulation outside the coordinative institutional constraints of the EU.

REFERENCES

Bank of England (2012) *Lending to Individuals*. June. Available at: http://www.bankofengland.co.uk/statistics/Pages/li/2012/Jun/default.aspx. (accessed 30 July 2013).

Black, J. (2013) 'True Toll of Mass Migration on UK Life: Half of Britons Suffer under Strain Placed on Schools, Police, NHS and Housing', *Daily Mail*, 4 July. Available at: http://www.dailymail.co.uk/news/article-2355208/Toll-mass-migration-UK-life-Half-Britons-suffer-strain-places-schools-police-NHS-housing.html (accessed 30 July 2013).

Blair, T. (1994) Speech to the Labour Party Conference, Blackpool, 4 October.

Blair, T. (1995a) Speech to the Royal Institute of International Affairs, London, 5 April.

Blair, T. (1995b) Speech at the Fabian Society Commemoration of the 50th Anniversary of the 1945 General Election, 5 July.

Blair, T. (1995c) Speech to the Annual Conference of the Confederation of British Industry, 13 November.
Blair, T. (2000) Statement to the House of Commons on the Nice European Council,12 December.
Boffey, D. (2013) 'Labour still to Blame for Economy, say 46% in Opinion/Observerpoll', *The Observer*, 30 June.
British Medical Association News (2013) 'Privatisation Purpose of NHS Reform, say Juniors'. Available at: http://bma.org.uk/news-views-analysis/news/2013/may/privatisation-purpose-of-nhs-reform-say-juniors (accessed 8 August 2013).
Brown, G. (1997) Budget Speech, House of Commons, 2 July.
Brown, G. (2005) Speech at Chatham House, 13 December.
Brown, G. (2006) Budget Speech, House of Commons, 22 March.
Brown, G. (2007) Speech to the Mansion House, 20 June.
Brown, G. (2010) *Beyond the Crash: Overcoming the First Crisis of Globalisation*. London: Simon and Schuster.
Cameron, D. (2010) Speech at the Annual Conservative Party Conference, Birmingham, 6 October.
Cash, B. (2011) 'It's the EU Stupid', 5 September. London: European Foundation.
Chang, H.J. (2013) 'To Describe the Economy as on the Mend is Orwellian', *The Guardian*, 26 June. Available at: http://www.theguardian.com/commentisfree/2013/jul/26/george-osborne-economy-orwellian-on-mend (accessed 30 July 2013).
Chu, B. (2012) 'Cameron: EU Financial Tax would be Madness', *The Independent*, 27 January. Available at: http://www.independent.co.uk/news/world/europe/cameron-eu-financial-tax-would-be-madness-6295396.html (accessed 30 July 2013).
Clift, B. and J. Tomlinson (2006) 'Credible Keynesianism? New Labour Macroeconomic Policy and the Political Economy of Coarse Tuning', *British Journal of Political Science* 37 (1): 47–69.
Conservative Party (2010) *Invitation to Join the Government of Britain. The Conservative Manifesto*. East Sussex: Pureprint.
Cribb, J., A. Hood, R. Joyce and D. Phillips (2013) *Living Standards, Poverty and Inequality in the UK: 2013*. IFS Report R81. London: Institute for Fiscal Studies.
Crouch, C. (2009) 'Privatised Keynesianism: An Unacknowledged Policy Regime', *British Journal of Politics and International Relations* 11 (3): 382–399.
Denman, R. (1997) *Missed Chances: Britain and Europe in the Twentieth Century*. London: Idigo.
European Commission (2012a) *Standard Eurobarometer 78 National Report UK*. Brussels: EU.
European Commission (2012b) *Standard Eurobarometer 78 National Report Czech Republic*. Brussels: EU.
European Commission (2013) *Standard Eurobarometer 79*. Brussels: EU.
Eurostat (2013a) *Real GDP Growth Rate – Volume*. Available at: http://epp.eurostat.ec.europa.eu/tgm/table.do?tab=table&init=1&plugin=1&language=en&pcode=tec00115 (accessed 30 July 2013).
Eurostat (2013b) *General Government Deficit/Surplus Percentage of GDP*. Available at: http://epp.eurostat.ec.europa.eu/tgm/table.do?tab=table&init=1&language=en&pcode=tec00127&plugin=1 (accessed 30 July 2013).
Eurostat (2013c) *General Government Gross Debt*. Available at: http://epp.eurostat.

ec.europa.eu/tgm/table.do?tab=table&init=1&language=en&pcode=tsdde410&plugin=1 (accessed 30 July2013).
Eurostat (2013d) *Gini Coefficient of Equalised Disposable Income*. Available at: http://epp.eurostat.ec.europa.eu/tgm/table.do?tab=table&language=en&pcode=tessi190 (accessed 13 March 2013).
Eurostat (2013e) *Unemployment Rate by Age Group*. Available at: http://epp.eurostat.ec.europa.eu/tgm/table.do?tab=table&init=1&language=en&pcode=tsdec460&plugin=1 (accessed 30 July 2013).
Eurostat (2013f) *In-Work At-Risk-of-Poverty-Rate*. Available at: http://epp.eurostat.ec.europa.eu/tgm/table.do?tab=table&init=1&language=en&pcode=tesov110&plugin=1 (accessed 30 July 2013).
Gamble, A. (2009) *The Spectre at the Feast: Capitalist Crisis and the Politics of Recession*. Basingstoke: Palgrave Macmillan.
George, S. (1998) *An Awkward Partner: Britain in the European Community*. Oxford: Oxford University Press.
Gowland, D. and A. Turner (eds) (2000) *Britain and European Integration 1945–1998: A Documentary History*. London: Routledge.
Hall, M. (2012) 'EU wants Migrants to take our Jobs', *Daily Express*, 15 November. Available at: http://www.express.co.uk/news/uk/358279/EU-wants-migrants-to-take-our-jobs (accessed 30 July 2013).
Hall, P. and D.W. Gingerich (2004) *Varieties of Capitalism and Institutional Complementarities in the Macroeconomy: An Empirical Analysis*. Cologne: MPIfG Discussion Paper 04/5.
Hall, P.A. and D. Soskice (2001) *Varieties of Capitalism: The Institutional Foundations of Comparative Advantage*. Oxford: Oxford University Press.
Hay, C. (2007) 'Whatever Happened to Thatcherism?', *Political Studies Review* 5 (2): 183–201.
Hay, C. (2013) 'Treating the Symptom not the Condition: Crisis Definition, Deficit Reduction and the Search for a New British Growth Model', *British Journal of Politics and International Relations* 15 (1): 23–37.
Heffernan, R. (2000) 'Beyond Euroscepticism? Labour and the European Unions Since 1945', in B. Brivati and R. Heffernan (eds) *The Labour Party: A Centenary History*. Basingstoke: Macmillan, pp. 383–401.
HM Treasury (2009) 'Public Expenditure and Statistical Analyses'. Available at: http://www.official-documents.gov.uk/document/cm76/7630/7630.pdf (accessed 3 August 2013).
Höpner, M. (2007) *Coordination and Organization: The Two Dimensions of Non-Liberal Capitalism*. Cologne: MPIfG Discussion Paper 07/12
Hutton, W. (2002) *The World We're In*. London: Little/Brown (Time Warner Books).
Hutton, W. (2003) 'New Keynesianism and New Labour', in A. Chadwick and R. Heffernan (eds) *The New Labour Reader*. Cambridge: Polity Press, pp. 116–119.
Hutton, W. (2011) *Them and Us: Changing Britain – Why we Need a Fair Society*. London: Abacus.
Jenkins, S. (2007) 'Thatcher's Legacy', *Political Studies Review* 5 (2): 161–171.
Labour Party (1997) *New Labour: Because Britain Deserves Better*. Surrey: HH Associates.
Levitas, R. (2005) *The Inclusive Society? Social Exclusion and New Labour*. Basingstoke: Palgrave Macmillan.

Mandelson, P. (1998) 'We are Extremely Relaxed about People Getting Filthy Rich', *Financial Times*, 23 October.
Mason, R. (2013) 'David Cameron: I love the NHS but it has deep problems', *Daily Telegraph*. Available at: http://www.telegraph.co.uk/health/10161543/David-Cameron-I-love-the-NHS-but-it-has-deep-problems.html (accessed 30 July 2013).
McCann, D. (2010) *The Political Economy of the European Union*. Malden: Polity Press.
McDermot, J. (2013) 'Zero-Hours Work for Britain's Zero-Hours Economy', *Financial Times*, 6 August.
Miliband, E. (2012) Speech on the Living Wage, Islington, London, 5 November.
National Audit Office (2010) *Maintaining the Financial Stability of UK Banks: Update the Support Schemes*. London: HM Treasury.
Norton, P. (2012) 'Opt-Out: Britain's Unsplendid Isolation', in J. Hayward and R. Wurzel (eds) *European Disunion: Between Sovereignty and Solidarity*. Basingstoke: Palgrave Macmillan, pp. 252–266.
OECD (2013a) 'Jobs and Wages', *OECD Factbook 2013: Economic, Environmental and Social Statistics*. OECD Publishing. Available at: http://www.oecd-library.org/economics/oecd-factbook-2013_factbook-2013-en (accessed 6 August 2013).
OECD (2013b) 'Income Distribution and Poverty Report', 15 May. Available at: http://www.oecd.org/els/soc/OECD2013-Inequality-and-Poverty-8p.pdf (accessed 6 August 2013).
Rawnsley, A. (2008) 'A Golden Age, and Other Things They Wish They'd Never Said', *The Observer*, 19 October. Available at: http://www.theguardian.com/commentisfree/2008/oct/19/gordonbrown-davidcameron-economic-policy (accessed 6 August 2013).
Redwood, J. (1999) *The Death of Britain?* Basingstoke: Macmillan.
Sanders, D. (1990) *Losing an Empire, Finding a Role: British Foreign Policy Since 1945*. London: Macmillan.
Sky News (2013) 'Sky News Poll on Europe', 5 June. Available at: http://news.sky.com/story/1099455/sky-news-poll-reveals-huge-divide-on-europe (accessed 31 July 2013).
Tapsfield, J. (2013) 'David Cameron Hits out at "Frustrating" EU', *The Independent*, 28 June. Available at: http://www.independent.co.uk/news/uk/politics/david-cameron-hits-out-at-frustrating-eu-8677867.html (accessed 30 July 2013).
Thatcher, M. (1993) *The Downing Street Years*. London: HarperCollins.
Thatcher, M. (2002) *Statecraft: Strategies for a Changing World*. London: HarperCollins.
The Times (2000) 'Blair: We Can't go on Like This' 12 December.
Watson, M. (2013) 'New Labour's Paradox of Responsibility', *British Journal of Politics and International Relations* 15 (3): 6–22.
Whyte, P. (2013) *Do Britain's European Ties Damage its Prosperity?* London: Centre for European Reform.
Wolf, M. (2013) 'Britain Must Fix its Banks – Not its Monetary Policy', *Financial Times*, 6 June. Available at: http://www.ft.com/cms/s/0/dff3364a-cddb-11e2-a13e-00144feab7de.html#axzz2sSGUiHQ8 (accessed 30 July 2013).
Young, H. (1998) *This Blessed Plot: Britain and Europe from Churchill to Blair*. London and Basingstoke: Macmillan.
Young, J.W. (2000) *Britain and European Unity 1945–1999*. Basingstoke and London: Macmillan.

5. Germany: the *Modell Deutschland* between stagnation and reform

The German economy has traditionally been presented as the classic contrast model to the liberal market capitalism of the US and the UK. Following Hall and Soskice's firm-based approach, it is emphasised that coordinated market economies are characterised by an institutional set-up which 'reflects higher levels of non-market coordination' than liberal models. This includes a system where companies are less reliant on stock market finance and are generally orientated towards a consensual approach in relations between the management and workers (Hall and Soskice 2001: 19 and 24). Coordinated economies also usually show 'incremental' innovation and change, which stands in stark contrast to the 'radical' changes to the economy in liberal models (Ibid.: 38). This is because the emphasis lies on building up a reputation for innovative and high quality production through 'product differentiation and niche production' (Ibid.: 27). Workers in these models tend to have higher skills levels than in liberal models as a result of a sophisticated education and training system which includes the availability of in-house apprenticeships for trainee workers (Ibid.: 25).

The Varieties of Capitalism (VoC) approach has lost nothing of its value in supporting the analysis of the German economy. It adequately determined the obvious competitive advantage of Germany as an export-orientated model which is based on product innovation and reputation of quality in the form of the renowned *Made in Germany* label. Like in the British case outlined in the previous chapter, Hall and Soskice however offer only a very limited account of the institutional surroundings of the national political economy in which firms are embedded. This is particularly noticeable in the case of Germany, whose economic model is fundamentally grounded in and significantly shaped by a complex system of the division of powers between multiple levels. Like in the British case, domestic attitude towards the process of institutionalised European integration also played, and continues to play, a significant role in determining the core features of the *Modell Deutschland.*

The foundations of the German economy are substantially rooted in the country's post-Second World War political culture. The traditional post-war *Rhenish* model of social market capitalism was built on West

Germany's '*semisovereign*' polity (Katzenstein 1987). The founders of the West German Federal Republic had drawn conclusions from both the experience of the *Weimar Republic* in 1920s, which was characterised by political and economic instability and the subsequent concentration of executive power under the Nazi dictatorship. The characterisation of West Germany's polity as *semisovereign* therefore referred as much to the need to coordinate its foreign policy with the three Western Allied Powers (the US, Britain and France), who had occupied the Western half of the country in 1945, as to the fact that the West German political system was characterised by the existence of multiple veto points. The latter was defined by Katzenstein as 'three nodes' which characterise the West German polity (Katzenstein 2005: 285).

First, the electoral system of mixed proportional representation with the 5 per cent entry hurdle for parties in order for them to be represented in parliament favours power-sharing in the form of multi-party coalitions. Second, the sophisticated system of federalism decentralises power towards the regions (*Länder*), which have sovereign state character with their own constitutions, parliaments and governments. They are also extensively involved in the legislative process at the federal level in the Federal Council (*Bundesrat*). Third, the variety of 'parapublic' institutions (Katzenstein 1987: 58) in the West German polity, which connected the state with the private sector. Examples for 'parapublic' institutions are the central bank (*Bundesbank*) and the semi-public healthcare providers (*Krankenkassen*). They also include policy principles such as that of co-decision between trade unions and employers, which manifest themselves institutionally in the form of work councils in companies and sector-wide wage-agreements. Essentially the West German Basic Law (*Grundgesetz*) had established a consensus democracy with multiple veto points against centralised decision-making. As consensus became the paramount principle for the political process and also economic interaction, the *Modell Deutschland* become synonymous with path-dependent and slow incremental change. The 'high equilibrium trap' of the West German model consequently tended to be slow in responding to challenges and favoured system stability over radical reform (Kitschelt and Streeck 2004: 1). The inherent stability was also noticeable in the West German economy. The Bonn Republic had developed a cooperative industrial system with high levels of trade union and worker representation, co-decision between workers and the management in company work councils and predominantly consensual wage industry-wide wage setting in the form of binding general wage agreements. The internal stability of the West German economic model, which stood in stark contrast to the polarised industrial relations in other European countries, such as France and the UK, helped Germany

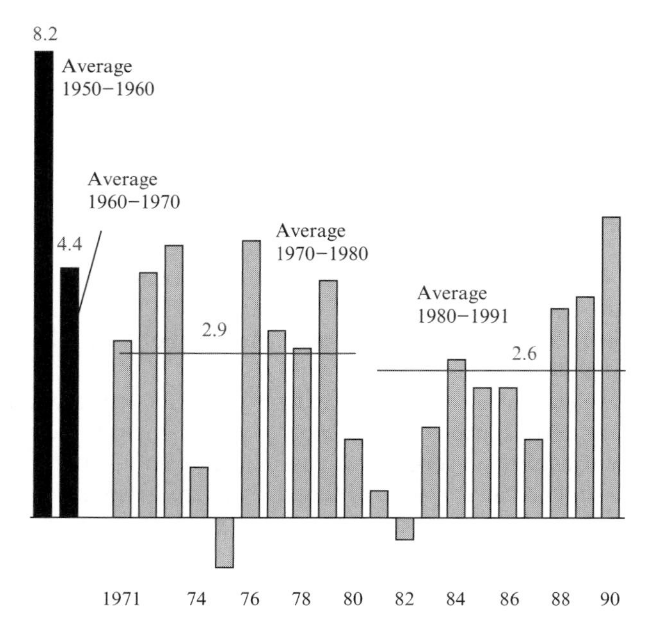

Source: Statistisches Bundesamt (2013a).

Figure 5.1 GDP growth in West Germany 1950–1990 (annual percentage)

to steadily rebuild its economic power. By the 1950s West Germany had turned into the economic miracle in Europe (*Wirtschaftswunder*) with very high average growth rates of above 8 per cent in the decade between 1950 and 1960 (Figure 5.1).

Externally, West Germany moved increasingly into the role of the economic locomotive of the newly established Common European Market. The embedment into the Common Market and the institutional setting of the European Economic Community (EEC) turned out to be beneficial for the Federal Republic in many respects. The multilateral framework of the Common Market allowed West Germany to grow its economy on the basis of a thriving export market and without raising fears of a German Europe. By having positioned itself at the heart of the emerging multilateralism of institutionalised European integration at the side of France, West German leaders also secured a relatively large scope for exercising external influence under the conditions of their country's *semisovereign* foreign policy. The political consensus beyond party lines in the Federal Republic was that full and constructive engagement in the EEC would ensure that Germany would be able to remain on a course of economic prosperity and political stability. Successive German governments from Adenauer in the 1950s to Kohl in 1980s consequently strongly promoted deepening political and economic integration in Europe (Anderson 1997: 82).

An essential feature of the Federal Republic's political culture was a preference for building its external influence in Europe and the world on 'soft' power in the form of economic power. The multilateralism, in which the West German state was rooted on the basis of the 1949 Basic Law, also became characteristic for the country's foreign policy. Due to having been socialised in a multi-level polity with a constant need for compromise between various interests, West German political elites showed a much more positive attitude towards European integration than most of their neighbours. The pooling of sovereignty at the European institutional level was considered to be an opportunity rather than a threat to the sovereignty of the state (Webber 2001: 4). The structure of the European Community (EC) as an emerging multi-level system of governance between Brussels, the national and regional levels resembled the state structure of the Federal Republic. West German political elites were hence overall comfortable with operating within the boundaries of Community institutions (Katzenstein 1997: 40) and managed to substantially influence their shape over the years (Bulmer et al. 2000: 40–46). In practice the overall comfort with the country's integration in the EC had the somewhat bizarre consequence that West German leaders refrained from defining external national interests. The official line became that the wider European interest would be identical with German interests. This amounted to a quasi default multilateralism (Jeffery and Paterson 2001: 180) which could not however conceal the fact that Germany was exercising power in Europe. This power may have been, as Simon Bulmer argues, 'unintentional' (Bulmer 1997: 75). It was certainly real and noticeable, even if West German Chancellors tended to act strictly in tandem with their French counterparts and strictly distinguished between their country's economic and political influence in Europe. From the West German perspective, the country had become an economic giant but remained a political dwarf, to use the words of the former Social Democratic Chancellor Willy Brandt. The importance of the economy for West Germany's European policy was also shown by the fact that the government in Bonn had to accommodate its European policy priorities with those of the Federal Central Bank. The *Bundesbank* became effectively a passenger in the driving seat of West Germany's European policy, especially after the creation of the European Monetary System (EMS) in 1979 with its inherent European Exchange Rate Mechanism (ERM). Even before the creation of the ERM, the West German currency *Deutsche Mark* had become the anchor currency for economies of the Common Market. Its persistent strength resulted from a rigid stability policy pursued by the *Bundesbank* and reflected West Germany's economic primacy in the Common Market (Cole 2001: 92). The EMS de facto institutionalised this dependence and strengthened the role of the *Bundesbank* in exercising a monetary stability policy based on keeping interest rates low. The *Bundesbank* has therefore been frequently accused of having exercised a parallel European policy (Bulmer et al. 2000: 15), which was exclusively orientated towards price stability in Germany without much consideration for the impact on other economies in the Common Market (Le Gloannec 2001: 124). With the path towards monetary integration set under the EMS the role of the *Bundesbank* as a watchdog over monetary stability was increasingly considered to be controversial. The events leading up to Black Wednesday on 16 September 1992, when the British pound and the Italian lira were forced out of the European ERM after massive market speculation against those two currencies, were widely interpreted to having been the effect of the high interest rate levels the *Bundesbank* had maintained after German reunification. The former Chancellor Helmut Schmidt, a long-standing critic of the approach of the German Central Bank, subsequently accused the bank's governors of having pursued an irresponsible high interest rate policy in the aftermath of reunification in 1990. Schmidt emphasised that this had not only contributed to the recession which plagued Europe in the 1990s but had also risked undermining public support for monetary integration in the European Union (EU) (Schmidt 1993: 90 and 214). The dominant role of the *Bundesbank* in the Common Market could lead to the conception that the commitment of the unified Germany towards Economic and Monetary Union under Chancellor Helmut Kohl was a political price which the larger Germany had to pay in order to get French consent towards the reunification of the two German states. European Monetary Union (EMU) certainly turned out to be a test for public opinion in the unified Germany. West Germans, who had got used to the *Deutsche Mark* as a status symbol for their country's economic success and were subjected to a tabloid media campaign in support of a *Deutsche Mark* patriotism, were for the first time openly sceptical towards abandoning sovereignty in an area which they perceived as a vital part of their national culture (Anderson 1999: 47). In addition, citizens in the formerly Communist Eastern part of the country, considered the introduction of the *Deutsche Mark* as an achievement which they were as reluctant to give away as their neighbours in the West. East Germans initially showed much less enthusiasm for being part of the EC than Germans in West (Janning 1994: 275).

In spite of this predominantly negative public perception of impending EMU in the wake of the Maastricht Treaty it is a fact that the Kohl government managed to exercise substantial influence on the shape of

EMU. Particularly the design of the European Central Bank (ECB) is an example of at least partial direct German institutional export. Not only was Frankfurt chosen as the seat for the ECB, which already gave a hint at the strong German influence. The Kohl government joined forces with the *Bundesbank* in ensuring that the ECB would be substantially designed along the lines of the German central bank model and monetary union be based around the German perception of monetary stability (Bulmer 1997: 74). The Kohl government consequently semi-imposed the characteristic 'two pillar' strategy of the *Bundesbank*, which maintained monetary stability and low inflation through an interest base policy, at the European level. Although the ECB generally takes a wider approach in its monetary approach it essentially falls short of a comprehensive strategy of crisis intervention beyond monetary policy. In practice it pursues the *Bundesbank* focus on price stability (Heering 2007: 92–93). In addition, like the *Bundesbank,* whose statute determines that it is independent from political influence, the ECB is supposed to determine its policy without taking political orders from other EU bodies or member state governments (Busch 2005: 103 and 105). In addition, the Kohl government insisted on framing monetary union in the Stability and Growth Pact (SGP) which was supposed to introduce a culture of budgetary stability in the newly created eurozone. The SGP became the precondition for the Kohl government's acceptance of the weaker economies of Southern Europe into the eurozone, particularly Italy. The SGP was therefore profoundly a German design and an attempt to instil the German *Stabiltätspolitik* (policy of stability) into the eurozone, in sum 'an example of German institutional export of far-reaching significance for the future development of the EU' (Bulmer et al. 2000: 41–42).

Those who had expected that Germany's strong imprint on the design of the EMU would mean that the country's economy would benefit equivocally from being inside the eurozone were disappointed. The creation of the single European currency has certainly been beneficial for German industry as it has created a new export market within the Single Market for German goods. Once inside the eurozone, Germany faced the fact that while the ECB focused on price stability and kept the standard rate of interest for the currency area low, real interest rates in Germany were above those of other countries, especially those in Southern Europe. This facilitated credit-based consumer-led growth in countries such as Spain but depressed growth in Germany (Bibow 2007: 60).

The decline in Germany's position as the economic locomotive of Europe in the 1990s and early 2000s had predominantly domestic reasons. By the 1980s cracks in the structure of the former economic role model started to appear but these were largely ignored. Supported by the strong performance of its economy, the West German Federal Republic was able to substantially expand the foundations of the welfare system which Bismarck had originated. The Bismarckian principle of state-sponsored life standard guarantee for the unemployed became the core of the West German welfare state. Workers in the Federal Republic became used to a generous social insurance system with high wage replacement rates for the unemployment, generous pension provision and universal high quality healthcare provided by a system of semi-public healthcare providers, the *Krankenkassen.* All this was only possible because of the acceptance of the solidarity principle which determines that the cost of the social insurance is equally shared by employers and employees. The costly insurance system became the heart of the German typology of coordinated capitalism. Determined in the German constitution, the Basic Law, in article 20, paragraph 1, the social character of the German market economy is irrevocable and determines that the state has a responsibility to protect economically disadvantaged people and ensure them a decent standard of living (Kommers and Miller 2012: 623). While the Basic Law does not determine what this means in terms of determining micro-level welfare policies it is clear that the scope for the reform of the German welfare state is limited. A severe limitation of state provision in the area of social security remains a remote and unlikely possibility as it would stand in contradiction to the essential character of the social market economy. This explains why reforms to the social insurance system have always been a controversial issue. This was the result of the rising levels of unemployment which for first time ever since the end of the Second World War exceeded 2 million in the period between 1983 and 1989 (Figure 5.2). This unprecedented situation was bolstered by a wave of early retirements which were generously supported by the Kohl government on the basis of an early retirement law passed in 1984 (Czada 2005: 167). In turn social insurance contributions for workers and employers increased steadily to around 13 per cent of the GDP in the late 1980s (Streeck 2009a: 43) while the number of people in work with social insurance contributions had dropped by between 0.4 and 1.9 per cent in the years 1981–1984.

As a result of the 'corporatist' institutional framework of the Bonn Republic (Funk 2000: 21) labour costs in the Federal Republic had become expensive by European comparison. It was however usually only the Employers' Association and the neoliberal wing of the West German Free Democrats (FDP) who called for changes of the German welfare system. The overall political climate in West Germany in the 1980s had become complacent and anti-reformist. The political slogan promoted by the Kohl government in the 1987 general election campaign was to leave things as they are in the country (*'Weiter so, Deutschland'*) (CDU/CSU 1987). This

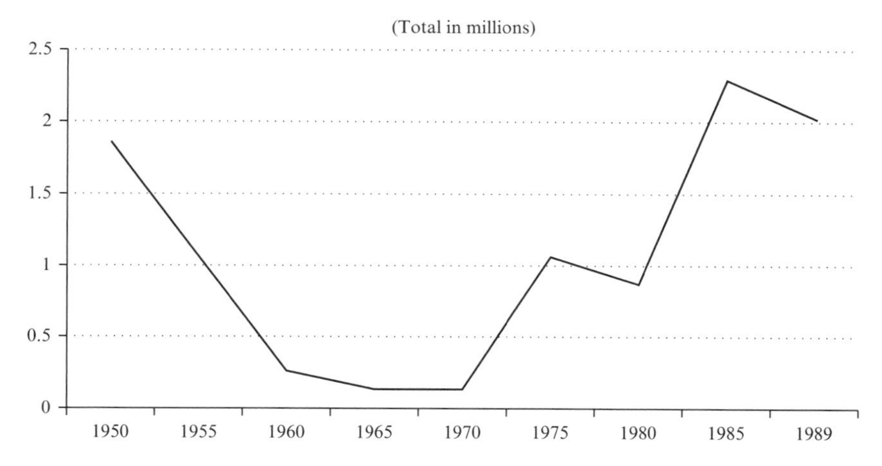

Source: Statistisches Bundesamt (2013b).

Figure 5.2 Unemployment in West Germany 1950–1989

can be explained by the fact that in spite of its overall weaker economic performance, West Germany maintained a higher standard of living and social cohesion than most of its neighbours in Europe. The West German welfare state was still able to produce cohesive results when it came under pressure from declining contribution levels and a rising number of welfare claimants in the 1980s. That it did not slide into a major funding crisis was the result of the 'subtle interaction between the welfare state, the system of collective bargaining and the federal budget' (Streeck and Trampusch 2007: 62). The consensus between the government and stakeholders to use welfare mechanisms to weaken the social effects of rising unemployment reflects the coordinative character of the West German *Rhineland* model. Hall and Soskice emphasised that in the coordinated model central actors (governments, business associations and trade unions) tend to work towards collective solutions to emerging problems by engaging in a dialogue with one another (Hall and Soskice 2001: 11 and 47). The West German model had started to show crisis symptoms but it was not yet in an existential crisis. It is however important to note the structural problems the West German economy had started to encounter, as these at least partly explain the crisis the *Modell Deutschland* slid into after reunification (Steingart 2004).

The speedy process with which the two German states moved towards their reunification in the course of 1989–1990 laid the foundation for the economic malaise the larger Germany would slide into within the next decade. The unique external conditions, where a faltering Soviet Union under Gorbachev was in principle willing to allow Germans on both sides of the former iron curtain to determine their future, probably made it inevitable to bring the process of unification to a swift conclusion. After all it was what most Germans, especially those in the East, desired. The internal design of the unification process between the two German states nevertheless contained major flaws. The biggest one was the full transformation of the West German state structure towards the former East German GDR. On 3 October 1990 the citizens in East Germany became almost overnight subjects to the West German Basic Law. Already in July 1990 both German states had signed a treaty on their economic, monetary and social union, which essentially fully transferred the West German economic and social model with its complex industrial relation and generous welfare system to the East. In economic terms this amounted to a merger between a Western market economy and a Communist command economy. In practice it meant that the already stretched West German social security system now had to shoulder the burden of providing for an approximately additional 14 million people, many of them pensioners, who had never paid any social insurance contributions in the past. The Kohl government expected that unification would boost investment in Germany and that the swift privatisation of East Germany's former state-owned industries under the supervision of the *Treuhandanstalt* would boost their competitiveness. Kohl spoke of his vision that the five new *Länder* would turn into 'blooming landscapes' within a short period of time. In reality this turned out to be a severe misjudgement of the de facto state of the East German economy. The Kohl government's optimistic view of East German industry stemmed from the GDR's relatively good export performance. However this did not result from the quality of East German products but from the provision of an artificial export market within the Communist Council for Mutual Economic Assistance (COMECON). In return for coordinating its annual production plans with Moscow, the GDR was therefore able to sell its products to neighbouring Warsaw Pact States in Eastern Europe and most of all to the large market in the Soviet Union. East German products only seemed to be competitive under the COMECON system's 'preference for self-sufficiency' (Kaser 2007: 233) but in reality they had never been exposed to the competition in Western markets. The lack of competitiveness of industries in the East was further aggravated by the introduction of the West German *Deutsche Mark* on the basis of a 1:1 exchange for the East German currency. Politically this may have been an important step to counter the rising number of East Germans who were migrating to the West. For East Germans the introduction of the *Deutsche Mark* was considered to be a symbol of inner unity. In the short term it therefore had a positive psychological effect on the confidence of the new citizens in the East that they had acquired equal status in the unified Germany (Brauburger 1994: 669). East Germans rewarded Kohl by giving him a substantial political mandate in the first general election in the unified Germany in December 1990. However the short-term political goal and the overall unification euphoria was soon overshadowed by the dire economic consequences the 1:1 monetary exchange had for East German industry. An industry which struggled to sell its products on the open market now was faced with a substantial wage inflation due to the fact that the real exchange value of the East German *Mark* in relation to the *Deutsche Mark* was estimated to have been 0.23 (Grosser 1999: 805; Sinn 1992: 64). Wages in actual fact went up by around 400 per cent (Münter and Sturm 2002: 187) and this was further aggravated by the introduction of the West German collective bargaining practices (Kaser 2007: 235; Sinn 1996: 114). The collapse failure of the *Treuhand* to establish a viable industrial sector in East Germany after 1990 resulted in the loss of thousands of workplaces. In the manufacturing industry, which was East Germany's most important industrial sector, more than 1 million jobs were lost between 1990 and 1997. This amounted to 66 per cent of all the jobs that had previously existed in the GDR in this sector (Statistisches Bundesamt 2010: 33). Moreover, it pushed the unified Germany into recession. Growth in Germany slowed down substantially after an immediate post-unification peak in 1990 and 1991. By the 1992 the country was in recession and only managed to return to sluggish growth rates for the rest of the decade (1.6 per cent yearly average) which was substantially below the average growth levels West Germany had managed to achieve in previous decades (Figure 5.3).

The five new *Länder* quickly developed a structural unemployment problem which pushed the German economy into a vicious circle from which it did not emerge until the mid-2000s, after the Schröder government had implemented controversial structural reforms. Sluggish growth and rising unemployment resulted in spiralling welfare costs which pushed the already overstretched welfare system to breaking point. The Kohl government had ruled out tax increases to shoulder the financial burden of reunification which Kohl himself describes as 'pocket money'. In reality a substantial financial effort had to be made to manage not just the inclusion of the citizens in the East but into Germany's pension, healthcare and unemployment insurance system. The new *Länder* in the East also lagged substantially behind in terms of their infrastructure. If there was any hope to transform economic fortunes in the region it was essential to invest in the infrastructure. Substantial sums have therefore been transferred from West to East, around €1.25 trillion only in the period between 1999 and 2003

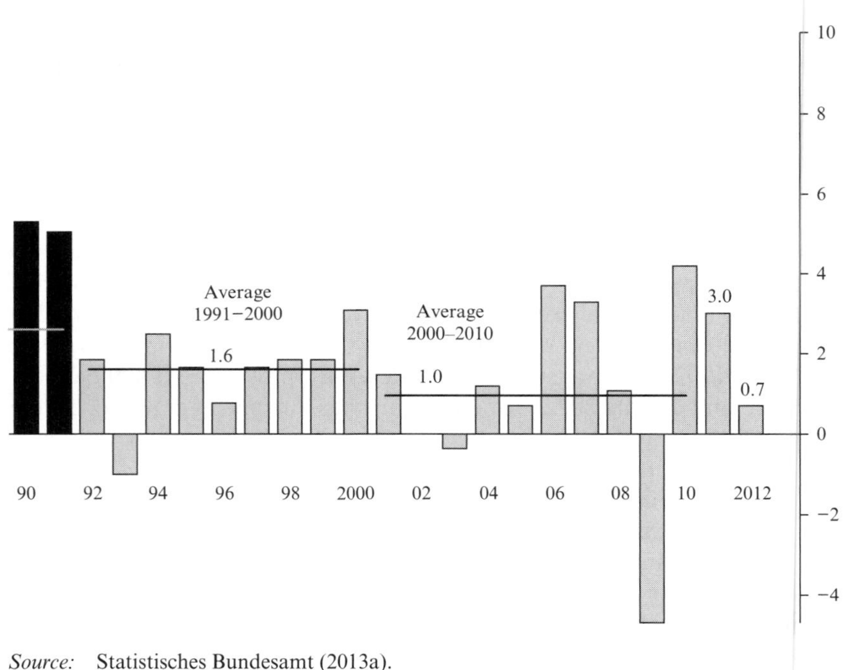

Source: Statistisches Bundesamt (2013a).

Figure 5.3 GDP growth in the unified Germany 1990–2012

(Jansen 2004: 2). The combined sum of all financial transfers to the five Eastern *Länder* since reunification, including financial transfers under the financial solidarity system between the regions (*Länderfinanzausgleich*), is estimated to be around €1.3 trillion (*The Economist* 2012; Vail 2010: 69). Social insurance expenditure consequently more than doubled from €218 million in 1990 to €446 million in 2001 (Figure 5.4).

The Kohl government shifted the financial burden predominantly on the social security system in order to avoid unpopular tax rises in the West (Streeck 2009a: 42). The exception was the introduction of a solidarity tax for West Germans in 1991 at a rate of an additional 7.5 per cent (currently 5.5) of the income tax rate of each taxpayer with the exemption of low-wage earners, and to maintain the West German support for unification. Figure 5.5 shows that the overall tax rate in relation to the GDP has hardly risen in Germany since reunification and remains below those of France and even the UK and Ireland, the two most liberal economies in the EU. The Federal Finance Ministry is therefore keen to point out that Germany is not a high tax economy.

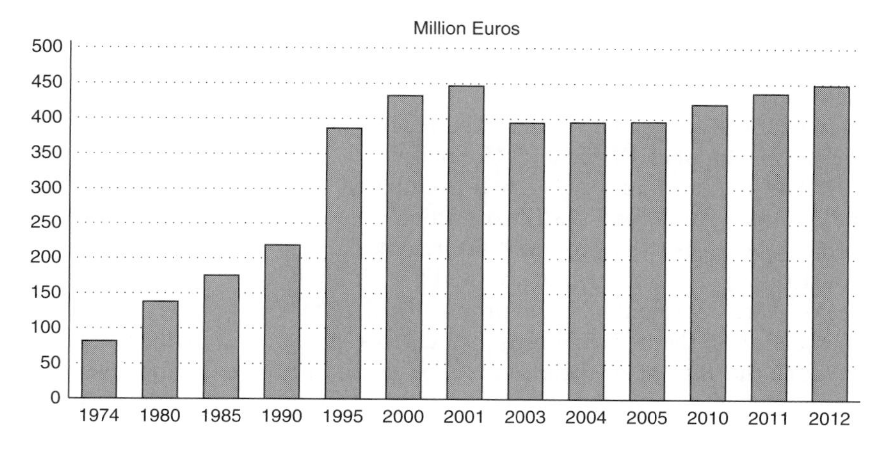

Source: Statistisches Bundesamt (2013c).

Figure 5.4 Social insurance expenditure 1974–2012

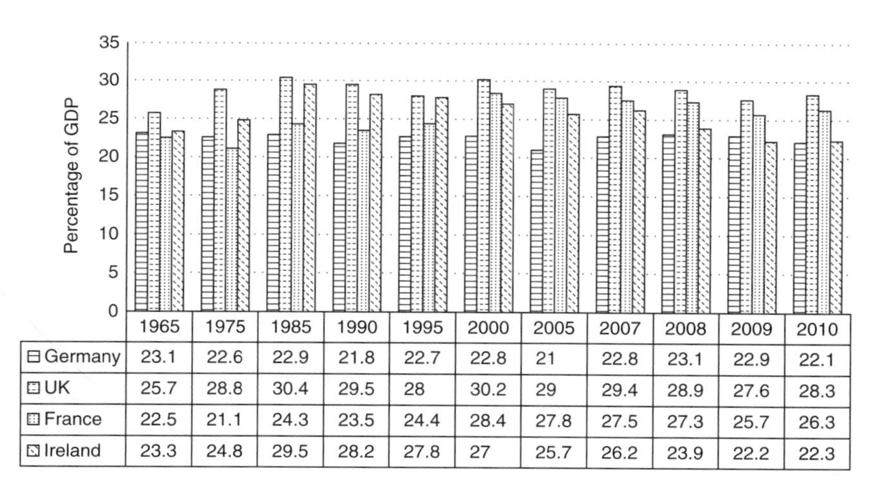

	1965	1975	1985	1990	1995	2000	2005	2007	2008	2009	2010
Germany	23.1	22.6	22.9	21.8	22.7	22.8	21	22.8	23.1	22.9	22.1
UK	25.7	28.8	30.4	29.5	28	30.2	29	29.4	28.9	27.6	28.3
France	22.5	21.1	24.3	23.5	24.4	28.4	27.8	27.5	27.3	25.7	26.3
Ireland	23.3	24.8	29.5	28.2	27.8	27	25.7	26.2	23.9	22.2	22.3

Source: Bundesministerium der Finanzen (2012).

Figure 5.5 Tax rates in comparison

The recession in the early 1990s and the slower levels of growth in successive years lead to a debate on the affordability of the German welfare state and the potentially negative effect of the comparatively high costs of labour in West Germany on the competitiveness of the *Modell Deutschland* in Europe ('*Standortdebatte*') (Seitz 1993). The debate was mainly initiated by economists and employers who feared for their competitive advantage. Cautious attempts made by the Kohl government in the mid-1990s to reform the increasingly costly German welfare system bore little fruit in a constant power game between the federal government and the second legislative chamber, the Federal Council.

Between 1996 and 1998 it was dominated by the opposition parties SPD, Greens and the PDS/Linke, which allowed them to block government policies like the proposed reform of the tax system. The German constitution determines that the Federal Council, the *Bundesrat*, where regions are represented by a proportional number of votes according to the size of their population, participates in the legislative process. In practice the *Bundesrat* therefore is a co-decision maker on any laws and policies which may affect the interests of the regions. Profound institutional reforms, such as changes to the employment, welfare, education and taxation system, have to pass the double hurdle of finding a majority in the national parliament (*Bundestag*) and the Federal Council. This mutual dependence between the federal government and the regions in practice frequently amounts to a 'joint decision trap' (Scharpf et al. 1976). If a federal government coalition faces a Federal Council, which is dominated by a majority of regional governments led by the opposition parties, the scope for the implementation of substantial policy change is limited. There are two ways to overcome this situation of 'divided government'. One is for the federal government to compromise with the opposition, which if both sides are far apart usually leads to a substantial watering down of its original policy agenda (Manow and Burkhart 2008: 365). This is the default approach in the German polity, which explains why radical institutional change is the exception and incremental change the rule (Green and Paterson 2008: 182). The inherent need for cooperation and consensus in the German polity hence has resulted in a de facto grand coalition state (Lehmbruch 1976) with a noticeably smaller ideological difference between the major political parties CDU/CSU and SPD than is the case in other countries, for example the UK. Change to the status quo tends to usually emerge somewhere in the middle between the positions of the CDU/CSU and SPD (König 2006: 524) and is substantially influenced by regional party interests, which are in a quasi permanent state of electioneering and are increasingly fiercely defending their financial positions (Jeffery 2005: 84; Scharpf 2005: 7). The core of Germany's consensus democracy hence lies in its 'cooperative' federalism with the inherent principle of financial solidarity between richer and poorer regions and the entangled web of decision-making between the federal and the regional level. The inherent emphasis on cooperation and stability in the German polity makes a rapid and profound response to

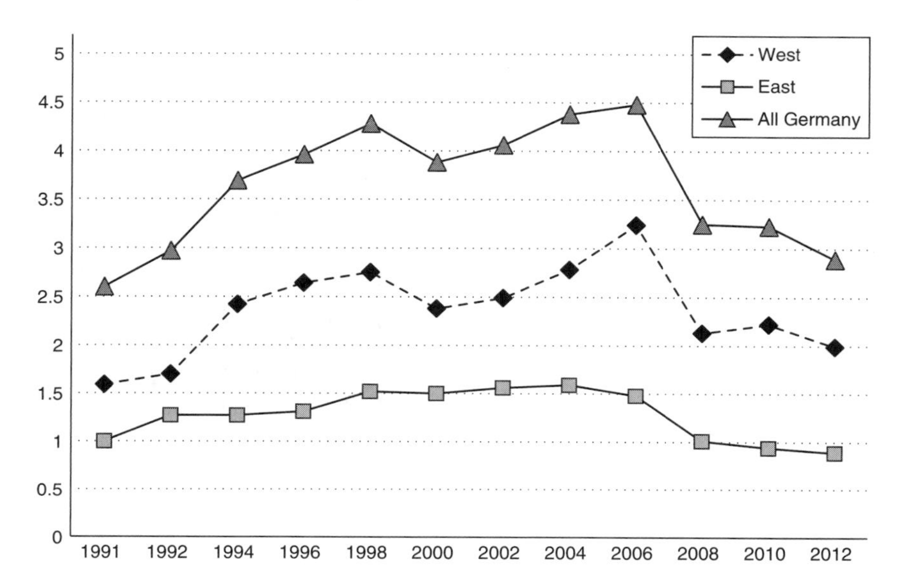

Source: Statistisches Bundesamt (2013c).

Figure 5.6 Unemployment in Germany

emerging systemic weaknesses difficult (Funk 2000: 28). Kitschelt and Streeck even characterised it as a 'catastrophic equilibrium' of inherent reform avoidance which would in the long run threaten the stability of the German state (Kitschelt and Streek 2004). This usually only occurs when 'tipping points', that is events which have a substantial systemic impact appear (Dyson 2005: 116)

The alternative is to try to weaken the opposition case by presenting an agenda which was developed by an independent commission of experts. This government by commission approach was most prominently adopted by the red–green coalition under Chancellor Gerhard Schröder in 2002 in order to be able to implement the controversial welfare reforms under the Agenda 2010. Schröder's red–green coalition inherited the effects which resulted from the failure to use the occasion of German reunification to develop a new constitution and to implement reforms to the German welfare system. Unemployment had been steadily rising since reunification and by 2002 the German economy was back in recession and unemployment approached the unprecedented peak of almost 4.5 million (Figure 5.6).

The rising costs of unemployment also caused Germany to break the budgetary criteria of the newly established eurozone by 2002. This

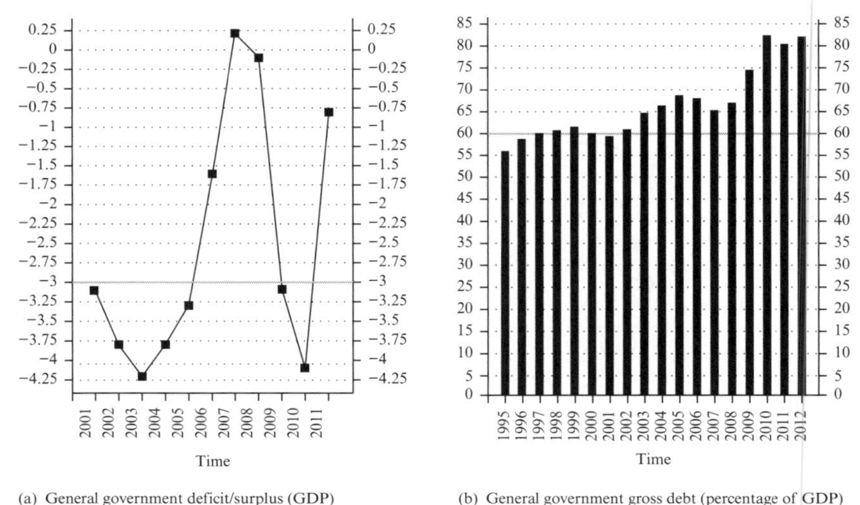

(a) General government deficit/surplus (GDP)

(b) General government gross debt (percentage of GDP)

Source: Eurostat (2013a) and (2013b).

Figure 5.7 Germany's performance under the SGP deficit criteria since 2001

was a rather embarrassing development, given the fact that the budgetary constraints under the EMU's SGP is profoundly a German design. Figure 5.7 shows that Germany exceeded the SGP 3 per cent annual deficit criteria between 2002 and 2005. It also shows that Germany broke through the ceiling of the second criteria, which limits the general level of government gross debt to 60 per cent, in 1999 and has done so constantly since 2002. Germany has therefore not managed to lead by example in the eurozone. This contributed substantially to an overall culture of budgetary laxity.

Initially the red–green coalition had considered this as a marginal problem. Chancellor Schröder tried to justify the breaking of the SGP criteria with the enormous financial burden the federal government had to shoulder in the wake of reunification. Schröder therefore successfully negotiated an exemption from the excessive deficit procedure under exceptional periods such as during periods of stagnant growth, when the need for public investment would become necessary. Schröder argued that the financial burden of reunification and the stagnant growth in Germany made it inevitable that the country would sooner or later not meet the SGP criteria:

> We have to transfer around 4 per cent of our GDP from West to East. The fact that these approximately 80 billion euro are missing from the annual investment budget was totally underestimated by the politics of the past. A pact was developed and pushed through which could only work under conditions which already then were no longer realistic (Schröder 2006: 88).

A change of course had become inevitable to break through the deepening vicious circle of stagnating growth, rising unemployment, spiralling social insurance costs and ultimately a deepening budgetary crisis. The dwindling public funds were less of a concern for Schröder's government than the psychological impact of reaching the critical watershed of 4.5 million people being unemployed. This was a massive setback for the Chancellor who had centred his 1998 general election campaign around the slogan that he would not deserve to be re-elected if he did not manage to substantially reduce unemployment. The support for Schröder's red–green coalition consequently plummeted in the opinion polls and there was very little prospect of his government winning another mandate in the upcoming 2002 general election. Schröder hence embarked on seeking expert advice on how to make the German labour market more flexible and to introduce welfare reforms which would support the reduction of structural unemployment. Economist Bert Rürup was put in charge of developing the proposals on the reform of the healthcare and pension system. Peter Hartz, the chief human resources executive at car manufacturer Volkswagen, formed a commission to propose labour market reforms. The aim of Schröder's approach was to introduce institutional reforms against the entrenched welfare corporatism of the German model, represented by the multiple veto points which ranged from the left-wing traditionalists in his own party to stakeholders such as trade unions and even the opposition parties CDU/CSU, FDP and the Party of the Left. The opposition were likely to oppose at least individual aspects of reform proposals in the *Bundesrat*, even if they opposed them for very different reasons. The CDU/CSU and FDP were calling for a fundamental liberalisation of the German economy while the Party of the Left, the successor to the Communist East German state party SED, vigorously defended the status quo of the German model. By asking renowned independent experts to make proposals Schröder pursued a strategy of delegitimising the various reform opponents. In addition however it was also a means for Schröder to enter the 2002 general election with a promise to defend the 'German way' against being reformed by uncontrolled market forces (Dyson 2007: 114). Schröder went into the 2002 general election campaign with the promise to combine limited reforms based on the recommendations made by the Hartz and Rürup commissions. Both had only published their recommendations relatively late in the campaign in August with the September election date looming. This allowed Schröder to centre his campaign around the vague slogan 'innovation and justice' and the promise to modernise but at the same time protect the core of Germany's social market economy. The government by commission approach was the result of a tipping point which made it obvious that the German model's inherent 'large scale inter-party consensus and corporatists politics' (Czada 2005: 186) was failing to respond to the apparent need to correct what had become a systemic failure. In 1998 Schröder came into government with the attempt to revitalise the coordination of macroeconomic policy under the concerted action between the government, employer federations and trade unions which had ended in the late 1970s. Schröder picked up his predecessor Kohl's attempt to revive the concerted action as an 'Alliance for Jobs', which had only lasted for a short period in the mid-1990s. The failure of Schröder to maintain the Alliance for Jobs pointed towards a decline in the consensus of the German industrial relations system which went hand-in-hand with a more confrontational attitude of the government, who was forced to find ways to limit welfare expenditure (Busch 2009: 65; Timmins 2000: 52). The failure of the red–green coalition to achieve reform by consensus hence represents a tipping point which 'discredited managed capitalism policy arguments, and made it likely that a crisis narrative would develop in ordo-liberal terms' (Dyson 2005: 120). This was more so the case as the alternative to the failing status quo in the *Modell Deutschland* could be compared to the relative success of the welfare-to-work reforms which Bill Clinton's New Democrats and Tony Blair's New Labour had implemented in the US and the UK. Schröder had been substantially inspired by Clinton's and Blair's 'Third Way' philosophy, which essentially promoted the activating state. During the 1998 general election campaign Schröder promoted himself as a pragmatic Social Democrat who would combine an entrepreneurial spirit with social justice. Schröder used the slogan *Die Neue Mitte* ('the new middle ground') which was essentially a rebuttal of the Keynesian ambitions of his inner-party rival Oskar Lafontaine (Schröder 1998: 39). The joint paper published by Schröder and Blair in 1999 enraged Lafontaine and the left wing of the SPD who considered it to be principally a concealed attempt to introduce neoliberal reforms by stealth (Lafontaine 1999: 185). In the paper Schröder and Blair reject the traditional Keynesian welfare state approach where 'achieving social justice became identified with ever higher levels of public spending, regardless of what they achieved' (Schröder and Blair 1999: 2). Both called for the reform of 'the safety net of entitlements into a springboard to personal responsibility' (Ibid.: 7). Schröder and Blair also called on governments in Europe to engage in mutual policy learning and best-practice benchmarking under the European Employment Strategy (EES), for which the EU had just started to promote the open method of coordination (OMC) as a mechanism to promote best practice and policy learning amongst member states. The proposals made by the Hartz Commission on the reform of the German employment system clearly followed the spirit of the Schröder–Blair paper (Funk 2007a: 129). In its report the commission called for a necessary 'paradigm shift from an active towards an activating labour market policy which would have to be in line with European employment guidelines' (Hartz Kommission 2002: 20). Therefore the labour market reforms which Schröder's red–green coalition implemented after its narrow re-election in 2002 have to be clearly considered as an example of policy learning in the European context. For Schröder personally the reform discussions with other centre-left governments from around the world within the Progressive Policy Network, which was initiated in 2000, were probably the most crucial inspiration (Schweiger 2010: 246). Overall policy learning occurred on the basis of the success of labour market activation policies which had been implemented not just by the UK but also by other European countries such as the Netherlands and the Scandinavian countries (Clasen 2011: 267). The changes the Schröder government implemented in the German labour market in 2003 therefore have to be seen in the context of the promotion of activating labour market policies in the EU (Büchs 2007: 75; De la Porte 2007: 31).

The Agenda 2010 which Gerhard Schröder announced in the German parliament in March 2003 represented a rather radical shift in the context of the German welfare state tradition. This explains why the core Hartz IV labour market reforms, which were part of the Agenda 2010, continue to be a matter of public controversy in Germany. Although they were relatively modest when observed from an external perspective, the Agenda 2010 did not alter the consensual industrial relations model of the German economy by leaving the right against unfair dismissal, the principle of collective bargaining and co-decision within work councils practically untouched. Its main focus was to make the labour market more flexible and to reduce the number of people who remain on benefit. Schröder spoke of the need to 'promote personal responsibility and to demand more individual effort from everyone' (Schröder 2003). The Agenda 2010 was hence instilling the principle of individual responsibility, which is characteristic of liberal economies, into the German model. It was a deliberate attempt to move away from the principle of welfare dependency towards a culture where welfare should become an activation measure rather than a long-term mechanism for living support. For this purpose it was necessary to follow the example of other European countries in offering a more personalised and effective service to jobseekers. As a first step, the Hartz I package introduced personal service agencies for jobseekers and the Hartz II package introduced measures to facilitate flexible employment (January 2003). The former was the first step towards a large-scale merger of the German unemployment offices and social insurance offices into a Federal Labour Agency with regional centres and jobcentre branches all over Germany, which came into effect in January 2004 under the Hartz III package. Jobseekers are hence offered a single point of contact for all enquiries regarding job vacancies, training opportunities and benefits. The Hartz II package on flexible employment made employment with a salary below €400 exempt from taxes and social insurance contributions, even if this employment exceeded 15 hours per week. Employers in the business sector who offer such 'mini jobs' are paying 25 per cent of regular taxes and contributions, private households who employ below this limit pay only 12 per cent.

Since January 2013 this limit was raised to €450 and those who are employed under this limit which is now classified as 'marginal employment' have to now also pay pension contributions. 'Mini jobs' are now also centrally administered by a nationwide central agency as a point of contact for jobseekers. This is to ensure that mini jobs, which are subject to the same legal standards as regular employment, including the right against unfair dismissal, are properly administered.[1] Hartz II also introduced the so-called 'Ich AG' scheme under which jobless people who set up their own business received state funding for a maximum of three years (€600 in the first year, €360 in the second year and €240 in the third year). The scheme was abandoned by the CDU/CSU–SPD grand coalition under Chancellor Merkel in 2006 and was replaced by one offering the unemployed a one-off starting capital payment.

The most controversial part of the Hartz reforms was the fourth package. It was aimed at tackling the core problem of the German employment system which Wolfgang Streeck described as the 'Keynesian reflation state' (Streeck 2005: 146). The problem basically boiled down to the simple fact that with a rising number of people out of work and a changing demographic factor with an expected sharp increase in the number of retired people in the decades to come, workers in the German employment system would have faced spiralling social insurance contributions if nothing had been done (Funk 2000: 26–27). The traditional post-war welfare approach, which Martin Seeleib-Kaiser branded as the 'social transfer state', offered jobless people wage replacement rates of up to 68 per cent of their former earnings without the need to accept employment which was lower paid than previous earnings (Seeleib-Kaiser 2001: 104).

Hartz IV tried to break with this tradition by merging the former unemployment benefit and income support into a new unemployment subsidy (*Arbeitslosengeld II* – ALG II) which is set at the rate of the former income support. Anyone who is unemployed is still able to receive the traditional unemployment benefit (*Arbeitslosengeld I* – ALG I) but under the Hartz II package this is no longer linked to wage developments, and Hartz IV also makes it strictly limited in terms of the level and the duration an individual can receive it. The level of payments is set at 60 per cent of the net income (67 per cent for people with dependent children). The maximum duration for the receipt of ALG I is 24 months for anyone under 50 years of age and up to 48 months for the age group 50+ (Bundesagentur für Arbeit 2013a). Anyone who remains unemployed after this period moves towards the new ALG II. The monthly payments under ALG II are set deliberately low to encourage the unemployed to take on additional employment and to make every effort to return to full-time employment at the earliest opportunity. Additional employment during the receipt of ALG II is limited to 15 hours per week. Anyone who takes on employment above this limit is considered to be in full-time employment and is no longer eligible to receive any unemployment support. The ALG II rates were initially separate for the Western and Eastern regions of Germany and have been continuously increased as a result of an ongoing debate about the impact on the living standards of recipients. Since July 2008 the ALG II has a unitary rate across Germany which was then set at €351 for a single unemployed person, €316 for a partner, €211 for a child under 14 and €281 for a child over 14 who all live in the same household. In the meantime the rates were increased several times and the latest levels are as follows: €382 (single person), €345 (partner), €306 (child aged 18–25), €289 (child aged 14–17), €255 (child aged 6–13), €224 (child aged 0–5) (Bundesministerium für Arbeit und Soziales 2013).

The most controversial aspect of the ALG II is the rigorous means-testing which applicants who apply for this type of support are subjected to. Hartz IV operates on the basis of a 'household community' which has more recently been redefined as 'community in need', which includes the applicant, the spouse or legal partner and any dependent children under the age of 25. All of these have to list their financial assets and other possessions such as property, jewellery and cars which are taken into account when a decision on the application for support under the ALG II is made. The principle is that financial assets or possessions which fall into these categories in the community have to be used before the state provides support (Bundesagentur für Arbeit 2013b).

The implementation of the Hartz reforms was followed by discussions on how they affect the nature of Germany's social market economy. Critics of the reforms argued that the Hartz package opened the floodgates to transform German welfare from the Bismarckian life standard guarantee, which determined the level of welfare provision on the basis of the contributions an individual had made, towards the Anglo-Saxon principle of basic provision (Kemmerling and Bruttel 2006: 96). The central criticism was that Hartz had shifted the German welfare from its previous emphasis on aspiring to maintain a decent standard of living for unemployed persons towards keeping them just above the poverty line (Burkhardt et al. 2011: 20). German trade unions reacted to the Hartz reforms by organising mass protests predominantly in cities across the Eastern part of Germany. These were supported by the Party of Left and many other social groups in what was classified as a new civil rights movement reminiscent of the demonstrations that had taken place against the Communist regime in the East German GDR. The widespread opposition to the Hartz reforms occurred in spite of the fact that even under the ALG II the state still covers the social insurance contributions for anyone who receives unemployment benefits, including healthcare, pensions and old age care insurance.

The Hartz reforms also gave a boost to those who continued the *Standortdebatte* and questioned the general viability of the German model. Those on the neoliberal side of the argument criticised Schröder's package for not having been radical enough. This was in spite of the fact that the Agenda 2010 also included an income and business tax reform package, a moderate relaxation of the right against unfair dismissal for smaller businesses, the relaxation of the regulations for temporary employment and the controversial raising of the retirement age to 67 (Busch 2009: 71). The changes to the retirement age were already preceded by the introduction of the so-called *Riester* pension reform, named after the then Employment Minister Walter Riester. The reform introduced a private pension scheme which encourages people to make additional savings for their retirement which are state-sponsored. Calls for a further liberalisation of the model and the weakening of its core industrial relations principles such as collective bargaining, co-decision and the right against unfair dismissal followed. The opposition parties CDU/CSU and FDP proposed to use the Agenda 2010 as a starting point for further and more substantial reforms (Stiller 2010: 154). The CDU leader Angela Merkel called for the fundamental liberalisation of the German model along the lines of the liberal market economies of the UK and Ireland. Particularly the supposed success of the liberalised Irish 'Celtic Tiger' economy was considered as a role model for creating growth and jobs on the basis of low levels of corporation tax and social contributions. At the 2003 CDU Party Conference in Leipzig, Merkel presented the proposals of the reform commission which was spearheaded by the former German President Roman Herzog (Merkel 2003). The commission proposed a systemic change in the social insurance system by introducing a flat rate healthcare premium for everyone. This became the core part of the CDU's manifesto for the 2005 general election and was accompanied by the proposal for a flat tax rate system which

Professor Paul Kirchhof, a former judge in the Federal Constitutional Court, had developed for Merkel (Green 2013: 55). The CDU manifesto for the 2005 general election also proposed a fundamental overhaul of the core features of the German model. The manifesto announced that once in government the CDU would make the system of collective bargaining and wage setting more flexible, remove the right against unfair dismissal in companies with less than 20 employees, allow employers to pay ALG II recipients less than 10 per cent of statutory wages and to relax the regulations for the employment under short-term contracts. Corporation tax was to be lowered to 22 per cent (CDU/CSU 2005).

Merkel's CDU had adopted the stance of those economists in Germany who argued that the German model of coordinated capitalism would in the long run be unsustainable in the era of globalisation. Hans-Werner Sinn from the Institute for Economic Research in Munich called Germany the 'sick man of Europe'. He most prominently presented Ireland as an example of an economy which had the become the 'economic miracle of Europe' by combining low tax rates with 'an extremely liberal economic policy modelled along the lines of the American example, which kept the level of regulation of businesses small and also largely dispensed with welfare state institutions' (Sinn 2004: 36).

Wolfgang Streeck detected a gradual shift of the German social market economy from coordination towards liberalisation in the form of the 'disorganisation' or gradual retreat of the state (Streeck 2009b: 158). This fundamental criticism of the coordinated nature of the German economy was not shared by the majority of the public. Merkel herself suffered a bitter defeat at the 2005 general election where all the previous opinion polls, which had predicted a clear majority for a reformist centre-right coalition between the CDU/CSU and the FDP, turned out to be wrong. Schröder's SPD managed to get almost the same amount of votes as the CDU/CSU. Most commentators put this down to the fact that the radical reform programme Merkel had proposed to implement was a step too far not just for the electorate but also for many within her own party (Clemens 2013: 202), most of all in the Bavarian CSU, which is traditionally more welfare orientated than the CDU. Merkel had completely underestimated the anti-reformist climate in Germany. The campaign she ran in favour of shifting the German model towards further liberalisation went against the overall anti-reformist sentiment in the country (Green and Paterson 2008: 192), which seemed to have increased after the Hartz reforms. This allowed Schröder to portray himself as the protector of the social market economy and to regain support, in spite of the widespread hostility to his Agenda 2010 reform programme (Schmitt-Beck and Faas 2007: 403). Although Schröder narrowly failed to win another mandate for his red–green coalition, he managed to force the CDU into a grand coalition in which the SPD took over key ministries (finance, employment, health, justice, environment, foreign affairs and international development). Since the 2005 general election the calls for further fundamental reforms to the German model have gradually faded away. Opinion polls show that there is little support amongst the public for further welfare state reforms, especially in the Eastern regions of the country (Gabriel and Trüdinger 2011: 280). The systemic change towards the liberal model which the advocates of the globalisation convergence hypothesis had predicted has certainly not occurred.

Since unification the German economy has witnessed changes towards greater flexibility without having witnessed a fundamental systemic change. The flexibilisation in the labour market through Hartz was accompanied by a decentralisation of the once rigid industrial relations model. Exemptions from industry-wide collective wage agreements have become more widespread in recent years, particularly in East Germany (Bosch 2008; Funk 2007b). Equally, the traditional system of corporate financing by a house bank, which provided a relatively sheltered environment for companies, has increasingly been replaced by stock market capitalisation. This is the result of the adoption of the principle of shareholder value in companies and a changing nature of the banks towards investment and securities operations.

The modifications the German model has witnessed are an example of the adaptation of existing institutions and central actors rather than of systemic failure. The German system of coordinated capitalism, most prominently represented by the principle of co-decision in industrial relations, showed enough flexibility to cope with the changes of globalisation to ensure that the country's export-orientated economy remains successful. The changes in the system of corporate finance occurred predominantly under state supervision. However the state did not act as a hurdle to the liberalisation of corporate finance and the restructuring of the banking industry but rather as a supervisory agent who facilitated and managed change (Lütz 2007: 35). In industrial relations both workers and trade unions have been willing to maintain a consensual approach with employers by showing substantial flexibility on pay settlements and working conditions. As a result work councils maintained an important role as a forum to negotiate 'concessions on wages or working hours in exchange for employment guarantees' (Jackson 2005: 248). The core institutions of Germany's industrial relations model have therefore shown to be more adaptable to change than was widely assumed. Rather than to act as veto points against change, they have tried to adapt to it by changing their purpose (Menz 2007: 91). The focus of the German model on non-market regulation and political consensus, which Busch emphasised as an asset for an export-orientated economy which has to compete on the basis of product innovation and quality (Busch 2007: 19–20), has indeed turned out to be a competitive advantage. The German social market economy was able to prove this under the extremely adverse external conditions of the 2008–2009 financial crisis when the ability to maintain internal consensus turned out to be a major advantage. This was supported by the fact that Germany was governed by a grand coalition between 2005 and 2010 during the bulk of the financial crisis. Crucial decisions in response to the crisis could therefore be made swiftly and without the usual delay due to the need to find a compromise between a minimum winning coalition in parliament and an opposition majority in the regional chamber. The grand coalition reacted prudently to the crisis by taking measures to limit a potential banking and employment crisis. The German banking industry is amongst the most capitalised in Europe (OECD 2012: 15). It was therefore substantially less exposed to the crisis in the US financial industry than other economies. Social Democratic Finance Minister Peer Steinbrück nevertheless ensured that the government provided €480 in support of potentially failing banks and made a joint announcement with Merkel in October 2008 that it would offer a guarantee for all private bank accounts. The aim of this was to prevent a run on unstable banks similar to the events the UK had witnessed with Northern Rock in the autumn of 2007. Even more importantly the grand coalition took an active stance to prevent a large-scale loss of jobs which could be expected as a result of the decline in exports to countries in the European neighbourhood who were embroiled in a sovereign debt crisis. The grand coalition hence worked with trade unions and employers to ensure that workers would be kept on contracts with reduced hours and subsidised salaries rather than to be sacked (Zolnhöfer 2011: 236). In this way the grand coalition managed to sustain the positive effects the Hartz labour market reforms started to have on unemployment rates in Germany after 2005.

This has resulted in lower unemployment figures which started to drop significantly after about 2006 and continued to fall even during the period of the global financial crisis. They have now reversed to below 3 million in the whole of Germany. Most significant is the decline in unemployment figures in the East, which are now below the 1991 figures before the collapse of East German industries (see Figure 5.7 above). Another important factor in Germany's surprisingly stable performance even during the most adverse economic conditions is the culture of wage restraint which trade unions reluctantly accepted in return for job guarantees from the employers. Part of this was also a decline of collective wage agreement coverage, particularly in public and private services where workplace agreements are

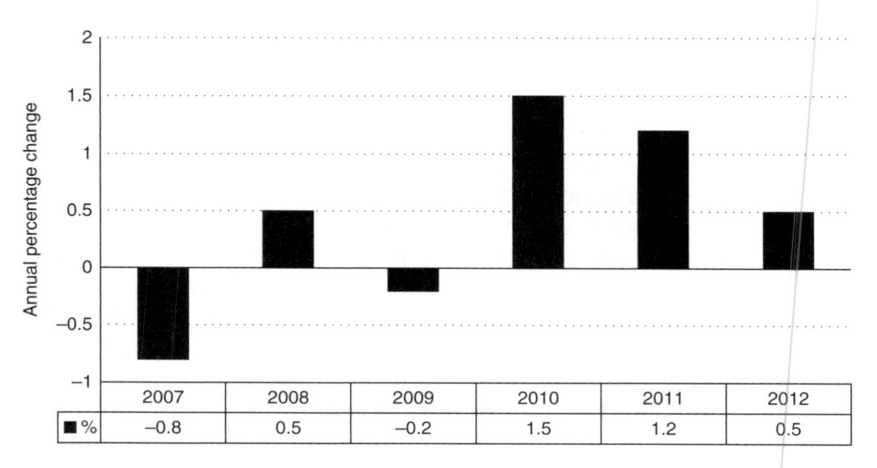

■ %	2007	2008	2009	2010	2011	2012
■ %	–0.8	0.5	–0.2	1.5	1.2	0.5

Source: Statistisches Bundesamt (2013d).

Figure 5.8 Real wage index in Germany

widespread and union coverage sparse. Overall the level of collective wage agreements in Germany dropped by 10 per cent between 1998 and 2006, with an overall coverage of 65 per cent (54 per cent industry wide). While the overall level of coverage is still relatively high, it is substantially lower in East Germany (54 per cent) (Lehndorff et al. 2009: 121). Real wages rose by less than 1 per cent before the crisis and then fell during the onset of the sovereign debt crisis. Since 2010 wages have risen again but only by a modest margin of between 0.5 and 1.5 per cent (Figure 5.8). The latest OECD economic survey on Germany emphasises that prior to the crisis unit labour costs in Germany decreased by 2 per cent (2000–2007) while they rose substantially by an average of 22 per cent in the whole of the OECD (OECD 2012: 44).

Some have blamed the German culture of wage restraint over the past decade for the structural crisis in the eurozone. The argument is that Germany boosted its export performance by limiting production costs through wage restraint rather than through a competitive advantage regarding its manufacturing standards. It is claimed that Germany would therefore have undermined the changes of competitors in Southern Europe who were unable to restrict wages to the same extent and instead resorted to growth based on a domestic credit boom, which was fuelled further by the support of German credit (Lapavitsas et al. 2012: 2 and 29; Wolf 2013). This issue has now become the subject of debate between German economists. Sinn has categorically rejected the notion that Germany was the main beneficiary of the eurozone at the expense of other countries. He argues that Germany's entry into the eurozone led to an outflow of capital which undermined domestic demand and substantially contributed to the weakness of the economy at the turn of the century (Sinn 2013).

Young and Semmler also reject the notion that low German wages secured Germany's export 'miracle' and point out that German export figures during the crisis remained strong because of growing demand in Asia (Young and Semmler 2011: 19). With around 16 per cent of German exports currently going to Asia this region has growth potential for the German economy. However at present 70 per cent of exports go to Germany's immediate neighbourhood in Europe. Out of German exports, 37.6 per cent go to other eurozone countries, 19.8 per cent to EU member states outside the euro and 11.9 per cent to countries in Europe who are not EU members (Statistisches Bundesamt 2013e).

In spite of some setbacks Germany has definitely benefited from being at the heart of the European currency union which has provided a relatively stable environment for its export-orientated economy. Germany's good economic performance in recent years in spite of a deepening sovereign debt crisis shows that the institutions of Germany's coordinated model of capitalism are adaptable to change without putting the model itself in question. The relatively stable performance of the German economy and continuous improvement of labour market figures after the implementation of limited structural reforms and during a period of adverse external conditions is a positive sign. It points towards the likelihood that the German model will continue to be viable under the conditions of globalisation without having to completely eradicate the consensual culture of its managed capitalism.

Germany's strong economic position in the wake of the financial crisis nevertheless should not distract from the fact that the model in its current shape still has structural weaknesses which could in the long run undermine its economic performance. The first risk lies in the future of Germany's budgetary position. In spite of Schröder's Agenda 2010 reforms the German welfare state remains costly when compared with other economies. Consequently the average tax burden on workers in Germany remains comparatively high. The reforms managed to maintain the level of taxation on the average worker (including other employee and employer contributions) as a percentage of total labour cost at around 50 per cent during the last decade. The tax burden on workers in Germany nevertheless remains beyond the OECD average and amongst the highest in the whole of the OECD. In the EU context it is only surpassed by France. It only decreased marginally after 2004 (from 52.2 to 49.8 per cent in 2012) when the effects of the Agenda 2010 reforms set in (Figure 5.9).

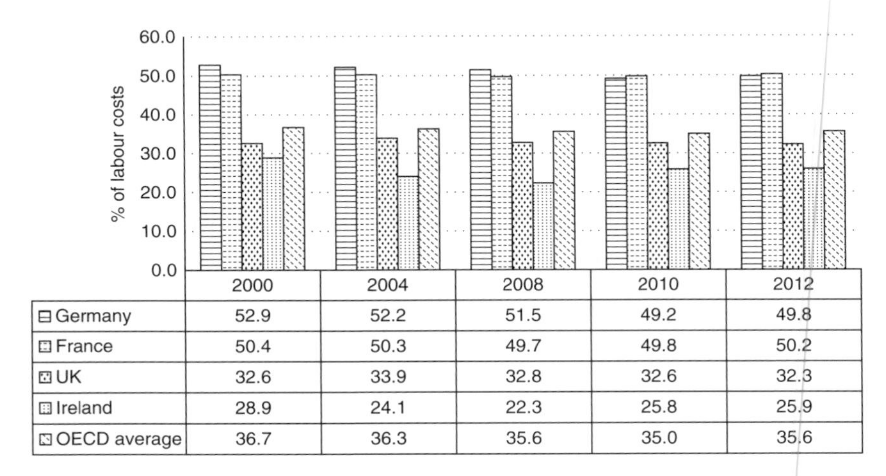

	2000	2004	2008	2010	2012
Germany	52.9	52.2	51.5	49.2	49.8
France	50.4	50.3	49.7	49.8	50.2
UK	32.6	33.9	32.8	32.6	32.3
Ireland	28.9	24.1	22.3	25.8	25.9
OECD average	36.7	36.3	35.6	35.0	35.6

Source: OECD (2013a).

Figure 5.9 Tax burden single person without children

Although the German state currently receives a record level of tax revenues, the country's budgetary position continues to be stretched from within and externally due to the strong financial involvement in the European Financial Stability Facility (EFSF) and the successor European Stability Mechanism (ESM). Germany's capital subscription at the ESM alone amounts to €190 billion (ESM 2013). Consequently the structural level of public debt in Germany keeps on rising and is forecast to reach 81.3 per cent in 2013 (OECD 2012). The risk of budgetary overstretch is real for Germany and could worsen if economic growth should stall as a result of declining exports. This leads straight to the second weakness of the model, which lies in its overreliance on the export of high quality manufacturing products. The sluggish level of domestic demand in Germany, both in terms of government investment but even more so due to a culture of spending restraint amongst private consumers and the weak services sector, leaves little alternative room for growth in case exports should decline. Germany has amongst the weakest services trade balance in the whole of the OECD and especially in Europe (OECD 2013b). Germany's continuing strong reliance on export trade with the rest of Europe, especially the countries in the eurozone, makes it extremely vulnerable to the effects of the sovereign debt crisis (Tilford 2012). If purchasing power amongst Germany's European neighbours declines further, it will almost inevitably have a profound effect on the German export balance.

The third major weakness lies in the structure of the German labour

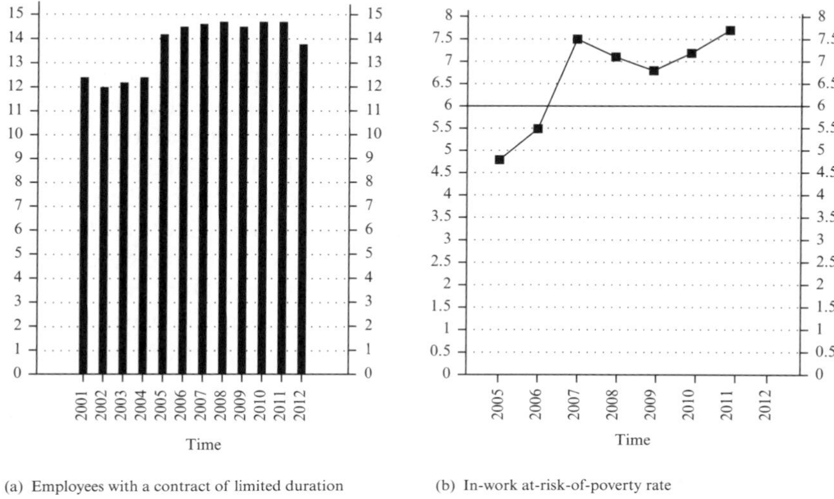

(a) Employees with a contract of limited duration

(b) In-work at-risk-of-poverty rate

Source: Eurostat (2013c and 2013d).

Figure 5.10 The increase of precarious employment in Germany

market. The increase in employment figures in the aftermath of the Hartz reforms came with a substantial increase in precarious jobs. Employers have made substantial use of the mini job regulation and the relaxation of the regulations for temporary job agencies, particularly in sectors like the services industry where trade unions are tolerating a move towards wage-setting at the individual company level. The number of people who are employed on a temporary contract has risen steadily since 2005 and now stands at over 14 per cent of the workforce. At the same time Germany saw a steep rise of people who have a job but are nevertheless considered to be at the risk of poverty because their income is below the 60 per cent of the national median equivalised income. The percentage of those classified as working poor has risen from 4.8 per cent in 2005 to 7.7 per cent in 2011 (Figure 5.10). Around 11 per cent of part-time workers are considered to be working poor.

The debate about the negative effects of the Agenda 2010 reforms on the German model hence continues. Those who argued that the liberalisation of the employment system would lead to a fall in living standards and less security for workers feel vindicated. The criticism concentrates on the increasing fragmentation of the German labour market, where particularly the services industry seems to turn into a sector where low pay and short-term contracts or agency work has become widespread (Lehndorff et al. 2009: 126). The increase in precarious employment became a major issue in the 2013 general election campaign where the SPD made the introduction of a standard minimum wage one of its core election pledges. The move is supported by the Green Party and the Party of the Left but rejected by the CDU/CSU and FDP who argue that a standard minimum wage for all industries may damage the competitiveness of the German economy. Instead the CDU calls for the introduction of low wage limits in individual economic sectors which are not determined by the government but through negotiations between the social partners (CDU/CSU 2013: 7).

The major challenge for Germany policy-makers is to ensure that the country's economic model can combine economic dynamism with social cohesion. The Bonn Republic used to be a role model for both. In the unified Germany the coordinated social market economy has come under severe internal and external pressures which it has so far managed surprisingly well. The institutions of the coordinated economy have adapted to these challenges by allowing incremental change towards the flexibilisation of the labour market, the welfare state, industrial relations and corporate financing to occur. In the context of the German cultural affiliation with consensus and social cohesion these changes are nevertheless perceived as rather radical. The substantially increased poverty risk for people in low wage and temporary jobs and the failure to provide sufficient opportunities for young people to move into a full-time employment on a living wage, after they finish training or education, represent crucial flaws in the reformed German model. The European Commission highlights these weaknesses in its reform recommendations to the German government in the response to Germany's 2013 national reform programme under the European Semester. The European Commission especially underlines the need to lower the tax burden for low-wage earners and to develop measures to assist people who only find marginal or short-term employment to move towards more sustainable full-time employment. The European Commission also calls on the German government to end the culture of wage restraint and to allow wage growth with the purpose of stimulating domestic demand (European Commission 2013: 4–5).

These internal challenges are accompanied by a fundamental external challenge for Germany regarding its role in the EU. The unified Germany has maintained the European policy legacy of the Bonn Republic by engaging constructively in the multilateral European diplomacy. The reflective Europeanism, which characterised the Bonn Republic, has gradually been replaced by a more pragmatic attitude (Wittlinger 2010: 98), where the German national interest is openly articulated and a cost-benefits analysis of individual European issues is performed. In spite of this the overall pro-European consensus has never been an issue of controversial domestic debate in Germany. The emergence of Germany as the new 'reluctant hegemon' in the aftermath of the financial crisis nevertheless challenges the traditional parameters of the country's European policy. Chancellor Merkel seems to have been overburdened by the depth of the sovereign debt crisis and the lack of leadership support from the economically weakened France. Merkel has failed to use Germany's new dominant leadership position to present a future vision for the EU which goes beyond the narrow focus on budgetary stability. Instead she has given the impression that she lacks an emotional affiliation with the European project (Paterson 2011: 66). Merkel's lack of emotional engagement with the rising social costs of the sovereign debt crisis in the eurozone risks undermining the still predominantly positive attitudes towards Germany's central role amongst the other EU-27 countries. If German leadership is predominantly perceived as an austerity dictate by the rest of the EU, one can expect a significant rise in Euroscepticism. Merkel's 'policy dictate' (Hübner 2012: 161) can also be seen internally, where the lack of a transparent discussion on the extent and the purpose of the financial stabilisation mechanisms is noticeable. Merkel's unwillingness to be transparent about the full extent of the financial burden on the German taxpayer, which results from the country's strong financial engagement in the EFSF and ESM, poses the significant risk of overstretching the general pro-European attitude of the German electorate. Equally, Merkel's government sends conflicting signals when it comes to determining the future institutional shape of the eurozone and the EU as a whole. She recently contradicted her Finance Minister Wolfgang Schäuble who put forward the vision of the European Commission to be turned into a European executive with a directly elected president. Merkel emphasised that the current circumstances would not make it necessary to equip the Commission with further powers. Instead she called for the better coordination of central policy areas between the EU member states (*Der Spiegel* 2013: 30). The Chancellor's retreat on deepening the EU politically may result from her increasing awareness of the limited scope for the federal government to abandon national sovereignty in key policy areas.

Based on the ruling made by the German Federal Constitutional Court in 2009, steps towards deeper political union would demand a new constitution backed by public referendum, especially if decision-making in core economic policy areas such as fiscal and social policy is transferred at the European level (Paterson 2011: 66–67). The public debate on the vision of a political union for the eurozone and beyond this still has to take place in Germany and hardly featured in the 2013 general election campaign.

Germany's, at present, strong economic and political position in Europe is undoubtedly the result of the ability of the social market economy to embrace change when it is necessary. The inherent culture of the German model to adapt incrementally and to achieve consensus between multiple veto players has not prevented the country from making essential modifications to the German economy under the conditions of emerging systemic weakness. Consequently the German coordinated economy is not generally a stagnant model. The lower level of reliance on market forces than it is the case in liberal economies has turned out to be a strength at a time of global financial turmoil. Because of the stronger dependence on the state and political leadership, the future of the German economy strongly depends on decisive political leadership which addresses the current internal and external weaknesses. Without the political will to address the internal structural imbalances in the economy (labour market, taxation system, weakness of the services sector) and the external challenge of leading the EU towards a comprehensive future vision beyond the austerity crisis Germany's 'moment in the sun' (Tilford 2011) may indeed sooner or later turn out to be a temporary occurrence.

NOTE

1. For further details see: http://www.minijob-zentrale.de/DE/0_Home/01_mj_im_gewerblichen_bereich/20_arbeitsrecht/node.html.

REFERENCES

Anderson, J.J. (1997) 'Hard Interests, Soft Power and Germany's Changing Role in Europe', in P.J. Katzenstein (ed.) *Tamed Power: Germany in Europe*. Ithaca: Cornell University Press, pp. 80–107.

Anderson, J.J. (1999) *German Unification and the Union of Europe*. Cambridge: Cambridge University Press.

Bibow, J. (2007) 'Bad for Euroland, Worse for Germany – the ECB's Record', in J. Hölscher (ed.) *Germany's Economic Performance: From Unification to Euroization*. Basingstoke: Palgrave Macmillan, pp. 42–65.

Bosch, G. (2008) 'Auflösung des deutschen Tarifsystems', *Wirtschaftsdienst* 1: 16–20.

Brauburger, S. (1994) 'Verträge zur deutschen Einheit', in W. Weidenfeld and K.R. Korte (eds) *Handbuch zur deutschen Einheit*. Frankfurt a.M.: Campus, pp. 667–681.

Büchs, M. (2007) *New Governance in European Social Policy: The Open Method of Coordination*. Basingstoke: Palgrave Macmillan.

Bulmer, S. (1997) 'Shaping the Rules? The Constitutive Politics of the European Union and Germany', in P.J. Katzenstein (ed.) *Tamed Power: Germany in Europe*. Ithaca: Cornell University Press, pp. 49–79.

Bulmer, S., C. Jeffery and W.E. Paterson (2000) *Germany's European Diplomacy: Shaping the Regional Milieu*. Manchester: Manchester University Press.

Bundesagentur für Arbeit (2013a) 'Merkblatt für Arbeitslose'. Available at: http://www.arbeitsagentur.de/zentraler-Content/Veroeffentlichungen/Merkblatt-Sammlung/MB-f-Arbeitslose.pdf (accessed 2 September 2013).

Bundesagentur für Arbeit (2013b) 'Anrechnung von Vermögen auf das ArbeitslosengeldII'. Available at: http://www.arbeitsagentur.de/nn_549800/Navigation/zentral/Buerger/Arbeitslos/Grundsicherung/Vermoegen/Vermoegen-Nav.html (accessed 2 September 2013).

Bundesministerium für Arbeit und Soziales (2013) 'SGB II im Überblick'. Available at: http://www.bmas.de/DE/Themen/Arbeitsmarkt/Grundsicherung/SGB-II-Uebersicht/inhalt.html (accessed 2 September 2013).

Bundesministerium der Finanzen (2012) '15 Steuerquoten im internationalen Vergleich', 21 June. Available at: http://www.bundesfinanzministerium.de/Content/DE/Monatsberichte/2012/06/Inhalte/Kapitel-4-Statistiken/4–1-15-steuer quoten-im-internationalen-vergleich.html?view=renderPrint (accessed 23 August 2013).

Burkhardt, C., R. Martin, S. Mau and P. Taylor-Gooby (2011) 'Differing Notions of Social Welfare? Britain and Germany Compared', in J. Clasen (ed.) *Converging Worlds of Welfare? British and German Social Policy in the 21st Century*. Oxford: Oxford University Press, pp. 15–32.

Busch, A. (2005) 'Shock-Absorbers under Stress: Parapublic Institutions and the Double Challenges of German Unification and European Integration', in S. Green and W.E. Paterson (eds) *Governance in Contemporary Germany: The Semisovereign State Revisited*. Cambridge: Cambridge University Press, pp. 94–115

Busch, A. (2007) 'Globalisation and National Varieties of Capitalism: The Contested Viability of the "German Model"', in K. Dyson and S. Padgett (eds) *The Politics of Economic Reform in Germany: Global, Rhineland or Hybrid Capitalism?* Abingdon: Routledge, pp. 11–25.

Busch, A. (2009) 'Schröder's Agenda 2010: From "Plan B" to Lasting Legacy?', in A. Miskimmon, W.E. Paterson and J. Sloam (eds) *Germany's Gathering Crisis: The 2005 Federal Election and the Grand Coalition*. Basingstoke: Palgrave Macmillan, pp. 64–79.

CDU/CSU (1987) *Weiter so, Deutschland für eine gute Zukunft: Das Wahlprogramm von CDU und CSU für die Bundestagswahl 1987*. Bonn: Konrad-Adenauer-Haus.

CDU/CSU (2005) 'Regierungsprogramm 2005–2009. Deutschlands Chancen nutzen. Wachstum. Arbeit. Sicherheit'. Available at: http://www.hss.de/fileadmin/migration/downloads/BTW_2005–09–18_01.pdf (accessed 30 July 2013).

CDU/CSU (2013) 'Gemeinsam erfolgreich für Deutschland: Regierungsprogramm 2013–2017'. Available at: http://www.cdu.de/sites/default/files/media/dokumente/cdu_regierungsprogramm_2013–2017.pdf (accessed 23 August 2013).

Clasen, J. (2011) 'From Unemployment Programmes to "Work First": Is German Labour Market Policy Becoming more British?', in J. Clasen (ed.) *Converging Worlds of Welfare? British and German Social Policy in the 21st Century*. Oxford: Oxford University Press, pp. 266–281.

Clemens, C.M. (2013) 'Beyond Christian Democracy? Welfare State Politics and Policy in a Changing CDU', *German Politics* 22 (1–2):191–211.

Cole, A. (2001) *Franco-German Relations*. Essex: Pearson.

Czada, R. (2005) 'Social Policy: Crisis and Transformation', in S. Green and

W.E. Paterson (eds) (2005) *Governance in Contemporary Germany: The Semisovereign State Revisited.* Cambridge: Cambridge University Press, pp. 165–189.

De la Porte, C. (2007) 'Good Governance via the OMC? The Cases of Employment and Social Inclusion', *European Journal of Legal Studies* 1 (1): 1–43.

Der Spiegel (2013) 'Wir sitzen in einem Boot'. Interview with German Chancellor Angela Merkel, *Der Spiegel* Issue 23: 28–30.

Dyson, K. (2005) 'Economic Policy Management: Catastrophic Equilibrium, Tipping Points and Crisis Interventions', in S. Green and W.E. Paterson (eds) *Governance in Contemporary Germany: The Semisovereign State Revisited.* Cambridge: Cambridge University Press, pp. 115–137.

Dyson, K. (2007) 'Binding Hands as a Strategy for Economic Reform: Government by Commission', in K. Dyson and S. Padgett (eds) *The Politics of Economic Reform in Germany: Global, Rhineland or Hybrid Capitalism?* Abingdon: Routledge, pp. 110–133.

European Commission (2013) *Recommendation for a Council Recommendation on Germany's 2013 National Reform Programme and Delivering a Council Opinion on Germany's Stability Programme for 2012–2017.* COM (2013) 355 final. Available at: http://ec.europa.eu/europe2020/pdf/nd/csr2013_germany_en.pdf (accessed 7 September 2013).

European Stability Mechanism (ESM) (2013) 'ESM Factsheet'. Luxembourg: ESM. Available at: http://www.esm.europa.eu/pdf/ESM%20Factsheet%20 29012013.pdf (accessed 15 March 2013).

Eurostat (2013a) 'General Government Deficit/Surplus Percentage of GDP'. Available at: http://epp.eurostat.ec.europa.eu/tgm/table.do?tab=table&init=1& language=en&pcode=tec00127&plugin=1 (accessed 30 July2013).

Eurostat (2013b) 'General Government Gross Debt'. Available at: http://epp.eurostat.ec.europa.eu/tgm/table.do?tab=table&init=1&language=en&pcode=tsdde 410&plugin=1 (accessed 30 July 2013).

Eurostat (2013c) 'Employees with a Contract of Limited Duration (Annual Average)'. Available at: http://epp.eurostat.ec.europa.eu/tgm/table.do?tab=t able&init=1&language=en&pcode=tps00073&plugin=1 (accessed 30 July 2013).

Eurostat (2013d) 'In-Work At-Risk-of-Poverty Rate'. Available at: http://epp. eurostat.ec.europa.eu/tgm/table.do?tab=table&init=1&language=en&pcode= tesov110&plugin=1 (accessed 30 July 2013).

Funk, L. (2000) 'Economic Reform of the *Modell Deutschland*', in R. Harding and W.E. Paterson (eds) *The Future of the German Economy: An End to the Miracle?* Manchester: Manchester University Press, pp. 16–35.

Funk, L. (2007a) 'Convergence in Employment-Related Public Policies? A British-German Comparison', *German Politics* 16 (1): 116–136.

Funk, L. (2007b) 'Current Structural Changes: Challenges for the German Labour Market and Collective Bargaining', in J. Hölscher (ed.) *Germany's Economic Performance.* Basingstoke: Palgrave Macmillan, pp. 175–196.

Gabriel, O.W. and E.M. Trüdinger (2011) 'Embellishing Welfare State Reforms? Political Trust and the Support for Welfare State Reforms in Germany', *German Politics* 20 (2): 273–292.

Green, S. and W.E. Paterson (2008) 'Last Orders: Semisovereignty and Cost Containment', in A. Miskimmon, W.E. Paterson and J. Sloam (eds) *Germany's Gathering Crisis.* Basingstoke: Palgrave Macmillan, pp. 181–201.

Green, S. (2013) 'Societal Transformation and Programmatic Change in the CDU', *German Politics* 22 (1–2): 46–63.
Grosser, D. (1999) 'Verhandlungen zur deutschen Einheit: Ökonomischer Prozeß', in W. Weidenfeld and K.R. Korte (eds) *Handbuch zur deutschen Einheit*. Frankfurt a.M.: Campus, pp. 804–817, 2nd edn.
Hall, P.A. and D. Soskice (2001) *Varieties of Capitalism: The Institutional Foundations of Comparative Advantage*. Oxford: Oxford University Press.
Hartz Kommission (2002) 'Moderne Dienstleistungen am Arbeitsmarkt'. Available at: http://www.bmas.de/DE/Service/Publikationen/moderne-dienstleistungen-am-arbeitsmarkt.html (accessed 30 August 2013).
Heering, W.W. (2007) 'Monetary Targeting by the German Bundesbank: Some Reflections on Conceptual Issues', in J. Hölscher (ed.) *Germany's Economic Performance: From Unification to Euroization*. Basingstoke: Palgrave Macmillan, pp. 66–100.
Hübner, K. (2012) 'German Crisis Management and Leadership – From Ignorance to Procrastination to Action' *Asia Europe Journal* 9 (2–4): 159–177.
Jackson, G. (2005) 'Contested Boundaries: Ambiguity and Creativity in the Evolution of German Codetermination', in W. Streeck and K. Thelen (eds) *Beyond Continuity: Institutional Change in Advanced Political Economies*. Oxford: Oxford University Press, pp. 229–254.
Janning, J. (1994) 'Europäische Integration und deutsche Einheit', in W. Weidenfeld and K.R. Korte (eds) *Handbuch zur deutschen Einheit*. Frankfurt a.M.: Campus, pp. 269–276.
Jansen, H. (2004) 'Transfers to Germany's Eastern Länder: A Necessary Price for Convergence or a Permanent Drag?' ECFIN Country Focus, 8 October. Available at: http://ec.europa.eu/economy_finance/publications/publication1437_en.pdf (accessed 28 August 2013).
Jeffery, C. (2005) 'Federalism: the New Territorialism', in S. Green and W.E. Paterson (eds) *Governance in Contemporary Germany*. Cambridge: Cambridge University Press, pp. 78–93.
Jeffery, C. and W.E. Paterson (2001) 'Germany's Power in Europe', in H. Wallace (ed.) *Interlocking Complexities of European Integration*. Basingstoke: Palgrave Macmillan, pp. 179–215.
Kaser, M. (2007) 'East Germany's Economic Transition in Comparative Perspective', in J. Hölscher (ed.) *Germany's Economic Performance: From Unification to Euroization*. Basingstoke: Palgrave Macmillan, pp. 229–243.
Katzenstein, P. (1987) *Policy and Politics in Germany: the Growth of a Semisovereign State*. Philadelphia, PA: Temple University Press.
Katzenstein, P. (1997) 'United Germany in an Integrating Europe', in P. Katzenstein (ed.), *Tamed Power: Germany in Europe*. Ithaca and London: Cornell University Press.
Katzenstein, P. (2005) 'Conclusion: Semisovereignty in United Germany', in S. Green and W.E. Paterson (eds) *Governance in Contemporary Germany*. Cambridge: Cambridge University Press, pp. 283–307.
Kemmerling, A. and O. Bruttel (2006) '"New Politics" in German Labour Market Policy? The Implications of the Recent Hartz Reforms for the German Welfare State', *West European Politics* 29 (1): 90–112.
Kitschelt, H. and W. Streeck (2004) *Germany: Beyond the Stable State*. London: Frank Cass.
Kommers, D.P. and R.A. Miller (2012) *The Constitutional Jurisprudence of the*

Federal Republic of Germany. Durham and London: Duke University Press, 3rd edn.
König, T. (2006) 'The Scope for Policy Change after the 2005 Election: Veto Players and Intra-Party Decision Making', *German Politics* 15 (4): 520–532.
Lafontaine, O. (1999) *Das Herz schlägt links*. Munich: Econ.
Lapavitsas, C., A. Kaltenbrunner, G. Labrinidis, D. Lindo, J. Meadway, J. Mitchell, J.P. Painceira, E. Pires, J. Powell, A. Stenfors, N. Teles and L. Vatikiotis (2012) *Crisis in the Eurozone*. London and New York: Verso.
Le Gloannec, A.M. (2001) 'Germany's Power and the Weakening of States in a Globalised World: Deconstructing a Paradox', in D. Webber (ed.) *New Europe, New Germany, Old Foreign Policy?: German Foreign Policy since Unification*. London: Frank Cass, pp. 117–135.
Lehmbruch, G. (1976). *Parteienwettbewerb im Bundesstaat*. Stuttgart: Kohlhammer.
Lehndorff, S., G. Bosch, T. Haipeter and E. Latniak (2009) 'From "Sick Man" to the "Overhauled Engine" of Europe? Upheaval in the German Model', in G. Bosch, S. Lehndorff and J. Rubery (eds) *European Employment Models in Flux: A Comparison of Institutional Change in Nine European Countries*. Basingstoke: Palgrave Macmillan, pp. 105–130.
Lütz, S. (2007) 'The Finance Sector in Transition: A Motor for Economic Reform?', in K. Dyson and S. Padgett (eds) *The Politics of Economic Reform in Germany*. Abingdon: Routledge, pp. 26–42.
Manow, P. and Burkhart S. (2008) 'Delay as a Political Technique under Divided Government? Empirical Evidence from Germany 1976–2005', *German Politics* 17 (3): 353–366.
Menz, G. (2007) 'Old Bottles – New Wine: The New Dynamics of Industrial Relations', in K. Dyson and S. Padgett (eds) *The Politics of Economic Reform in Germany: Global, Rhineland or Hybrid Capitalism?* Abingdon: Routledge, pp. 82–93.
Merkel, A. (2003) Speech at the 2003 CDU Party Conference in Leipzig.
Münter, M. and R. Sturm (2002) 'Economic Consequences of German Reunification', *German Politics* 11 (3): 179–194.
OECD (2012) 'OECD Economic Surveys Germany'. February. Available at: http://www.keepeek.com/Digital-Asset-Management/oecd/economics/oecd-economic-surveys-germany-2012_eco_surveys-deu-2012-en#page1 (accessed 6 September 2013).
OECD (2013a) 'Tax Burden Trends Between 2000 and 2012'. Available at: http://www.oecd.org/ctp/tax-policy/TW_2013_Part_2_Table2a.xls (accessed 23 August 2013).
OECD (2013b) 'Factbook 2013: International Trade in Services'. Available at: http://www.oecd-ilibrary.org/economics/oecd-factbook-2013/international-trade-in-services-billion-us-dollars_factbook-2013-table78-en (accessed 6 September 2013).
Paterson, W. (2011) 'The Reluctant Hegemon? Germany Moves Centre Stage in the European Union', *Journal of Common Market Studies* 49 (Annual Review): 57–75.
Scharpf, F. (2005) 'No Exit from the Joint Decision Trap? Can German Federalism Reform Itself?' Cologne: Max Planck Institute for the Study of Societies Working Paper 05/8.
Scharpf, F.W., B. Reissert and F. Schnabel (1976) *Politikverflechtung: Theorie und Empirie des kooperativen Föderalismus in der Bundesrepublik*. Berlin: Cornelsen.

Schmidt, H. (1993) *Handeln für Deutschland*. Rowohl: Berlin.
Schmitt-Beck, R. and T. Faas (2007) 'The Campaign and its Dynamics at the 2005 German General Election', *German Politics* 15 (4): 393–419.
Schröder, G. (1998) *Und weil wir unser Land verbessern: 26 Briefe für ein modernes Deutschland*. Hamburg: Hoffmann and Campe.
Schröder, G. (2003) Speech in the German *Bundestag* on the *Agenda 2010*, 14 March.
Schröder, G. (2006) *Entscheidungen: Mein Leben in der Politik*. Hamburg: Hoffmann and Campe.
Schröder, G. and T. Blair (1999) *Europe – The Third Way / Die neue Mitte*. Joint Paper 8 June. Berlin/London: SPD/New Labour.
Schweiger, C. (2010) 'Towards Convergence? New Labour's *Third Way* and the SPD's *Agenda 2010* in Comparative Perspective', *Sozialer Fortschritt: German Review of Social Policy* 59 (9): 244–253.
Seeleib-Kaiser, M. (2001) 'Globalisation and the German Social Transfer State', *German Politics* 10 (3): 103–118.
Seitz, K. (1993) 'Die Standortdebatte geht am Wesentlichen vorbei', *FOCUS Magazin* 16. Available at: http://www.focus.de/politik/deutschland/standpunkt-die-standortdebatte-geht-am-wesentlichen-vorbei_aid_140965.html (accessed 21 August 2013).
Sinn, H.W. (1992) *Kaltstart: Volkswirtschaftliche Aspekte der deutschen Vereinigung*. Tübingen: Mohr-Siebeck, 2nd edn.
Sinn, H.W. (1996) 'Dann bricht das Chaos aus', *Der Spiegel* 50 (25): 114–115.
Sinn, H.W. (2004) *Ist Deutschland noch zu retten?* Munich: Econ.
Sinn, H.W. (2013) 'It is Wrong to Portray Germany as the Euro Winner', *Financial Times*, 22 July. Available at: http://www.ft.com/cms/s/0/bbb2176a-ed70-11e2-8d7c-00144feabdc0.html#axzz2e7p5tIDO (accessed 6 September 2013).
Statistisches Bundesamt (2010) *20 Jahre Deutsche Einheit: Wunsch oder Wirklichkeit*. Wiesbaden: Destatis.
Statistisches Bundesamt (2013a) 'Lange Reihen seit 1950'. Available at: https://www.destatis.de/DE/ZahlenFakten/GesamtwirtschaftUmwelt/VGR/Inlandsprodukt/Tabellen/Volkseinkommen1950.xls?__blob=publicationFile (accessed 15 August 2013).
Statistisches Bundesamt (2013b) 'Lange Reihen Arbeitsmarkt'. Available at: https://www.destatis.de/DE/ZahlenFakten/Indikatoren/LangeReihen/Arbeitsmarkt/lrarb003.html (accessed 20 August 2013).
Statistisches Bundesamt (2013c) 'Wirtschaft und Gesellschaft'. Available at: https://www.destatis.de/DE/Publikationen/WirtschaftStatistik/Archiv/WirtschaftStatistikArchiv.html (accessed 23 August 2013).
Statistisches Bundesamt (2013d) 'Reallohnindex'. Available at: https://www.destatis.de/DE/ZahlenFakten/GesamtwirtschaftUmwelt/VerdiensteArbeitskosten/RealloehneNettoverdienste/Tabellen/Reallohnindex.html (accessed 6 September 2013).
Statistisches Bundesamt (2013e) 'Zusammenfassende Übersichten für den Außenhandel'. Available at: https://www.destatis.de/DE/Publikationen/Thematisch/Aussenhandel/Gesamtentwicklung/ZusammenfassendeUebersichtenM2070100131064.pdf?__blob=publicationFile (accessed 6 September 2013).
Steingart, G. (2004) *Deutschland: Der Abstieg eines Superstars*. Munich: Piper.
Stiller, S. (2010) *Ideational Leadership in German Welfare State Reform*. Amsterdam: Amsterdam University Press.

Streeck, W. (2005) 'Industrial Relations: From State Weakness as Strength to State Weakness as Weakness. Welfare Corporatism and the Private Use of the Public Interest', in S. Green and W.E. Paterson (eds) *Governance in Contemporary Germany: The Semisovereign State Revisited*. Cambridge: Cambridge University Press, pp. 138–164.

Streeck, W. (2009a) 'Endgame? The Fiscal Crisis of the German State', in A. Miskimmon, W.E. Paterson and J. Sloam (eds) *Germany's Gathering Crisis: The 2005 Federal Election and the Grand Coalition*. Basingstoke: Palgrave Macmillan, pp. 38–63.

Streeck, W. (2009b) *Re-Forming Capitalism: Institutional Change in the German Political Economy*. Oxford: Oxford University Press.

Streeck, W. and C. Trampusch (2007) 'Economic Reform and the Political Economy of the German Welfare State', in K. Dyson and S. Padgett (eds) *The Politics of Economic Reform in Germany: Global, Rhineland or Hybrid Capitalism*, pp. 60–81.

The Economist (2012) 'West v. East in Germany: A Ruhr Deal', 31 May. Available at: http://www.economist.com/node/21551512 (accessed 22 August 2013).

Tilford, S. (2011) 'Germany's Brief Moment in the Sun', *Centre for European Reform* essay. Available at: http://www.cer.org.uk/publications/archive/essay/2011/germanys-brief-moment-sun (accessed 7 September 2013).

Tilford, S. (2012) 'Germany's Own Goal: Why Berlin's Sense of Invulnerability will be its Undoing', *Centre for European Reform* Insight. Available at: http:/www.cer.org.uk/insights/germanys-own-goal-why-berlins-sense-invulnerability-will-be-its-undoing (accessed 6 September 2013).

Timmins, G. (2000) 'Alliance for Jobs: Labour Market Policy and Industrial Relations after the 1998 Elections', in R. Harding and W.E. Paterson (eds) *The Future of the German Economy: An End to the Miracle?* Manchester: Manchester University Press, pp. 36–53.

Vail, M.I. (2010) *Recasting Welfare Capitalism: Economic Adjustment in Contemporary France and Germany*. Philadelphia, PA: Temple University Press.

Webber, D. (2001) 'Introduction: German European and Foreign Policy Before and After Unification', in D. Webber (ed.) *New Europe, New Germany, Old Foreign Policy? German Foreign Policy Since Unification*. London: Frank Cass, pp. 1–18.

Wittlinger, R. (2010) *German National Identity in the Twenty-First Century: A Different Republic After All?* Basingstoke: Palgrave Macmillan.

Wolf, M. (2013) 'The German Model is not for Export', *Financial Times*, 7 May. Available at: http://www.ft.com/cms/s/0/aacd1be0-b637–11e2–93ba 00144feabdc0.html?siteedition=uk#axzz2e7p5tIDO (accessed 6 September 2013).

Young, B. and W. Semmler (2011) 'The European Sovereign Debt Crisis: Is Is Germany to Blame', *German Politics and Society* 29 (1): 1–24.

Zolnhöfer, R. (2011) 'Between a Rock and a Hard Place: The Grand Coalition's Response to the Economic Crisis', *German Politics* 20 (2): 227–242.

6. The new crisis paradigm: the GIIPS countries

The sovereign debt crisis in the eurozone makes it necessary to add a new category to the Varieties of Capitalism (VoC) in the European Union (EU). This paradigm consists of a group of countries who have shown severe crisis symptoms since the onset of the global financial crisis. Greece, Italy, Ireland, Portugal and Spain, the so-called GIIPS group, shared common structural weaknesses in their economies which existed prior to the crisis. Under adverse external circumstances these weaknesses have reached a tipping point. All of the countries involved display profound gaps in the capitalisation of their financial industries. Substantial government support hence became necessary to avoid the collapse of major banks which would have had unforeseen consequences for individual economies. None of them were able to shoulder this financial burden without external support from the International Monetary Fund (IMF) and EU. This dependency on external financial help in the form of loans inevitably has resulted in a loss of political autonomy for the governments of the countries in question. As long as they are recipients of loans from the IMF and the European Financial Stability Facility (EFSF)/European Stability Mechanism (ESM) they are in a situation where they have to accept the imposition of strict austerity measures. Drastic public spending cuts are hence inevitable with the effect of substantial job losses in the public sector, reduced welfare spending and an increase in the retirement age. In the case of Greece and Italy, the external influence from the EU level went as far as to apply pressure for democratically elected governments to be replaced by temporary technocratic administrations. In Greece Socialist Prime Minister George Papandreou made way in November 2011 for an unelected government of national unity, spearheaded by economist Lucas Papademos. The latter was subsequently replaced by Judge Panagiotis Pikrammenos. The subsequent elected government in Greece headed by Antonis Samaras's New Democracy did not take office until June 2012. In Italy the government coalition under long-term Prime Minister Silvio Berlusconi was replaced by a technocratic government headed by the former EU Commissioner Mario Monti in November 2011. The Monti administration governed Italy until April 2013 when it was replaced by an elected grand coalition led by

Social Democrat Enrico Letta. Ireland, Spain and Portugal refrained from installing unelected administrations. All three countries have nevertheless seen fundamental political change and in the case of Spain and Portugal ongoing domestic political turmoil.

This chapter offers a summary of the structural problems the countries in the GIIPS group have been facing since the advent of the global financial crisis. The GIIPS group is likely to remain part of the crisis paradigm in the medium term. If the sovereign debt crisis in the eurozone deepens further it is likely that more member states will have to be positioned in this group. As the latest country to ask for financial support from the ESM, Cyprus technically already belongs to this group. Slovenia is the first of the more recent eurozone members in Central and Eastern Europe (CEE) to slide into sovereign debt problems with its overall level of structural debt forecast to double from 35 per cent in 2009 to around 67 per cent of its GDP by 2014. Belgium has been in the budgetary danger zone for quite some time with a structural level of debt which approaches 100 per cent of its GDP (European Commission 2013a: 19).

6.1 THE IRISH REPUBLIC

The case of Ireland is treated separately in this chapter due to the fact that the background story of its economy is remarkably different from that of the crisis economies in Southern Europe. Ireland suffered from the same crisis symptoms as the Greece, Italy, Portugal and Spain and was actually the first eurozone country to be hit by severe banking and subsequent sovereign debt crisis in 2008. However in the Irish case this crisis emerged from a previously much stronger economic performance than any of the Southern European countries had witnessed. Ireland also had seen a fundamental transformation of its economy in the two decades prior to the crisis. While a number of aspects of this transformation were the direct cause of the subsequent crisis symptoms, the legacy of what was once called the 'Celtic Tiger' economy still puts Ireland in a better position to recover from the crisis in the long term than the countries in the South of Europe.

The economy of the Irish Republic has witnessed a remarkable roller-coaster ride since its accession to the European Community (EC) in 1973. Before it managed a remarkable turnaround of its economic fortunes in the early 1990s, Ireland was positioned at the bottom end of the economic league in Europe. Since the end of the Second World War, Ireland had been plagued by repeated episodes of recession, problems with increasing public debt and most of all high levels of structural unemployment, which caused many young Irish people to emigrate. When Ireland is today celebrated as one of the most open and globalised economies in Europe it is easily forgotten that it took the country almost two decades after the end of the Second World War to gradually move away from a predominantly protectionist stance. Before the 1960s the Irish economy was strongly dependent on trade with the UK, which was largely considered as a remnant of the colonial past which most Irish people despised and were keen to shake off. After Ireland had gained full independence from the UK in 1921 it pursued a predominantly inward-looking economic approach with only cautious attempts to open the national economy up to foreign investment. The dominant governing party Fianna Fáil and the strongly influential Catholic Church were keen on preserving what the Irish had achieved through independence and made little efforts to ensure that economic growth in the Irish Republic would be fostered. The nationalistic economic approach pursued by Fianna Fáil (Allen 2000: 17; Boylan 2002: 12) was most of all intended to cut off remaining links with the UK and to promote the development of an independent culture for the Irish Republic. Fianna Fáil believed that Ireland's strong agricultural sector would be sufficient to sustain an independent Irish economy. However in reality the UK remained an important trading partner for the Irish Republic, which was symbolised by the signing of the Anglo-Irish Free Trade Agreement in 1965. Irish policy-makers quickly realised that entry into the European Economic Community's (EEC) Common Market would allow the country to become more independent from the British economy by broadening its links with other European countries. Entry into the Common Market was believed to have the dual benefit of enhancing the Irish Republic's political independence from the UK while at the same time ensuring that access for Irish products to the British market could still be guaranteed (Fitzgerald and Girvin 2000: 273). This was because even by 1950 over 90 per cent of Irish exports still went to the British market (Bradley 2000: 29). While it took until 1973 for the six EEC members to allow Ireland to join as part of the first wave of enlargement, domestically the Irish Republic had started to initiate a transformation of its economic approach by the late 1950s. A severe economic crisis in the 1950s caused the Fianna Fáil government to announce the 'Plan for Economic Development', issued, in 1957, in which the government acknowledged that the time had come for Ireland to revise its predominantly protectionist economic approach which lacked a long-term strategic vision. Over the next decade Ireland would consequently start to transform its economy from a strong reliance on agriculture towards industrialisation. Right from the beginning Irish policy-makers tended to look towards attracting foreign direct investment (FDI) as the basis for growth in their country rather than to concentrate on building up a viable indigenous industrial sector (Coogan 2003: 392). Ireland hence pursued a strategy of 'dependent industrialisation' (Wickham 1983: 172), with an ever increasing number of foreign companies opening subdivisions in Ireland. By the late 1970s the majority of the Irish workforce was no longer predominantly employed by British-owned companies but by companies which originated in the US, Germany and other European countries, as well as Japan. As a result of the opening of the Irish economy towards FDI, growth started to accelerate rapidly in the 1960s and continued to grow throughout the 1970s at an average rate of 4 per cent. This was boosted by the government investing in the supply side of the economy and followed by a significant return of around 100,000 Irish emigrants to their home country (Fitz Gerald 2000: 43–44). When Ireland finally managed to join the EEC alongside Britain and Denmark in 1973 its strategy of dependent industrialisation was boosted further by having become part of a Common Market of now nine countries. Not only did entry into the EEC make it easier to attract FDI from across Europe but even more importantly, the generous financial support new member states received from the Community funds at the time supported Ireland in boosting its agricultural sector under the Common Agricultural Policy (CAP). Especially the payments under the European structural funds, which in combination with the agricultural payments amounted up to an average of between 5 to 6 per cent of its annual GDP (Fitzgerald 2004: 74), allowed Irish governments to invest in infrastructure and education. This was an important precondition for becoming attractive to foreign companies, especially those with the highest growth potential, such as computer technology. Ireland soon started to develop its own form of economic planning and corporatism. In 1949 it had established the Industrial Development Authority (IDA), which was initially a government organisation within the Department of Industry and Commerce that was put in charge to remove protectionist barriers in the Irish economy and to attract FDI. In 1969 the IDA became an independent state-sponsored body with the wider responsibility to supervise industrial relations as a whole. The IDA has ever since become an important agent for the promotion of the Irish Republic as an investment haven. In 1963 the National Industrial Economic Council (NIEC) was created to develop a strategy for Ireland's long-term economic development, followed by the establishment of the National Economic and Social Council (NESC) in 1973.

Both bodies were an attempt to gradually develop a consensus between the government and social partners on the long-term parameters for economic growth in the Irish Republic. The NESC offered a forum for nationwide negotiations between the government, employers and the trade unions on which basis it made recommendations for the economic and social policy priorities the country should pursue. The NESC only acts as an advisory body but it has supported the creation of a national consensus in Ireland which became the foundation for the fundamental transformation of the Irish economy from the late 1980s onwards (Turner 2002: 284).

By the late 1970s the government strategy of combining a gradual liberalisation of the economy with a Keynesian state intervention programme, which had previously shown modest results, started to fail. Between 1979 and 1987 economic growth in the Irish Republic slowed down substantially to an average of 1.5 per cent. At the same time unemployment rose to 17 per cent (O'Connell 2000: 61) and Irish budget debt started to increase. Irish elites realised that membership of the Common Market alone was not sufficient to sustain growth in the country without an economic strategy which went beyond significant state investment. As a result elites in the country unified under a new political consensus, which determined that the country would have to restore fiscal responsibility and enhance its attractiveness as a location for international investment. The new consensus was manifested in the 1987 Programme for National Recovery (PNR), a programme which mainly concentrated on introducing public spending cuts and tax reforms but also outlined wider goals such as broadening social cohesion and widening participation in education. This programme was the first step in what was to become Ireland's own form of 'semi-corporatism'. It was a compromise between the confrontational industrial relations which are characteristic of liberal economies and the social democratic corporatism of coordinated economies. By consenting to be part of the social partnership agreements trade unions became part of a national dialogue on the future strategic shape of Ireland's economy and society. The latter was possible because the extent of the social partnership agreements grew over time. The seven national partnership agreements which were signed since 1987 (1988 PNR; 1991 Programme for Economic and Social Progress (PESP); 1994 Programme for Competitiveness and Work (PCW); 1997 Partnership 2000 (P2000); 2000 Programme for Prosperity and Fairness (PPF); 2003 Sustaining Progress (SP); and 2006 Towards 2016: Ten Year Framework (TYF)) were characterised by an ever growing number of participants and consequently dealt with a growing number of issues, including wages, employment and workplace rights, fiscal, social environmental and infrastructure policies (Department of the Taoiseach 2006). The inclusion of more interest groups in the social partnership process resulted in the division of the social partners into four pillars after 2000: trade unions, employers and businesses, farming, community and voluntary sectors.

Ireland's particular form of social partnership was not uncontroversial in the country itself. Some considered it to be the symbol of Ireland's own particular brand of social democracy (Fitzgerald and Girvin 2000: 280). For the critics of the model it was simply a disguised neoliberal government strategy to limit the influence of the trade unions (Allen 2000: 15). Especially for trade unions the social partnerships represented a double-edged sword. On the one hand the deal offered trade unions direct access to the government but on the other hand they had to agree to a limitation of their direct influence on working conditions and wages. For the privilege of being accepted as full partners in the national dialogue on the future of the economy, trade unions accepted a reduction of their role in the industrial relations process under the Industrial Relations Act passed in 1990. The Act limited the power of unions to call strikes and use picketing, which is why it was regarded by some as a replica of the anti-union legislation Margaret Thatcher had introduced in the UK (Wallace and O'Sullivan 2002: 172). What trade unions received in return was more prominence on the national political stage, which did not necessarily amount to a greater influence on government policy-making. In contrast to the corporatist arrangements in many continental economies the Irish social partnership process produced consensual agreements which were supposed to determine a framework for policy-making on the variety of issues they covered. Because the agreements are not binding for governments, trade unions could only trust that the government would legislate in their spirit but had no guarantee that it would do so. Paul Teague therefore argued that this new form of inclusive national partnership created an awareness amongst the actors involved of the key economic challenges that the country was facing. Yet it also resulted in 'the weakening of the special public status conferred on organised labour and employer groups and a change in the style of economic and social policy-making' (Teague 2005: 9).

The post-1987 consensus in Ireland became a crucial basis for its successful promotion as a country that was open for business. The stable industrial relations framework combined with Ireland's position as a member of the emerging Single European Market (SEM) allowed the IDA to develop a successful strategy for the attraction of high-tech companies from the US, which witnessed a boom in the 1990s. Ireland already had a history of American investment but it was only a taste of what was to come in the course of the 1990s. FDI flows to the Irish Republic grew steadily throughout the 1990s. By the year 2000 FDI stocks in Ireland had reached an annual level of US$127 billion and subsequently doubled over the period up to 2009 (OECD 2012). Figure 6.1 shows that between 2000 and 2001 FDI stock in Ireland rose to more than 130 per cent of the country's GDP and subsequently fell to just under 70 per cent in 2006.

US multinational companies were attracted to Ireland for a number of reasons. Ireland offered foreign companies an attractive low-tax environ-

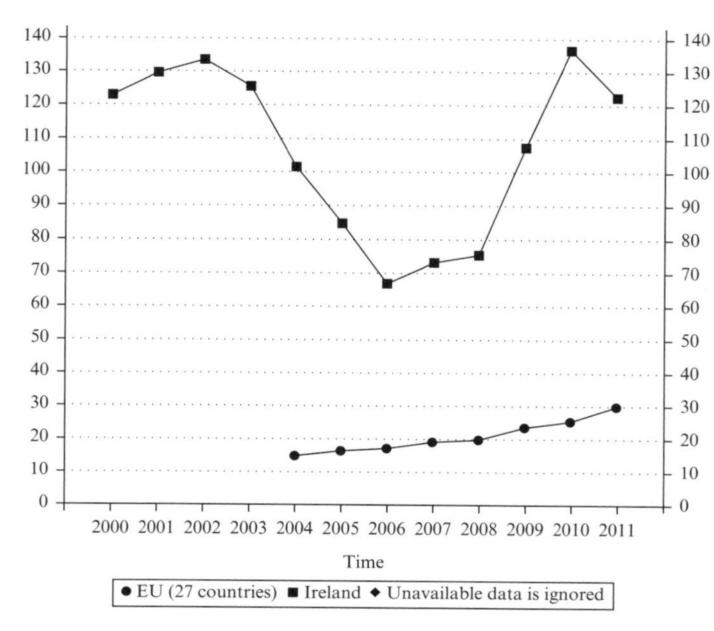

Source: Eurostat (2013a).

Figure 6.1 Direct investment stock as percentage of GDP (direct investment in the reporting economy)

ment with an increasingly skilled workforce in technical areas (mainly on the basis of non-academic third-level education in technical colleges), embedded in a consensus-orientated industrial relations climate. The Irish government prioritised its spending on education and infrastructure to support the FDI-based growth model. As a result substantial support was given to support a male breadwinner model based on tertiary education in industries such as computing science while vocational training was widely neglected (Wickham and Boucher 2004: 388). IDA Ireland has consistently been using the high share of young people with third-level qualifications ('60 per cent of students go to higher education') as a selling point to multinational companies (IDA Ireland 2012a). US companies in the information technology, pharmaceuticals and other healthcare products, as well as electrical engineering sectors used Ireland as the main distribution hub for their products in Europe. Between 1990 and 1999 $7.4 billion in US-based FDI flowed into Ireland (Collings et al. 2005: 128). By 2007 the IDA reported that 48 per cent of companies it had supported in making direct investments in Ireland were from North America. Major North

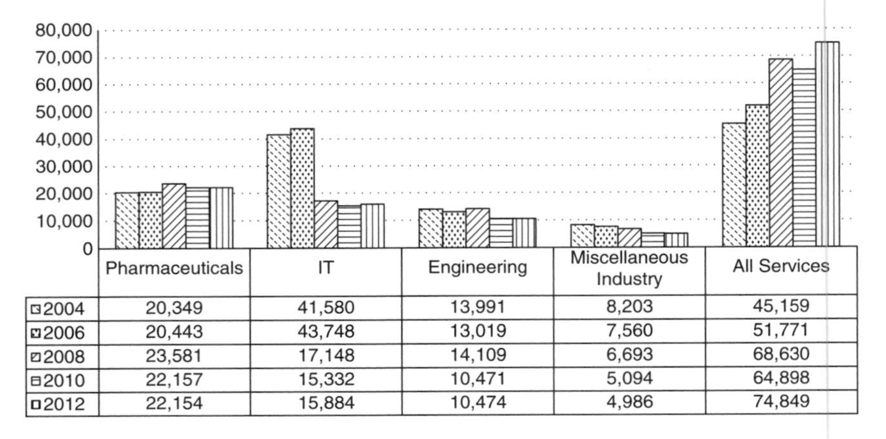

	Pharmaceuticals	IT	Engineering	Miscellaneous Industry	All Services
2004	20,349	41,580	13,991	8,203	45,159
2006	20,443	43,748	13,019	7,560	51,771
2008	23,581	17,148	14,109	6,693	68,630
2010	22,157	15,332	10,471	5,094	64,898
2012	22,154	15,884	10,474	4,986	74,849

Source: IDA Ireland (2013: 7).

Figure 6.2 Total employment by sector in IDA supported companies

American IT companies, amongst them Intel, IBM, Hewlett Packard, Dell, Microsoft, Google and Ebay and more recently even Facebook and Twitter opened their European headquarters in Ireland. These were clustered around business parks in the Eastern (greater Dublin) and the Southern part of the country. Before the financial crisis, the IDA listed 474 North American companies with branches in Ireland. These companies employed a total of 95,271 people in the country. The second largest share of companies originated from the rest of Europe (169), followed by Germany (113) and the UK (108). The foreign companies had created a total of 65,223 jobs in the East and 34,232 in the South of the country (IDA Ireland 2007: 7 and 27) but much less in other regions. By 2013, 74,440 were employed in foreign companies in the greater Dublin region in the East and 39,744 in the South, 25,071 in the West and only 8,410 in the structurally weaker North of the country (IDA Ireland 2012b: 6). Meanwhile the number of German companies based in Ireland has risen further to 531, but the number of British and German companies declined slightly. In the case of Germany from 113 to 95 and in the British case to 103. The IDA highlights that even after the crisis the Irish Republic hosts 'nine out of ten' global ICT and pharmaceutical companies, '12 out of 15' global medical device companies and more than 50 per cent of the leading global Financial Services Firms (IDA Ireland 2013).

Figure 6.2 shows the evolvement of sectoral employment figures in foreign companies in Ireland between 2004 and 2012. It is obvious that over time the bulk of employment has shifted from the IT sector (including electronic and optical equipment) to the service industry (including international, financial and software services).

The foreign-owned high technology sector became the backbone of what would be classified as the Irish 'Celtic Tiger' economy with high growth rates. Ireland's nominal GDP growth accelerated rapidly from the late 1980s onwards and stood at an average of 9.8 per cent between 1988 and 1998. At the same time Germany as the former economic powerhouse of Europe only grew by an average of 4.9. In 2000 Ireland's GDP rate peaked at 16.6 per cent, the highest level in the whole of the EU. Until the onset of the financial crisis in 2007 Ireland maintained a nominal level of GDP growth between 6–11 per cent (OECD 2013a). The basis for this was the sharp increase in exports of foreign high-tech products and increasingly also affiliated services, such as software and online-based applications. Between 2004 and 2006 exports of foreign products and services amounted to between €74 and €90 billion annually and increased to €122 billion in 2013 (IDA Ireland 2007 and 2013)

The strong dependence on North American FDI essentially tied Ireland closely to the US economy. It was argued what was described as the European form of the East Asian Tiger economies, was in principle a model whose success had become 'more dependent on US investment than, say Costa Rica and Honduras, which are often described as an American backyard' (Allen 2000: 27). Essentially the 'Celtic Tiger' became what has been classified as a 'developmental network state' with substantial weaknesses: an industrial relations and education system orientated towards solidarity with foreign investors, which broadly came at the expense of the development of the indigenous industry and failed to distribute equality beyond the beneficiaries of the job growth in the foreign-owned IT and services industry (Ó Riain 2004: 44 and 47).

This refers to the fact that the multinational companies as the biggest employers in Ireland were courted by the government by offering them the conditions of a flexible and deregulatory industrial relations environment. Ireland has persistently had the third lowest corporation tax in Europe. It was gradually lowered from 40 per cent in 1995 to the current level of 12.5 per cent. The Irish corporation tax rate below the current EU-27 average of 23.2 per cent is only surpassed by Bulgaria and Cyprus, who have both lowered their corporation tax to 10 per cent in recent years (Eurostat 2013b: 38). In industrial relations trade unions accepted a system where under the consensus umbrella of the social partnership agreements the foreign-owned high-growth sectors of the economy were increasingly characterised by the introduction of US-style management practices. Due to the non-binding character of the social partnership agreements, the Irish government was able to allow multinational companies to shut out trade unions in favour of company-based arrangements. Ireland's new economy of high-tech multinationals therefore displayed a picture of a low level of union density and US-style managerial human resources practices. Performance-related pay and 'delegative employee participation' became a widespread practice in companies which originated from the US (Roche and Geary 2002: 67). Those who studied the industrial relations practices in high-tech Greenfield sites argued that Ireland's new economy was in danger of becoming a 'union neutral environment' (Gunnigle et al. 2002: 250).

In its recent report on the Ireland's industrial relations, the European Industrial Relations Observatory (EIRO) pointed out that under the social partnership consensus collective bargaining declined significantly and was gradually replaced by individualistic employment law. The EIRO speaks of a breakdown of the social partnership process after 2010, when the government, employers and trade unions failed to reach an agreement on wages. Crucially it shows that trade union density in Ireland is likely to have fallen around 37 per cent. The highest level of union representation can be found in the public sector (80 per cent). The service sector is largely de-unionised, with 15 per cent trade union membership in the sales industry and only 6 per cent in the hotel and catering services industry, a sector which for a long time during the Celtic Tiger boom had a large foreign workforce (EIRO 2013).

Irish semi-corporatism set the country apart from other countries in the EU. The flexibilisation of industrial relations during the Celtic Tiger boom represents a compromise between the continental European form of corporatism, where trade unions have maintained a much larger influence under collective bargaining arrangements, and the anti-union approach of liberal economies such as the US and the UK (Boucher and Collins 1999: 314). Over time this compromise may have tilted too far towards favouring the interests of US multinationals and certainly reflected a dependence which posed risks. At the same time the changes in Ireland's industrial relations showed a degree of flexibility and willingness to achieve a consensus which is lacking in the economies of Southern Europe, where corporatist arrangements became so entrenched that they prevented the implementation of structural reforms.

The core problem of the Irish 'Celtic Tiger' growth model did not lie in its level of flexibility and ability to implement change, which are both fundamentally positive characteristics under the conditions of globalisation. It was rather the nature and extent of its dependency on external factors which turned out to be the undoing of the model as it developed in the early 1990s and 2000s. The Celtic Tiger essentially was characterised by multiple external dependencies:

1. The dependence on FDI, predominantly from the US, which to a large extent tied Ireland's economic fortunes to those of the economy across the Atlantic. By 2007 the OECD reported Ireland as the country with the highest level of employment in foreign-owned companies, over 45 per cent in manufacturing and over 25 in services (OECD 2010). It turned Ireland into a 'developmental network state' whose domestic policies had over time started to institutionalise the foreign investment regime (Ó Riain 2004: 171).
2. The dependence on membership of the EU's internal market and subsequently the European currency union as a crucial factor in assisting Ireland to become an investment hub for US companies. The EU significantly boosted Ireland's financial capability to improve its transport and general infrastructure in the cluster regions where multinational companies opened their headquarters and distribution branches. Some have argued that the developmental state under the 'Celtic Tiger' was significantly dependent on an EU which in effect allowed Irish governments to 'free ride' financially (Adshead and Robinson 2009: 18). Ireland's membership of the SEM, and after 2002 its entry into the eurozone, also offered foreign investors who located in the Irish Republic a prime location for trade with an integrated market (Kirby 2010: 47). In addition, the ambition of Irish elites to ensure that the country was able to be part of the founding group of eurozone members fundamentally contributed to the fiscal consolidation course which was pursued under the social partnership consensus from the late 1980s onwards (Allen 2000: 13–15; O'Hagan 1995: 194). The Irish budgetary restraint again was substantially facilitated by the EU's structural financial support to the country. Finally, when the financial crisis had severely hit the 'Celtic Tiger' after 2007, the EU once again came to the financial rescue by providing a loan which helped to stabilise Ireland's ailing banking system.
3. The dependence on migrant labour which was essential to fill the vacancies in parts of the Irish service industry, which employers could (or in some cases) did not want to fill with indigenous people (Ruhs 2005: 3). Ireland fully opened up its labour market to workers from the eight member states in CEE who joined the EU in 2004. Employers hence had the chance to choose from a growing pool of CEE migrant workers. Ireland's net immigration rate spiralled upwards from 17.3 per cent in 1999 to 53.4 per cent in 2005. Between 2000 and 2004 Ireland had the second highest net migration rate in the OECD (just after Spain), as even before the 2004 EU enlargement a continuous flow of migrants from outside Europe came to the country (OECD 2008a). In 2003 the Ahern government introduced the so-called

'Labour Market Test' under which employers are required to provide evidence that they could not recruit from the pool of native Irish or EU/European Economic Area (EEA) residents before they are allowed to employ workers from outside Europe. When the CEE-8 countries joined the EU in 2004 a large number of people from these countries came to Ireland to take up mainly low-skilled job vacancies in the services industry in general and particularly in catering, agriculture and the healthcare sector. Between 2004 and 2005 around 85,000 new social security numbers (PPS) were issued to nationals from the CEE-8. The bulk of these (40,000) were issued to workers from Poland (Immigration Council of Ireland 2003; Irish Department of Social Protection 2009). While the 'Celtic Tiger' provided record levels of employment for the highly skilled and foreign workers, low-skilled younger people were left behind. This was illustrated by an increase of the unemployment rate for young people. Equally women and older workers found it hard to set foot in a labour market which was geared towards workers who had the skills of a globalised high-tech export economy. While unemployment amongst young people under 25 had fallen considerably between 1993 and 2000, after 2001 it started to rise again, if only marginally. The employment rate amongst unskilled workers in Ireland never reached even 60 per cent during the whole period of the 'Celtic Tiger' boom from 1993 to 2006. This explains why the total employment rate in Ireland barely reached the 70 per cent Lisbon target before 2000 and has never managed to achieve the new 75 per cent target of the new Europe 2020 Strategy (Eurostat 2013c).

Irish politicians were and continue to be proud to advertise their economy as the most globalised economy in Europe (IDA Ireland 2007: 10). The risks of the level of openness and dependency on external factors were widely discussed. Before the onset of the financial crisis, critics of Ireland's new economy however emphasised most of all the persistence of social imbalances under extremely benign economic conditions (Allen 1999; Garvin 2005; O'Hearn 2000). This manifested itself in the struggle of the Irish Republic to match its role model levels of growth with the same levels of social cohesion as other economies in Europe had achieved. Ireland has had continuously higher rates of people who are considered to be at risk of poverty or social exclusion (between 22–25 per cent of the total population) than those in coordinated economies such as Germany, France and Sweden who remained at or below 20 per cent (Eurostat 2013d)). The former Irish President Mary McAleese admitted in 2005 that Ireland under the 'Celtic Tiger' boom had in fact

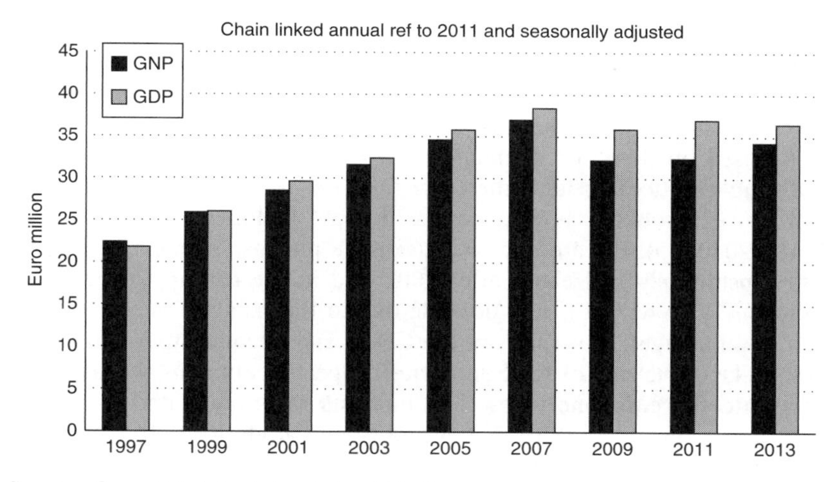

Source: Central Statistics Office Ireland (2013).

Figure 6.3 GNP and GDP at constant factor costs

become a tale of two societies: 'For those who seem to have missed the boat named the "Celtic Tiger", modern Ireland can be a very scary place, where all you can see in front of you are the far-off backs of those who are making rapid headway in this new time of opportunity' (McAleese 2005).

At the same time it failed to meet EU expectations on the making its booming labour market more inclusive, particularly for women. Ireland only reached the Lisbon target of 60 per cent employment rate for women for a brief period between 2005 and 2009. Before then, employment levels for women barely reached 50 per cent until the late 1990s and have been falling below 60 per cent again since the onset of the sovereign debt crisis (Eurostat 2013c). Even in Ireland's new globalised economy the male breadwinner model, which was traditionally favoured by the Catholic Church, therefore only shifted very slowly.

Critics also warned of the risk of economic decline if FDI stocks would be attracted to other locations in Europe or Asia. Figure 6.3 shows that Ireland has had a persistently lower Gross National Product (GNP) than its GDP since 2001 which indicated that the foreign multinational companies behind the boom tend to increasingly invest the business profits they gain inside Ireland elsewhere. The major risk for the Irish economy by the mid-2000s was hence considered to be pushed into a 'vicious circle of declining investment, rising inequality, and – ultimately – the weakening of coordination capacities and the social basis of the knowledge economy' (Ó Riain 2004: 234).

What received little attention was the fact that, once the levels of FDI started to slow down in the early 2000s, growth in Ireland became increasingly based on domestic demand which was extensively fuelled by risky financing practices. Ireland therefore followed the UK in developing its own property bubble as part of the 'frenzy in domestic consumption' (Kirby 2010: 35). Private borrowing, for the purpose of mortgage loans, rose substantially in Ireland after 2002 and in the run-up to the financial crisis. This was not only possible due to the rising incomes of those who had managed to set foot in the Celtic Tiger economy. A substantial factor, like in the case of the Southern European economies, was Ireland's entry into the eurozone whose low interests rates facilitated borrowing for private consumers (Shik Kang and Shambaugh 2013: 16). This was accompanied by a political culture which considered it essential for a flexible modern economy to give the financial sector a relatively free reign. The government of Prime Minister's Bertie Ahern's Fianna Fáil in coalition with the neoliberal Progressive Democrats, extended the liberalisation of the Irish economy towards the financial industry. One of the most prominent figures in this coalition was Charlie McCreevy, Irish Finance Minister between 1997 and 2004. McCreevy was an unequivocal and outspoken supporter of deregulation which he considered to be the backbone for economic success in the era of globalisation. O'Toole documents the mindset that was dominant amongst the political leaders in Dublin at the time, which he called the 'unregulated generation': 'McCreevy and many of his listeners were indeed from the "unregulated generation" that had planted the flag of freedom from Dublin to the Cayman Islands before boldly going into the uncharted virtual territories of ghost banks and brassplate companies' (O'Toole 2010: 145).

Because the Irish government maintained record levels of growth even when the rest of Europe was stalling in the early 2000s, Ireland was hailed as a role model economy. This substantially boosted the influence of the Ahern government in the EU and led to the appointment of McCreevy as Commissioner for the Internal Market and Services in Barroso's first Commission in 2004. Like Barroso, McCreevy subsequently relentlessly pushed towards the liberalisation and deregulation of national economies. The core of this was to promote a regulatory approach which essentially resorted to a basic framework rule-based approach at the expense of an active and precautionary regulatory approach to the regulation of business activity: 'We must ensure that our rules are effective and cause the minimum burden for business' (McCreevy 2005). Under the Ahern government a large part of financial assets made in Ireland were invested abroad as part of the property boom. O'Toole states that by 2007 Irish citizens had invested €1.3 billion abroad, a staggering amount for a small country (O'Toole 2010: 165). Wickham emphasises the asset boom the Irish banking industry witnessed in the wake of Ireland having joined the eurozone, which allowed Irish banks to provide record levels of credit to private customers (Wickham 2012: 67).

Ireland entered the crisis with sound budgetary conditions and a real GDP growth rate of 5.4 per cent in 2007. With the onset of the subprime mortgage crisis in the US and the subsequent turmoil in the US financial sector, the exposure of Ireland's open economy to external factors became obvious. The culture of self-regulation in the financial sector had unsustainable lending activities in a similar fashion as this was the case in the US and to a much wider extent than in the UK. The deregulatory culture, which the Ahern government had sold as the asset of Ireland's new economy, proved to be its undoing. When major US financial companies collapsed like a house of cards in the course of 2007–2008, Irish banks were unable to cover their financial liabilities. September 2008 turned out to become the decisive month for Ireland and other economies in Europe, whose banking system was closely interlinked with the US financial industry. The US administration of George W. Bush had to take drastic action to prevent the collapse of the mortgage lenders Fannie Mae and Freddie Mac that month only to find out that the major investment bank Lehman Brothers collapsed on 15 September 2008. The bankruptcy of Lehman Brothers set in motion a vicious circle of declining assets for financial institutions in Europe which were also pushed to the brink of collapse. Particularly those banks and mortgage lending institutions which had pursued subprime loans to customers found themselves unable to find assets on the asset markets which had gone into turmoil. They were also put under increasing pressure from rating agencies who substantially downgraded many major banks and mortgage lenders. Lending activity slowed down dramatically and there was the real risk that major banks would be unable to guarantee their customers' deposits. A run on banks in the way it had occurred in the UK in September 2007 when customers queued outside the troubled bank Northern Rock could have been replicated across Europe if governments had not taken swift and drastic action to restore customer and ultimately also market confidence. Europe had been hit by an adverse feedback loop where the economic downturn following the loss in market confidence deepened the liquidity problems of the banking sector and eventually the fiscal position of the countries affected.

After banking shares had plummeted by 26 per cent, the Irish government announced on 28 September 2008 that it would guarantee all retail, commercial, institutional and interbank deposits for major Irish banks who had run into severe asset liquidity problems for the period of two years. The offer covered Allied Irish Bank, Bank of Ireland, Anglo-Irish Bank, Irish Life and Permanent, Irish Nationwide Building Society and the Education Building Society (Department of Finance Ireland 2008). The total cost of this guarantee amounted to a staggering 225.2 per cent of Ireland's GDP (European Commission 2009: 62). As a result of the banking crisis the country that had managed to present a role model budgetary position for many years rapidly moved towards a sovereign debt crisis. It was clear from the beginning that Ireland would not be able to shoulder the financial burden of having to guarantee the assets of practically all its major banks without external support. Like the rest of Europe the Irish economy quickly plunged into a recession with the Irish GDP contracting by 2.1 per cent in 2009 and by 5.1 per cent in 2010. In 2008 Ireland borrowed at the level of 7.4 per cent of its GDP. The situation worsened in 2009 when borrowing increased to 13.9 per cent. However in 2010 things took a dramatic turn for the worse. The 2010 borrowing figure for Ireland stood at 30.8 per cent of the GDP and the overall budget deficit had risen from 44.5 per cent in 2008 to 92.1 per cent (Eurostat 2013e and 2013f). By September 2010 Irish bond yields had increased to 7 per cent and Irish banks, who were now no longer under the government asset guarantee scheme, severely struggled to repay their debts. Alarm bells started ringing in Brussels. The new Irish Fianna Fáil Prime Minister Brian Cowen, who replaced Bertie Ahern in 2008 in a period of political turmoil, attempted to avoid admitting that Ireland needed external support. On 16 November 2010 that the Irish government publicly declared that they would not seek any loans from the IMF or the EU because 'Ireland would be fully funded way until 2011' (McDonald 2010). Only a few days later, on 21 November, Cowen had to reverse his position under the gravity of the circumstances and officially requested assistance from the EU and the IMF. Ireland, which for many years had been the former poster boy of economic success and was hailed as a role model for economic transformation by politicians across Europe, amongst them Angela Merkel and George Osborne, was now at the mercy of the IMF and the solidarity of the rest of the eurozone. The joint EU/IMF financial assistance package for Ireland which was agreed in December 2010 reserved a total of €67 billion of external support for the country. €22.5 each are provided by the IMF and from the EU budget (financial stabilisation mechanism) and the European Financial Stabilisation Mechanism (EFSM). Individual EU member states also supported Ireland directly with bilateral financial support (UK €3.8 billion, Sweden €0.6 billion and Denmark €0.4 billion). The Irish government however also made its own €17.5 contribution by taking out money from its reserve funds. By the end of 2012 Ireland had received €75.7

billion of the total €85 set aside under the programme. Under the lending conditions Ireland has to embark on a fundamental reform of its financial industry with better levels of capitalisation, risk assessment and a reduction in the size of the sector as a whole. The Irish government was also asked to reduce public spending by €15 billion by 2014, which amounts to around 9 per cent of the country's GDP and introduce structural reforms to the country's employment and training system (European Commission 2011). The extent to which Ireland's finances had declined within a short time span since 2008 made the Cowen government extremely unpopular and led towards a stunning election victory for the opposition parties Fine Gael and Labour in the 2011 general election. The new Prime Minister Enda Kenny was adamant to convince the EU to ease the lending conditions for the country but with only limited success. In June 2013 the EU Council extended the maturities of the loans for Ireland and Portugal from 12.5 to 19.5 years, which lowers the pressure for both countries with regard to the repayment of the loans (Council of the European Union 2013). In its latest assessment of the country's progress on the economic adjustment programme the EU/IMF/European Central Bank troika sees some progress but highlights the large size of the structural deficit and the likely marginal fall of annual borrowing from 7.6 per cent to 7.5 per cent in relation to the GDP in 2013. The troika also criticises the Irish government for making only slow progress with the structural reforms in the labour market (European Commission 2013b).

6.2 THE GIPS-4 COUNTRIES GREECE, ITALY, PORTUGAL AND SPAIN IN COMPARISON

In which respect is the Irish case different from that of the other crisis economies in the South of Europe? In the final section of this chapter I want to shed some light on the specific weaknesses of the GIPS-4 without offering a comprehensive analysis of each of them. The complexity of the individual challenges Greece, Italy, Portugal and Spain each face in the coming years is so extensive that it could be the subject of a separate volume. For the purpose of my analysis I want to concentrate on emphasising why Ireland has the best chance of leaving this group in the medium to long term while the future perspective of the other four is substantially more gloomy. Esping-Andersen included Ireland in the Mediterranean cluster of welfare states in Europe and grouped it with Southern European countries because of the central role the Catholic Church and the family play in the provision of welfare (Esping-Andersen 1989). With a decline in the political influence of the Catholic Church this particular cul-

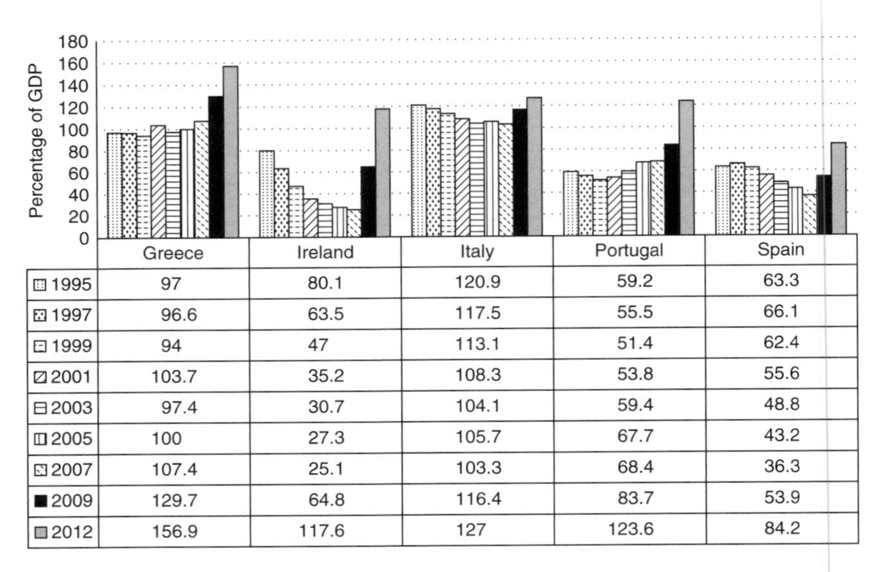

	Greece	Ireland	Italy	Portugal	Spain
1995	97	80.1	120.9	59.2	63.3
1997	96.6	63.5	117.5	55.5	66.1
1999	94	47	113.1	51.4	62.4
2001	103.7	35.2	108.3	53.8	55.6
2003	97.4	30.7	104.1	59.4	48.8
2005	100	27.3	105.7	67.7	43.2
2007	107.4	25.1	103.3	68.4	36.3
2009	129.7	64.8	116.4	83.7	53.9
2012	156.9	117.6	127	123.6	84.2

Source: Eurostat (2013f).

Figure 6.4 General government gross debt in the GIPPS countries

tural feature has weakened over recent years under the new Fine Gael government of Prime Minister Enda Kenny. The new Prime Minister was not afraid to publicly criticise the Church[1] and also to legalise abortion in 2013. Ireland nevertheless remains a society which is more traditional than others in Central and Northern Europe. Religion and a strong family community remain crucial features of Irish society. In this respect Ireland is still similar to Southern Europe and different from countries in other parts of the continent.

I would argue that the main difference lies in Ireland having substantially transformed its economy before the crisis while the Southern European countries were rather complacent in avoiding essential structural changes. Ireland has certainly made fundamental mistakes in shaping its 'Celtic Tiger' model but it nevertheless introduced some positive changes. These offer the country a much stronger foundation for lasting economic recovery than this is the case for Greece, Italy, Portugal or Spain.

The main difference in how Ireland and the GIPS-4 entered the financial crisis lies in the state of their national finances. Ireland managed to reduce the substantial public deficit it had accumulated by the end of the 1980s significantly. This was the result of the consensus to pursue a strategy of budgetary consolidation under the social partnership process. Figure 6.4 shows that Ireland reduced its structural debt from 80 per cent in 1995 to 25.1 per cent in 2007. Amongst the GIPS-4 countries only Spain managed to also pursue a budgetary consolidation course. Like Ireland, by the time of the introduction of the euro in 2002 Spain had brought down its deficit below the 60 per cent of the Stability and Growth Pact (SGP) limit. Spain also currently has the lowest deficit of all the GIPS-4 countries and is in a better position than Ireland, whose deficit levels continue to be above 100 per cent.

The situation in Greece and Italy is fundamentally different. Both were allowed to enter monetary union in spite of an excessive deficit but were never subject to an excessive deficit procedure which resulted in a financial penalty. Italy never managed to reduce its level of structural debt below 100 per cent since 1995. It took until June 2005 for the European Commission to initiate an excessive deficit procedure against Italy which was subsequently terminated without consequences after one year. Greece and Portugal were never put under an excessive deficit procedure before the financial crisis. This was in spite of the fact that both countries not only exceeded the SGP structural debt criteria but also borrowed in excess of 3 per cent of their annual GDP (for Portugal only from 2005 in both cases).

In terms of their fiscal position Greece, Italy and Portugal are the three countries which are of the most concern for the eurozone as they have little realistic prospect to escape from the current vicious circle of slow growth, rising unemployment and consequently increasing debt in the medium to long term. Ireland's structural deficit remains high but the Irish economy is forecast to return to growth in the coming years. The European Commission 2013 spring economic forecast predicts that Ireland's economy will grow by 2.2 per cent in 2014, while Greece, Italy, Spain and Portugal are all considered to grow by less than 1 per cent. The Organisation for Economic Co-operation and Development (OECD) also paints an overall positive picture of the prospect for Ireland's recovery from the crisis. In its 2013 economic survey of Ireland it emphasises the need for Irish policy-makers to address the weaknesses in the Irish model after the crisis. These weaknesses the OECD considers lie in the high level of public debt, a failure to provide training and employment opportunities for low-skilled workers (especially those in the construction sector) and the neglect of the indigenous industry which continues to show low levels of productivity. Overall the OECD is convinced that Ireland has a good chance to regain stable levels of growth due to the competitive advantages it built before the crisis: 'Ireland is endowed with a well-qualified workforce, flexible labour and product markets, a low and stable corporate tax rate and access to the EU Single Market, all of which attracts significant new foreign investment and will contribute to lifting growth' (OECD 2013b).

The OECD is slightly less optimistic than the EU about Ireland's level of

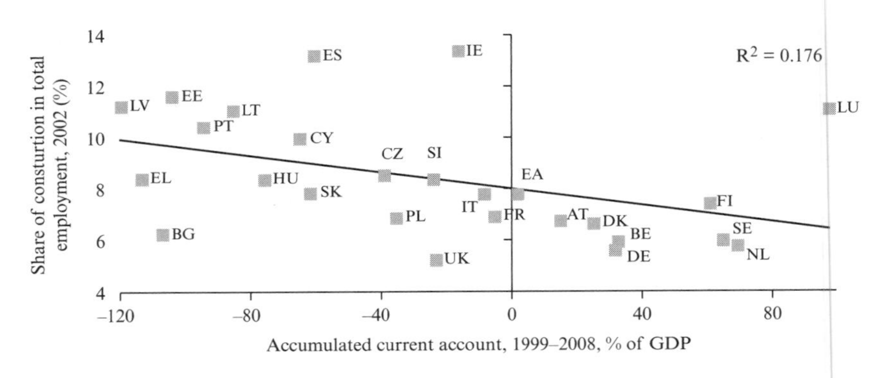

Source: European Commission (2009: 29).

Figure 6.5 Construction activity and current account position

growth in 2013 and 2014. The OECD growth forecast for Ireland in 2013 is 1 per cent and for 2014 is 1.9 per cent. The more cautious outlook is due to the fact that even after the financial crisis Ireland is likely to depend extensively on FDI and exports of foreign-owned products, 'making Ireland's outlook largely dependent on developments in trading partners' (OECD 2013c).

The GIPS-4 countries were all to a greater or lesser extent relying on a housing market bubble. Italy is to some extent the exception here. Figure 6.5 shows how important the housing market and the construction industry had become for some EU member states. Like some of the new member states in CEE (Bulgaria, Estonia, Latvia, Lithuania and to a lesser extent Hungary), Greece, Portugal and Spain are countries whose economies had developed what could be classified as an excessive dependence on a construction boom. Between 1999 and 2008 construction made up almost 120 per cent of Greece's GDP and over 8 per cent of its total employment. In Portugal the share of construction activity made up close to 100 per cent of its economy with around 11 per cent of employment. The construction sector made up a smaller percentage of the economy in Spain (around 60 per cent) and a lot less in Ireland (around 20 per cent) but the labour market in both countries was highly dependent on it (around 13 per cent in each case). Italy is the only country amongst the GIPS-4 who had a lesser dependence on the construction industry.

Risky and unfounded lending activities in connection with a housing bubble were a major factor in the decline of the GIPS-4 countries' economies. In connection with the weakness of the banking sector in the GIPS-4 countries this turned out to be a fatal risk, which was exposed by the onset

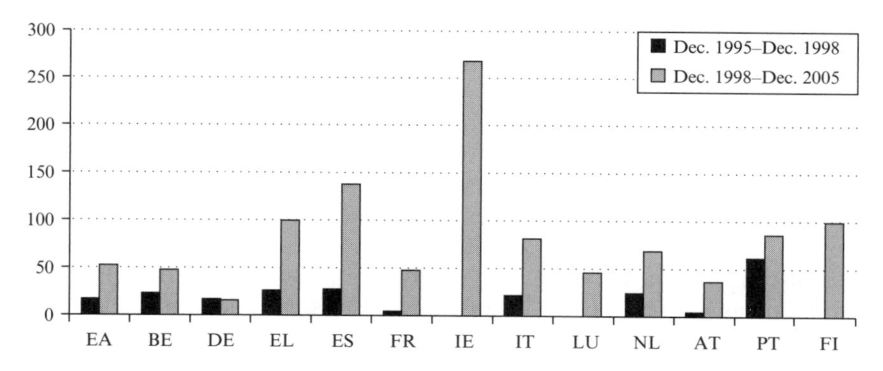

Source: European Commission (2006: 71).

Figure 6.6 Nominal credit growth rates in the euro area, 1995–1998 and 1999–2005

of the financial crisis. Before the crisis lending activities to private households grew substantially in the GIPS-4 countries. This was not limited to providing mortgages for house purchases but to meet the rising income expectations of consumers. In its assessment of lending activities in the EU in 2006, the European Commission came to the conclusion that in euro member states who witnessed a credit boom 'the resulting increased credit demand was willingly met by the banking sector, partly as the effective elimination of the exchange rate allowed them to refinance domestic credit operations abroad' (European Commission 2006: 70–71). Between 2002 and 2005 lending to private households grew by over 100 per cent in Greece and Ireland, by 90 per cent in Spain, by around 60 per cent in Italy. In Portugal the growth in this area was only around 20 per cent but the total level of nominal credit growth, which includes corporate loans, stood between 60 and 80 per cent. In Ireland it was a staggering 260 per cent (Figure 6.6).

The expansion of credit for consumers and businesses which led to a debt-fuelled growth bubble in these countries did not have a sound financial backing. The first section of this chapter outlined the fragility of the financial sector in the Irish Republic as the major factor for the collapse of the Celtic Tiger economy. The situation was not very different in Greece, Italy, Portugal and Spain. The latest financial stability report issued by the IMF shows that all the GIPS-4 countries remain in the red zone when it comes to the ranking of their banking systems. All of them have a banking system with inadequate financial buffers and negative asset quality. They all remain underfunded and have shown low levels of profitability (IMF 2013: 17).

The collapse of the construction sector and the inability to fund growth on the basis of domestic demand is a serious setback for all GIPS-4 economies. All of them share a relatively narrow orientation of their economies. Ireland relies extensively on FDI and continues to neglect the development of its indigenous industries and businesses. Italy has shown a narrow product specialisation on 'supplier-dominated products' in a low-skilled manufacturing industry whose decline in the era of globalisation could not be offset by a policy of moderate wage increases since the 1990s. It has also not managed to attract significant levels of FDI (Larch 2005: 4–5). Portugal's position declined in the early 2000s after a relatively good previous position. The country consequently shifted from the declining levels of exports of the once booming textile and footwear sector, which were unable to withstand increasing competition from Asia, towards a demand-driven growth on the basis of borrowing (Abreu 2006: 4). Spain witnessed a similar struggle in the competition for markets for the export of its exports, which concentrate in the low to medium technology sectors, amounting to 'products with a low degree of technological sophistication and limited degree of product differentiation, in which price competition is intense' (Bravo and Igal 2007: 5).

Greece and Ireland showed relatively good levels of productivity in their labour force in the 1990s but this has subsequently declined. Portugal's productivity witnessed a sharp decline by the turn of the century while Spain has had a consistent productivity problem (Figure 6.7). The low

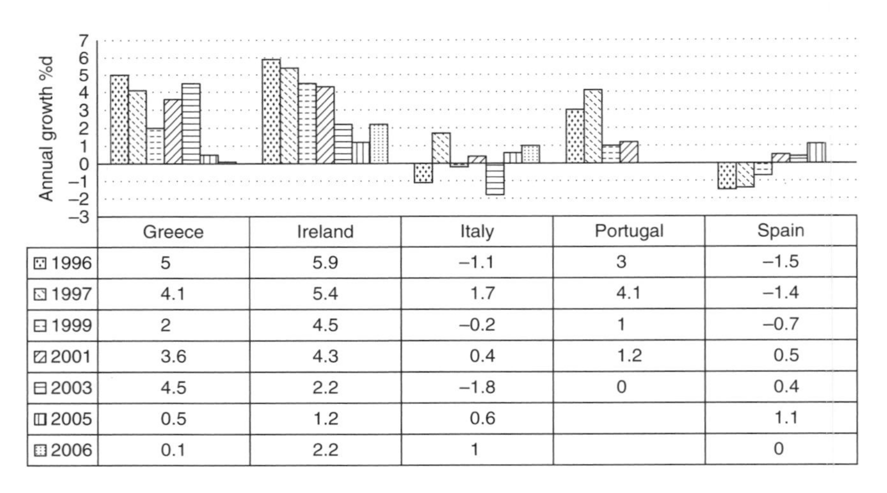

	Greece	Ireland	Italy	Portugal	Spain
1996	5	5.9	−1.1	3	−1.5
1997	4.1	5.4	1.7	4.1	−1.4
1999	2	4.5	−0.2	1	−0.7
2001	3.6	4.3	0.4	1.2	0.5
2003	4.5	2.2	−1.8	0	0.4
2005	0.5	1.2	0.6		1.1
2006	0.1	2.2	1		0

Source: OECD (2008b).

Figure 6.7 Labour productivity business sector

productivity levels which all these countries started to display by the mid-2000s stood in stark contrast to their unit labour costs. Spain, Greece, Italy and Ireland stood in seventh, eighth, ninth and eleventh place amongst all OECD countries when it came to the average annual growth of their unit labour costs between 2000 and 2006. They were surpassed by Norway, Iceland, the Slovak Republic and Turkey. In comparison, Germany and Poland were in the bottom league with a decline in labour costs (OECD 2008b: 283).

A crucial factor in the lack of progress in the Southern European economies are the high levels of government inefficiency, political instability and widespread clientelism and corruption, particularly in Greece and Italy. Italy has been plagued by continuous political instability since the end of the Second World War. Since 1946 Italy has gone through repeated episodes of political turmoil. The most significant was the experienced complete shake-up of its political system in the early 1990s when the dominant role of the of the Christian Democrats came to an abrupt end as a result of the disclosure of the ties between large parts of the country's political elite with organised crime and the mafia. Since 1946 Italy has seen 64 different government coalitions and has been dominated by the towering figure of media mogul Silvio Berlusconi, who managed to put a stranglehold on Italian politics. The short termism of Italian politics makes it practically impossible for any government to introduce structural reforms. This explains the stagnation in the Italian economy. Schmidt and Gualmini see the Italian model as being characterised by a state which hinders rather than coordinates and facilitates. This 'state-hindered' model consequently is unable to achieve reforms by following the normal democratic process and has to instead resort to the installation of technocratic expert-driven leadership, like in the case of the Monti government in 2011 (Schmidt and Gualmini 2013: 378).

Greece, which has even deeper structural problems and is currently caught in a spiral of economic decline which could last for a considerable amount of time, has even deeper domestic institutional flaws. It is without doubt that entry into a eurozone with low interest rates was an incentive for Greek governments to pursue reckless budgetary policies, in a similar fashion as was the case in Italy and to a lesser extent in Portugal and Spain. Where Greece is different from all the others is that it has a variety of complex structural domestic problems which will have to be overcome before there is a realistic prospect that the country's economy can get back on its feet. The sovereign debt crisis in Greece unveiled a system which is riddled by meritocratic practices. These result in widespread patronage and corruption in the country's labour market and the public sector in general. Manolopoulos (2011) documents how the mix of low interest rates in the eurozone paired with the domestic meritocracy created the toxic mix for a downwards spiral for the country. He emphasises that Greece has developed a culture where 'the elite and wider society have undermined those who wish to ensure compliance to the principles of probity and efficiency' (Manolopoulos 2011: 82). Manolopoulos considers the complacent reliance on the availability of cheap credit, a labour market characterised by clientelism, a culture of early retirement (at the legal retirement age of 58 and at an average wage replacement rate of 95.7 per cent) and a failure to establish an effective system of tax collection as the main weaknesses of the country before the crisis. His analysis amounts to a country which lived beyond its means and was kept on an artificial lifeline by EU funds and the cheap supply of credits which was supported by the low interest rate environment in the eurozone: 'Greece was a low-tax, low-public service economy, papered over by EU cohesion funds, bond market borrowings and a brain drain of those Greeks who would support meritocracy. This was always an unsustainable Ponzi system. The only question was: what took it so long to blow up?' (Manolopoulos 2011: 108).

Like with the other GIIPS countries, the EU Commission and the leaders of the EU-15 countries have to ask themselves why they let things in Southern Europe deteriorate to a point where a turnaround of fortunes has become increasingly difficult. Greece has now been in recession for six consecutive years and, like the other GIIPS countries, is unlikely to see its economy grow before 2013. The bursting of the credit bubble has effectively left Greece with declining shipping, agriculture and a currently faltering tourism sector. The sluggish GDP growth figure of 0.6 per cent, which the European Commission forecasts for Greece for 2014, is unlikely to be enough to lift the country out of its current vicious circle of rising unemployment, painful public spending cuts and sharply rising unemployment, especially amongst young people under 25. Overall unemployment levels in Greece have risen to a dramatic 24.3 per cent in 2012 and are estimated to go up further to 27 per cent in 2013. In 2012 over half of young people under 25 in Greece were registered as unemployed (55 per cent). A similar situation can be found in Spain, where the overall level of unemployment stood at 25 per cent in 2012 and is forecast to rise to 27 per cent in 2013, with youth unemployment at 53.2 per cent. In Ireland, Italy and Portugal youth unemployment has also risen to over 30 per cent (Figures 6.8 and 6.9).

This poses a major challenge to political elites in these countries which they are unlikely to be able to sort out without substantial external support from the EU. The EU Commission has reacted to the prospect of the emergence of a lost generation of long-term unemployed in the GIIPS countries with proposals of a €6 billion youth unemployment initiative

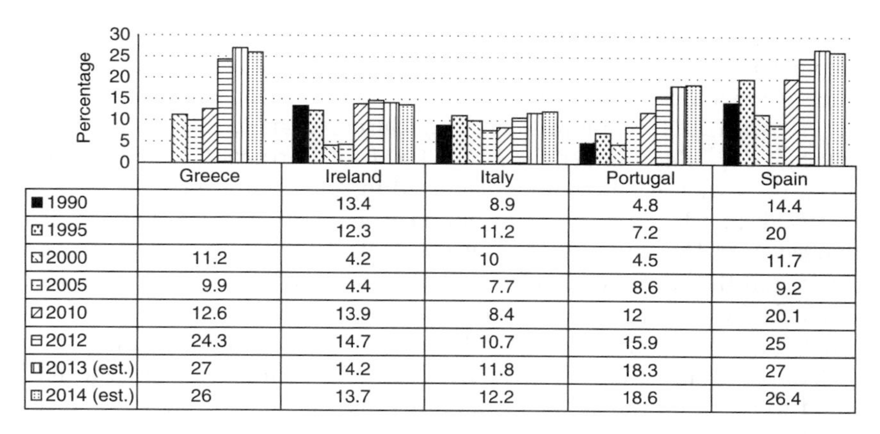

	Greece	Ireland	Italy	Portugal	Spain
1990		13.4	8.9	4.8	14.4
1995		12.3	11.2	7.2	20
2000	11.2	4.2	10	4.5	11.7
2005	9.9	4.4	7.7	8.6	9.2
2010	12.6	13.9	8.4	12	20.1
2012	24.3	14.7	10.7	15.9	25
2013 (est.)	27	14.2	11.8	18.3	27
2014 (est.)	26	13.7	12.2	18.6	26.4

Source: Eurostat (2013g).

Figure 6.8 Unemployment rate in the GIIPS countries

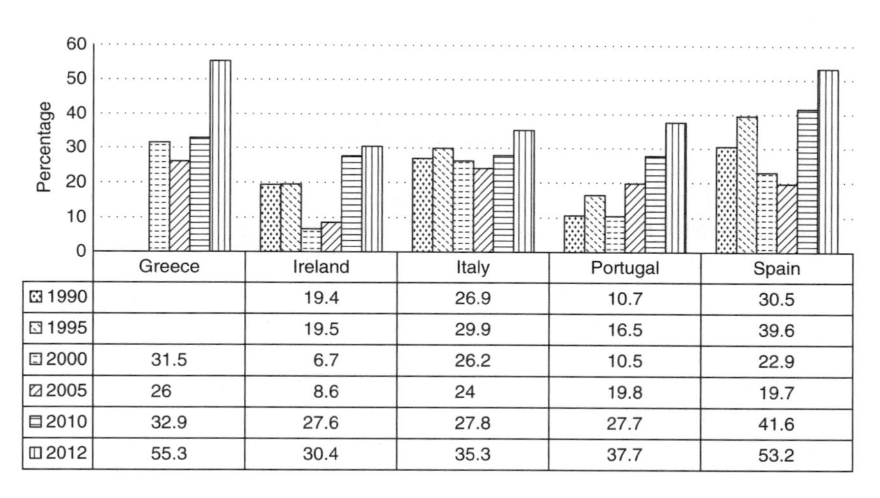

	Greece	Ireland	Italy	Portugal	Spain
1990		19.4	26.9	10.7	30.5
1995		19.5	29.9	16.5	39.6
2000	31.5	6.7	26.2	10.5	22.9
2005	26	8.6	24	19.8	19.7
2010	32.9	27.6	27.8	27.7	41.6
2012	55.3	30.4	35.3	37.7	53.2

Source: Eurostat (2013h).

Figure 6.9 Unemployment rate (age group less than 25)

and a youth alliance for apprenticeships, which is in the process of being negotiated with the Council (European Commission 2013c). If this will be enough to prevent a social crisis and a mass exodus of young people from these countries remains to be seen. Particularly young Greek and Spanish citizens currently face an extremely bleak perspective.

The GIIPS countries have all to a greater or lesser extent become dependent on the EU as a provider of external financial assistance during the sovereign debt crisis. Portugal requested financial assistance from the EU in April 2011, Spain in June 2012. The eurozone countries decided to allocate €52 billion under the EFSF/ESM for Portugal (plus €26 billion from the IMF), which will be disbursed in stages until mid-2013. Spain received an allocation of €100 billion from the EFSF/ESM to be disbursed until December 2013. It was signalled to Italy by Germany and France in the course of 2012 that the country could not expect external financial help from the eurozone. Merkel and Sarkozy insisted that Italy implements substantial structural reforms on its own. This eventually led to the resignation of Silvio Berlusconi as Prime Minister who had tried to patch up rather than to address the real state of Italy's finances (Fabbrini 2013: 167). Greece is the country amongst the GIPPS countries who has become the most dependent on external support from the rest of the eurozone. It has been receiving financial support from the EFSF and the IMF since May 2010 under two programmes. The first, issued in May 2010 ('Greek Loan Facility'), allocated a total of €77.3 billion from the eurozone to be disbursed until 2013 to Greece. This was a slight reduction from the original €80 after Slovakia refused to support the programme. It was complemented by €30 billion from the IMF. With Greece's financial situation worsening, the eurozone countries and the IMF decided to issue a second programme in March 2012, called the 'Economic Adjustment Programme for Greece'. The second programme allocates a total of €164.5 billion to Greece (€144.7 under the ESFS and €19.8 from the IMF), to be disbursed until the end of 2014. The programme is strictly conditional on the implementation of profound budgetary cuts and structural reforms. The austerity measures demanded under both programmes caused profound political turmoil in Greece and led to the collapse of the Socialist government of George Papandreou and elections in November 2011. It was replaced by two temporary unelected caretaker governments, who continued to oversee the structural reforms which are closely monitored by a designated EU Task Force for Greece. Since the general election of June 2013 a three party coalition under Prime Minister Antonis Samaras, consisting of the centre-right New Democracy, centre-left PASOK and the DIMAR, pursues profound reforms of the Greek labour and product market and also the financial sector. Moreover, the Greek government is expected to reduce annual borrowing levels to below 3 per cent by 2014 by reducing the public debt by 18 per cent of its GDP (European Commission 2010: 13). The Greek government has repeatedly asked for and been granted concessions on the conditions of the programme by the eurozone finance ministers and the IMF, particularly in relation to the deficit reduction targets and the interest rates charged on the loans it receives. The latest report by the troika on Greece's progress on the implementation of the structural adjustment programme sees slow but steady progress towards consolidation. It nevertheless highlights the pitfalls the Greek government faces in reducing the size of its public sector in the face of strong opposition from vested interests and also points towards the uncertainty about Greece returning to growth under generally fragile conditions in the eurozone (European Commission 2013d).

The uncertainty about the economic situation in the eurozone and the global economy poses a big question mark over the prospect of all the countries in the GIIPS group to move towards full economic and fiscal consolidation. Ireland, Portugal and Spain, and to a lesser extent, Italy have a better chance to return to sustainable growth than Greece. The complete disappearance of the crisis paradigm is however not in sight. Even if the existing countries manage to resolve their economic problems, other countries, such as Slovenia and Belgium, are developing budgetary crisis symptoms which make it likely that they could soon have to be listed in the crisis category of the new VoC in the EU. As much as the Commission and political leaders in the member states may want to suggest that the EU has moved towards a post-crisis phase, the crisis paradigm in the eurozone is likely to stay with us for the foreseeable future.

NOTE

1. Shortly after having taken office in 2011 Enda Kenny publicly criticised the Catholic Church for its secrecy in the abuse scandal in Irish schools and children homes. In his address to the Irish parliament on 20 July 2011 Kenny spoke of an end to Ireland's subservience to the Catholic Church: 'No Irish prime minister has ever talked to the Catholic Church before in this fashion. The obsequiousness of the Irish state toward the Vatican is gone. The deference is gone' (McDonald 2011).

REFERENCES

Abreu, O. (2006) 'Portugal's Boom and Bust: Lessons for Euro Newcomers'. Country focus 16 December. Brussels: European Commission Directorate General for Economic and Financial Affairs. Available at: http://ec.europa.eu/economy_finance/publications/publication1274_en.pdf (accessed 16 September 2013).

Adshead, M. and N. Robinson (2009) 'Late Development and State Developmentalism – Never the Twain? Towards a Political Economy of "Post-Celtic Tiger" Ireland', Paper Presented at the 2009 Annual Conference of the *Political Studies Association*, 8 April.

Allen, K. (1999) 'The Celtic Tiger, Inequality and Social Partnership', *Administration* 47 (2): 31–55.
Allen, K. (2000) *The Celtic Tiger: The Myth of Social Partnership*. Manchester: Manchester University Press.
Boucher, G. and G. Collins (1999) 'Having One's Cake and Being Eaten too: Irish Neo-liberal Corporatism', *Review of Social Economy* 61 (3): 295–316.
Boylan, T.A. (2002) 'From Stabilisation to Economic Growth – The Contribution of Macroeconomic Policy', in G. Taylor (ed.) *Issues in Irish Public Policy*. Dublin: Irish Academic Press, pp. 9–27.
Bradley, J. (2000) 'The Story of Ireland's Failure – and Belated Success', in B. Nolan, P.J. O'Connell and C.T. Whelan (eds) *Bust to Boom? The Irish Experience of Growth and Inequality*. Dublin: Institute of Public Administration, pp. 27–57.
Bravo, A.C. and J. Igal (2007) 'The Spanish External Deficit: Cyclical or Structural?'. Country Focus 01 January. Brussels: European Commission Directorate-General for Economic and Financial Affairs. Available at: http://ec.europa.eu/economy_finance/publications/publication_summary10077_en.htm (accessed 16 September 2013).
Central Statistics Office Ireland (2013) 'National Accounts Quarterly'. Available at: http://www.cso.ie/px/pxeirestat/Statire/SelectVarVal/Define.asp?maintable=NQQ17&PLanguage=0 (accessed 20 September 2013).
Collings, D.G., P. Gunnigle and M.J. Morley (2005) 'American Multinational Subsidiaries in Ireland: Changing the Nature of Employment Relations', in G. Boucher and G. Collins (eds) *The New World of Work: Labour Markets in Contemporary Ireland*. Dublin: Liffey Press, pp. 125–144.
Coogan, T.P. (2003) *Ireland in the Twentieth Century*. London: Arrow Books.
Council of the European Union (2013) 'Council Extends Maturities of EFSM Loans to Ireland, Portugal'. Press Release 21 June. Available at: http://www.consilium.europa.eu/uedocs/cms_data/docs/pressdata/en/ecofin/137563.pdf (accessed 14 September 2013).
Department of Finance Ireland (2008) 'Government Decision to Safeguard Banking System'. Available at: http://www.finance.gov.ie/viewdoc.asp?docid=5475 (accessed 14 September 2013).
Department of the Taoiseach (2006) 'Towards 2016: Ten-Year Framework Social Partnership Agreement 2006–2015'. Dublin. Available at: http://www.taoiseach.gov.ie/attached_files/Pdf%20files/Towards2016PartnershipAgreement.pdf (accessed 10 September 2013).
Esping-Andersen, G. (1989) *The Three Worlds of Welfare State Capitalism*. Cambridge: Polity Press.
European Commission (2006) 'The EU Economy: 2006 Review'. Available at: http://ec.europa.eu/economy_finance/publications/publication425_en.pdf (accessed 15 September 2013).
European Commission (2009) 'Economic Crisis in Europe: Causes, Consequences Responses'. European Economy 7. Available at: http://ec.europa.eu/economy_finance/publications/publication15887_en.pdf (accessed 14 September 2013).
European Commission (2010) 'The Economic Adjustment Programme for Greece'. Brussels: Directorate-General for Economic and Financial Affairs. Available at: http://ec.europa.eu/economy_finance/publications/occasional_paper/2010/pdf/ocp61_en.pdf (accessed 16 September 2013).
European Commission (2011) 'European Economy Occasional Papers 76: The Economic Adjustment Programme for Ireland'. Brussels: Directorate-General

for Economic and Financial Affairs. Available at: http://ec.europa.eu/economy_finance/publications/occasional_paper/2011/pdf/ocp76_en.pdf (accessed 14 September 2013).

European Commission (2013a) 'Report on Public Finances in EMU'. European Economy 4. Available at: http://ec.europa.eu/economy_finance/publications/european_economy/2013/pdf/ee-2013–4.pdf (accessed 8 September 2013).

European Commission (2013b) 'Economic Adjustment Programme for Ireland: Spring 2013 Review'. Available at: http://ec.europa.eu/economy_finance/publications/occasional_paper/2013/pdf/ocp154_en.pdf (accessed 14 September 2013).

European Commission (2013c) 'Youth Employment Initiative: Questions and Answers'. 2 April. Available at: http://ec.europa.eu/social/main.jsp?langId=en&catId=89&newsId=1829&furtherNews=yes (accessed 16 September 2013).

European Commission (2013d) 'The Second Economic Adjustment Programme for Greece – Third Review July 2013'. Available at: http://ec.europa.eu/economy_finance/publications/occasional_paper/2013/pdf/ocp159_en.pdf (accessed 16 September 2013).

European Industrial Relations Observatory (EIRO) (2013) 'Ireland: Industrial Relations Profile'. Available at: http://www.eurofound.europa.eu/eiro/country/ireland.pdf (accessed 12 September 2013).

Eurostat (2013a) 'Foreign Direct Investment Stocks as % of GDP'. Available at: http://epp.eurostat.ec.europa.eu/tgm/table.do?tab=table&init=1&language=en&pcode=tec00047&plugin=1 (accessed 12 September 2013).

Eurostat (2013b) 'Taxation Trends in the European Union: Data for the EU Member States, Iceland and Norway'. Available at: http://ec.europa.eu/taxation_customs/resources/documents/taxation/gen_info/economic_analysis/tax_structures/2013/report.pdf (accessed 10 September 2013).

Eurostat (2013c) 'Employment Rate by Sex'. Available at: http://epp.eurostat.ec.europa.eu/tgm/table.do?tab=table&init=1&language=en&pcode=tsdec420&plugin=1 (accessed 10 September 2013).

Eurostat (2013d) 'People at Risk of Poverty or Social Exclusion'. Available at: http://epp.eurostat.ec.europa.eu/tgm/table.do?tab=table&init=1&language=en&pcode=t2020_50&plugin=1 (accessed 10 September 2013).

Eurostat (2013e) 'General Government Deficit/Surplus Percentage of GDP'. Available at:http://epp.eurostat.ec.europa.eu/tgm/table.do?tab=table&init=1&language=en&pcode=tec00127&plugin=1 (accessed 30 July 2013).

Eurostat (2013f) 'General Government Gross Debt'. Available at: http://epp.eurostat.ec.europa.eu/tgm/table.do?tab=table&init=1&language=en&pcode=t sdde410&plugin=1 (accessed 30 July 2013).

Eurostat (2013g) 'Unemployment Rate by Sex'. Available at: http://epp.eurostat.ec.europa.eu/tgm/table.do?tab=table&init=1&language=en&pcode=tsdec450&plugin=1 (accessed 30 July 2013).

Eurostat (2013h) 'Unemployment Rate by Age Group'. Available at: http://epp.eurostat.ec.europa.eu/tgm/table.do?tab=table&init=1&language=en&pcode=t sdec460&plugin=1 (accessed 30 July 2013).

Fabbrini, S. (2013) 'The Rise and Fall of Silvio Berlusconi: Personalization of Politics and its Limits', *Comparative European Politics* 11 (2): 153–171.

Fitz Gerald, J. (2000) 'The Story of Ireland's Failure and Belated Success', in B. Nolan, P.J. O'Connell and C.T. Whelan (eds) *Bust to Boom? The Irish Experience of Growth and Inequality*. Dublin: Institute of Public Administration, pp. 27–58.

Fitzgerald, G. (2004) 'The Economics of EU Membership', in J. Hourihane (ed.) *Ireland and the European Union: The First Thirty Years, 1973–2002*. Dublin: Liliput Press, pp. 67–80.

Fitzgerald, R. and B. Girvin (2000) 'Political Culture, Growth and the Condition for Success in the Irish Economy', in B. Nolan, P.J. O'Connell and C.T. Whelan (eds) *Bust to Boom? The Irish Experience of Growth and Inequality*. Dublin: Institute of Public Administration, pp. 268–285.

Garvin, T. (2005) *Preventing the Future: Why Ireland was so Poor for so Long?* Dublin: Gill and Macmillan.

Gunnigle, P., M. O'Sullivan and M. Kinsella (2002), 'Organised Labour in the New Economoy: Trade Unions and Public Policy in the Republic of Ireland' in D. D'Art and T. Turner (eds) *Irish Employment Relations in the New Economy*. Dublin: Blackhall, pp. 222–258.

IDA Ireland (2007) 'Annual Report 2007'. Available at: http://www.idaireland.com/news-media/publications/annual-reports/2001-present/pdf/IDA-Annual-Report-2007.pdf (accessed 11 September 2013).

IDA Ireland (2012a) 'Why Ireland?'. Available at: http://www.idaireland.com/invest-in-ireland/why-invest-in-ireland/index.xml (accessed 13 September 2013).

IDA Ireland (2012b) 'Annual Report 2012'. Available at: http://www.idaireland.com/newsmedia/publications/annualreports/2012/IDA_Annual_Report_2012.pdf (accessed 11 September 2013).

IDA Ireland (2013) 'Foreign Investment in Ireland', June. Available at: http://www.idaireland.com/invest-in-ireland/fdi-in-ireland-2013/ (accessed 11 September 2013).

IMF (2013) 'Global Financial Stability Report: Old Risks, New Challenges'. Available at: http://www.imf.org/External/Pubs/FT/GFSR/2013/01/pdf/text.pdf (accessed 15 September 2013).

Immigration Council of Ireland (2003) 'Labour Migration into Ireland'. Available at: http://www.immigrantcouncil.ie / research-publications / archive ? start = 20 (accessed 15 September 2013).

Irish Department of Social Protection (2009) 'Total Allocation of PPS Numbers by Nationality'. Available at: https://www.welfare.ie/en/downloads/ppsn_all_years.pdf (accessed 15 September 2013).

Kirby, P. (2010) *Celtic Tiger in Collapse: Explaining the Weaknesses of the Irish Model*. Basingstoke: Palgrave Macmillan.

Larch, M. (2005) 'Stuck in a Rut? Italy's Weak Export Performance and Unfavourable Product Specialisation', Country Focus 09 May. Brussels: European Commission Directorate-General for Economic and Financial Affairs. Available at: http://ec.europa.eu/economy_finance/publications/publication_summary11331en.ht (accessed 16 September 2013).

Manolopoulos, J. (2011) *Greece's "Odious" Debt: The Looting of the Hellenic Republic by the Euro, the Political Elite and the Investment Community*. London: Anthem Press.

McAleese, M. (2005) Opening Address of the Céifin Conference 'Filling the Vacuum?', West Country Hotel, Ennis, Co. Clare, 8 November.

McCreevy, C. (2005) 'The Way Ahead in the Internal Market', Speech to the Legal Affairs Committee of the European Parliament, Brussels, 2 February.

McDonald, H. (2010) 'Irish Prime Minister Denies any Application for Euro Bailout', *The Guardian*, 16 November. Available at: http://www.theguardian.

com/business/2010/nov/16/cowen-denies-bailout-application (accessed 12 September 2013).

McDonald, H. (2011) 'Irish Prime Minister Attacks Vatican', *The Guardian*, 20 July. Available at: http://www.theguardian.com/world/2011/jul/20/irish-prime-minister-attacks-vatican (accessed 12 September 2013).

O'Connell, P. (2000) 'The Dynamics of the Irish Labour Market in Comparative Perspective', in B. Nolan, P.J. O'Connell and C.T. Whelan (eds) *Bust to Boom? The Irish Experience of Growth and Inequality*. Dublin: Institute of Public Administration, pp. 58–89.

O'Hagan, J.W. (1995) *The Economy of Ireland: Policy and Performance of a Small European Country*. Basingstoke: Macmillan.

O'Hearn, D. (2000) 'Globalization, "New Tigers", and the End of the Developmental State? The Case of the Celtic Tiger', *Politics and Society* 28 (1): 67–92.

Ó Riain, S. (2004) *The Politics of High-Tech Growth: Developmental Network States in the Global Economy*. Cambridge: Cambridge University Press.

O'Toole, F. (2010) *Ship of Fools: How Stupidity and Corruption Sank the Celtic Tiger*. London: Faber and Faber.

OECD (2008a) 'Factbook 2008: Net Migration Rate OECD'. Available at: http://dx.doi.org/10.1787/272370046012 (accessed 12 September 2013).

OECD (2008b) 'Factbook 2008: Unit Labour Costs, Labour Productivity and Labour Compensation'. Available at: http://dx.doi.org/10.1787/factbook-2008–100.en (accessed 15 September 2013).

OECD (2010) 'Factbook 2010: Employment in Foreign Affiliates'. Available at: http://www.oecd-ilibrary.org/employment/oecd-factbook-2010/employment-in-foreign-affiliates_factbook-2010–29-en (accessed 12 September 2013).

OECD (2012) 'Factbook 2012: Outward and Inward FDI Stocks'. Available at: http://dx.doi.org/10.1787/888932707420 (accessed 10 September 2013).

OECD (2013a) 'Economic Outlook Volume 2013'. 1 (93). Available at: http://dx.doi.org/10.1787/888932838368 (accessed 10 September 2013).

OECD (2013b) *Economic Surveys: Ireland 2013*. Paris: OECD.

OECD (2013c) 'Ireland – Economic Forecast Summary May 2013'. Available at: http://www.oecd.org/economy/irelandeconomicforecastsummary.htm (accessed 15 September 2013).

Roche, W.K. and J.F. Geary (2002) '"Collaborative Production" and the Irish Boom: Work Organisation, Partnership and Direct Involvement in Irish Workplaces', in D. D'Art and T. Turner (eds) *Irish Employment Relations in the New Economy*. Dublin: Blackhall, pp. 58–92.

Ruhs, M. (2005) *Managing the Immigration and Employment of Non-EU Nationals in Ireland*. Dublin: The Policy Institute Blue Paper.

Schmidt, V. and E. Gualmini (2013) 'The Political Sources of Italy's Economic Problems: Between Opportunistic Political Leadership and Pragmatic, Technocratic Leadership', *Comparative European Politics* 11 (3): 360–382.

Shik Kang, J. and J.C. Shambaugh (2013) 'The Evolution of Current Account Deficits in the Euro Area Periphery and the Baltics: Many Paths to the Same Endpoint'. IMF Working Paper 13/169. Available at: http://www.imf.org/external/pubs/ft/wp/2013/wp13169.pdf (accessed 13 September 2013).

Teague, P. (2005) *Social Partnership and the Enterprise Lessons from the Irish Experience*. Dublin: The Policy Institute Working Paper.

Turner, T. (2002) 'Corporatism in Ireland: A Comparative Perspective', in D. D'Art and T. Turner (eds) *Irish Employment Relations in the New Economy*. Dublin: Blackhall, pp. 275–300.

Wallace, J. and M. O'Sullivan (2002) 'The Industrial Relations Act 1990: A Critical Review', in D. D'Art and T. Turner (eds) *Irish Employment Relations in the New Economy*. Dublin: Blackhall, pp. 169–195.

Wickham, J. (1983) 'Independence and State Structure: Foreign Firms and Industrial Policy in the Republic of Ireland', in O. Höll (ed.) *Small States in Europe and Dependence*. Vienna: Wilhelm Braumüller, pp. 165–183

Wickham, J. and G. Boucher (2004) 'Training Cubs for the Celtic Tiger: the Volume Production of Technical Graduates in the Irish Educational System', *Journal of Education and Work* 17 (4): 377–395.

Wickham, J. (2012) 'After the Party's Over: the Irish Employment Model and the Paradoxes of Non-Learning', in S. Lehndorff (ed.) *A Triumph of Failed Ideas: European Models of Capitalism in the Crisis*. Brussels: European Trade Union Institute, pp. 59–78.

7. Central and Eastern Europe: from transition towards new risk

The Central and Eastern European (CEE) economies can be classified as a 'transition model' with some common challenges but with noticeably differences in the culture and development of their economies and welfare states. It is therefore justified to speak of an emerging new Varieties of Capitalism (VoC) in this region, which warrants further detailed investigation over the coming years. The countries of the CEE-8 (2004) and CEE-2 (2010) accession group share the common and ongoing challenge of shedding the legacy of centralised state planning of their economies under Communism, which lasted for more than four decades after the end of the Second World War.

The European Union (EU) was instrumental in setting the CEE countries on the path towards liberal market economies by promoting the principles of the Washington Consensus (Cernat 2006: 29). As a result, the emerging policy consensus in the CEE region is generally favourable towards economic liberalisation. In practice this manifests itself in following the example of dependent growth for which Ireland became the role model amongst the EU-15, as it is outlined in Chapter 6. Like in the Irish case, foreign direct investment (FDI) hence became a crucial factor in the development of economies in CEE. Germany, which has been a longstanding political and economic partner for all CEE member states in the EU, plays a crucial role in this respect.

While the CEE countries show distinctive differences in their economic development since the end of the Cold War, they all have been facing the same challenges in the process of profound economic, political and social transformation since the early 1990s. The main challenges for the CEE countries have been threefold:

1. Accession to the EU based on the Copenhagen membership criteria demanded that all of them prepared their political, legal and economic systems for entry into the EU's *acquis*. In addition, all of the CEE countries have shown an ambition to become members of the eurozone. Budgetary consolidation has therefore been a major priority for governments in the region and continues to be of prime importance,

both for those CEE countries who are already inside the eurozone but even more so for those on the outside.
2. All CEE countries continue to be in process of economic, political and social transformation with the aim of shaking off the remainders of the *totalitarian* legacy of decades of state-imposed socialism. The progress made in this respect varies in each individual country.
3. The global financial crisis turned out to be a major setback for the CEE countries in this transformation process, particularly in respect of the progress they had previously made on reducing unemployment and consolidating their budgets.

All CEE countries entered the EU with a GDP per capita which was below the EU-15 average. The EU-15 countries were consequently concerned about the potential impact of the historic wave of enlargement to eight post-Communist countries in 2004. Concerns concentrated on the financial burden the inclusion of this new group of member states was thought to impose on Western Europe. Most of all on the potential impact of mass labour migration from the economically disadvantaged East was an issue of profound concern (Grabbe 2004: 6).

The new member states had a lot of ground to make up to lift their economic strength up to the EU-15 level. In contrast to most expectations they nevertheless soon embarked on the path towards growth. Between 2003 and 2007 average GDP growth rates in the EU-15 remained below 3 per cent, while all of the new member states and even Bulgaria and Romania, who would only join the EU in 2007, grew at between 3 and over 10 per cent (Figure 7.1). The high growth rates in CEE countries substantially boosted sluggish growth in the Single Market and to a certain degree calmed the concerns of Western European governments that the eastward enlargement would be detrimental to the competitiveness of the Single Market.

In addition, the new member states accepted that at the time of their accession, many of the EU-15 governments were unwilling to exercise the same financial generosity they had granted during past waves of enlargement, particularly those to the Southern European countries in the 1980s. The Agenda 2000, which was decided under the German EU presidency, determined a total of €3,120 million pre-accession aid to be made available to the CEE-8 accession countries between 2000 and 2006 under the PHARE programme and €58 billion of support under the structural funds for the new member states (European Commission 2001: 14 and 26). The fears that the new member states would not be able to integrate swiftly into the EU's complex legal and institutional framework also turned out to be unfounded. By the end of 2005 the European Commission reported that the CEE countries, apart from the Czech Republic, were amongst

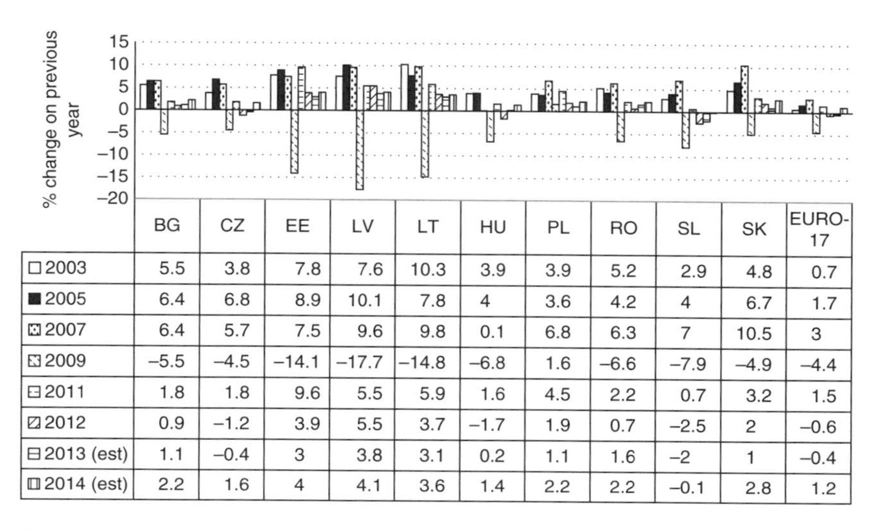

	BG	CZ	EE	LV	LT	HU	PL	RO	SL	SK	EURO-17
2003	5.5	3.8	7.8	7.6	10.3	3.9	3.9	5.2	2.9	4.8	0.7
2005	6.4	6.8	8.9	10.1	7.8	4	3.6	4.2	4	6.7	1.7
2007	6.4	5.7	7.5	9.6	9.8	0.1	6.8	6.3	7	10.5	3
2009	−5.5	−4.5	−14.1	−17.7	−14.8	−6.8	1.6	−6.6	−7.9	−4.9	−4.4
2011	1.8	1.8	9.6	5.5	5.9	1.6	4.5	2.2	0.7	3.2	1.5
2012	0.9	−1.2	3.9	5.5	3.7	−1.7	1.9	0.7	−2.5	2	−0.6
2013 (est)	1.1	−0.4	3	3.8	3.1	0.2	1.1	1.6	−2	1	−0.4
2014 (est)	2.2	1.6	4	4.1	3.6	1.4	2.2	2.2	−0.1	2.8	1.2

Source: Eurostat (2013a).

Figure 7.1 Real GDP growth rate

the best performers in the implementation of Single Market directives, while many of the EU-15, most of all the Southern European countries, had a slow and incorrect implementation record (European Commission 2005). Romania and Bulgaria followed the CEE-8 countries in their good performance once both countries had joined the EU. Both are frequently listed amongst the top performers when it comes to the implementation of Single Market directives (European Commission 2013a).

The main concern about the impact of the 2004 and 2007 waves of enlargement has centred on the impact of potentially large waves of labour migration from countries with high levels of unemployment and poverty. The labour markets of Latvia, Lithuania, and especially Poland and Slovakia, gave cause for concern as they seemed to offer little prospect for unemployed people, most of all young people, to find employment opportunities. Both Slovakia and Poland had an unemployment rate which approached 20 per cent, Latvia and Lithuania almost 10 per cent when they joined the EU in 2004 (Figure 7.2). All EU-15 countries except the UK, Ireland and Sweden, consequently introduced transitional periods, which limited the access of workers from the 2004 CEE-8 accession group to their labour markets for a period of up to a maximum of seven years. Eight member states, amongst them the UK and Germany restricted the free movement of workers from Bulgaria and Romania to the maximum possible duration of seven years after 2007. This means that Bulgarians

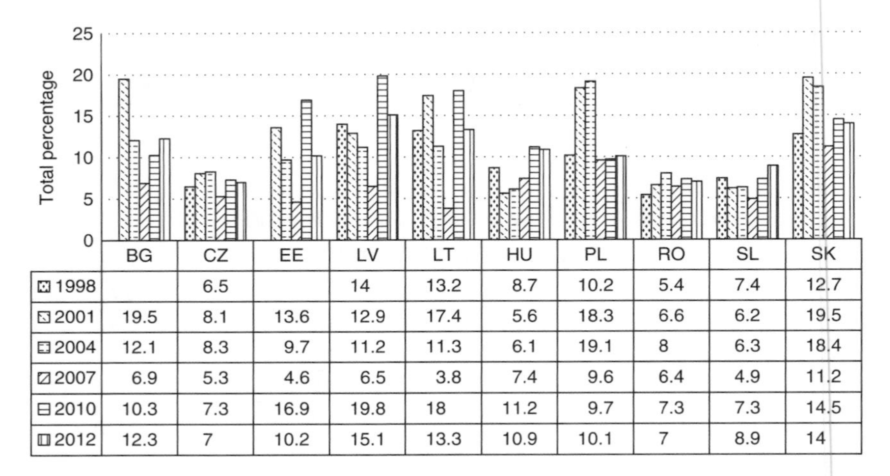

	BG	CZ	EE	LV	LT	HU	PL	RO	SL	SK
1998		6.5		14	13.2	8.7	10.2	5.4	7.4	12.7
2001	19.5	8.1	13.6	12.9	17.4	5.6	18.3	6.6	6.2	19.5
2004	12.1	8.3	9.7	11.2	11.3	6.1	19.1	8	6.3	18.4
2007	6.9	5.3	4.6	6.5	3.8	7.4	9.6	6.4	4.9	11.2
2010	10.3	7.3	16.9	19.8	18	11.2	9.7	7.3	7.3	14.5
2012	12.3	7	10.2	15.1	13.3	10.9	10.1	7	8.9	14

Source: Eurostat (2013b).

Figure 7.2 Unemployment rate in the CEE countries

and Romanians only have full access to the labour markets of all other 26 member states from January 2014 (European Commission 2012). This occurred in spite of the fact that Bulgarian and Romanian unemployment rates were relatively modest by comparison at the time of accession (6.9 and 6.4 per cent respectively) and have only grown noticeably in Bulgaria since the onset of the global crisis.

Before the effects of the financial crisis hit them in 2007 the CEE-8 countries, with the exception of Hungary, had not only maintained good levels of GDP growth but most of all had started to reduce their unemployment rates. This was especially significant in the cases of Latvia, Lithuania and Poland, where double digit unemployment rates were substantially reduced. Lithuania managed to reduce its unemployment rate from 17.4 per cent in 2001 to only 3.8 per cent in 2007. Latvia's decreased from 14 per cent in 1998 to 6.5 per cent in 2007. Most remarkable was however Poland's recovery. The Polish unemployment rate decreased from a peak of 19.1 per cent in 2004 to 9.6 per cent within a period of just three years in 2007.

This was partly the result of a dramatic wave of outward migration of Polish workers to the UK and Ireland after accession to the EU. However most of all this was the effect of profound employment policy reforms which have increased labour flexibility in Poland. As a result the number of temporary jobs and self-employed workers increased substantially. In 2001 only 11.7 per cent of all workers were employed on a contract with limited duration. By 2007 this had risen to 28.2 per cent (Eurostat 2013c). Poland has also maintained a high number of self-employed people and a number of jobs in the public sector were transformed into self-employed contractor positions (Funk 2009: 564). Between 2004 and 2008 approximately 900,000 workers emigrated to work in the labour markets of the UK, Ireland and Sweden which were fully open to workers from the new member states (Central Statistics Office Poland 2009: 458). Under the conditions of contracting labour markets in these countries since 2007 many Polish workers have either started to return home or moved to other EU member states. In 2007 and 2008 alone around 100,000 Poles returned to their country of origin (Ibid.: 449). The employment growth in Latvia and Lithuania can to a large extent be explained by the two countries' basing their post-accession economic growth predominantly on financial services. Both established strong links with financial systems across Europe. Like Estonia, both managed to attract a large portion of FDI in the banking sector, particularly from Nordic countries. This boosted economic growth and led to bubble economies driven by domestic demand similar to that of Ireland in the late stages of the Celtic Tiger. Private credit in these countries spiralled towards levels which were neither sustainable nor backed by the strength of the economies. The result was a strong dependence on foreign lenders, especially in Scandinavia, which turned out to be detrimental for the Baltic economies during the onset of the financial crisis after 2007 (Deroose et al. 2010: 3–5). This explains why the contraction of the Baltic countries' GDP growth was more severe than for the rest of the CEE countries. Estonia's GDP declined by 14.1 per cent in 2009, Lithuania's by 14.8 and Latvia's even by 17.7 per cent, the deepest recession in the whole of the EU-27. The situation in the Latvian banking sector became so severe under the crisis conditions that it was forced to ask for external financial assistance. In December 2008 Latvia received a €7.5 billion joint loan from the EU, the IMF, the World Bank, the European Bank for Reconstruction and Development (EBRD) with individual contributions from EU member states (Czech Republic, Poland, Sweden, Denmark, Finland, Norway and Estonia), to be disbursed until January 2012. The conditions of the programme were tied to fundamental reform of the Latvian financial sector towards greater transparency and better funding in addition to the introduction of a more efficient system of fiscal governance in the country (European Union 2009). Myant and Drahokoupil have classified the Baltic economies as 'peripheral market economies' in the varieties of transitional capitalism in the CEE region, which are characterised by 'financialized growth and significant dependence on remittances' (Myant and Drahokoupil 2011: 311). This makes them extremely vulnerable towards external shocks.

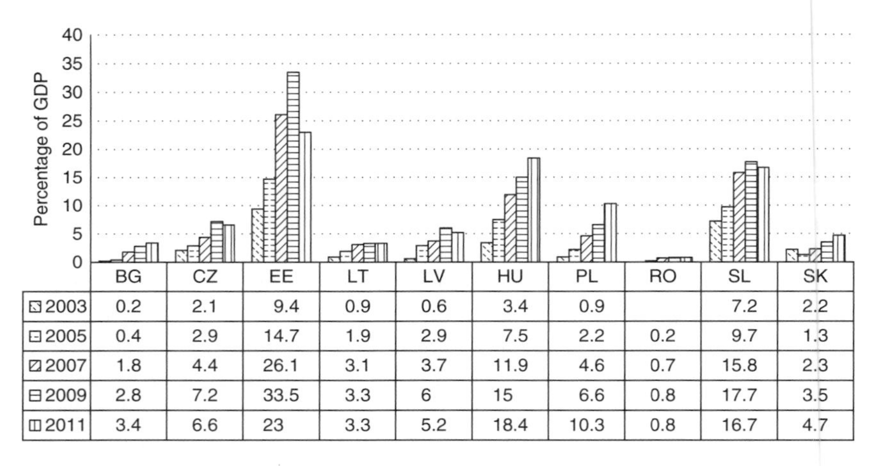

	BG	CZ	EE	LT	LV	HU	PL	RO	SL	SK
2003	0.2	2.1	9.4	0.9	0.6	3.4	0.9		7.2	2.2
2005	0.4	2.9	14.7	1.9	2.9	7.5	2.2	0.2	9.7	1.3
2007	1.8	4.4	26.1	3.1	3.7	11.9	4.6	0.7	15.8	2.3
2009	2.8	7.2	33.5	3.3	6	15	6.6	0.8	17.7	3.5
2011	3.4	6.6	23	3.3	5.2	18.4	10.3	0.8	16.7	4.7

Source: Eurostat (2013d).

Figure 7.3 FDI stocks CEE countries

Estonia is the country amongst the CEE member states with the highest level of FDI stocks which even continued to grow during the crisis. The FDI stocks in Estonia increased from 9.4 per cent of its GDP in 2003 to over 33 per in 2009. FDI has been an important growth factor for all economies in the region but most significantly for Estonia, Hungary and Slovenia (Figure 7.3).

In their initial assessment of the emerging VoC in the CEE region following the first wave of enlargement in 2004, Lane and Myant classified all the economies of the CEE-8 member states and the accession candidates Bulgaria and Romania as being close to the continental type of coordinated market capitalism. In Bulgaria, Romania, Latvia and Lithuania the authors' detected even greater levels of state coordination (Lane and Myant 2006: 35). It seems however that overall the direction of economic policy is less determined in the CEE member states than is the case in coordinated models in the West. Changes in government can bring substantial shifts in the taxation system and in employment and welfare policies. The fact that the state continues to play a substantial role in the economies of the CEE countries is partly a leftover from the culture of state-controlled socialism. A major influence has however also been the proximity to and strong dependence on Germany as a political and economic partner. Germany was a strong supporter of the process of eastward enlargement, which the former German Chancellor Gerhard Schröder famously promoted by stating that 'European integration can only succeed if this

Europe does not end at the borders of the former iron curtain' (Schröder 1999). The long-standing political ties between Germany and the countries of CEE reach back as far as the 1970s, during the period of détente in the Cold War, when West Germany signed bilateral agreements with Poland and the CSSR and intensified its political and cultural dialogue with the region. For most CEE countries Germany therefore had become a crucial point of reference in Europe. In political terms this is illustrated by the generally positive attitude towards German leadership in the EU. With the exception of the government led by Prime Minister Jarosław Kaczyński in Poland in 2006–2007 and the current Fidesz government of Prime Minister Viktor Orbán in Hungary, anti-German rhetoric in CEE has been sparse. Especially the current Polish and Slovak governments have been strongly in favour of a German leadership role in the EU and recently publicly stated this. Polish Foreign Minister Radosław Sikorski used the occasion of Poland's 2011 EU presidency to call on Germany to show more leadership in developing major EU policy areas, such as security and defence policy, further (Sikorski 2011). The Slovak Foreign Minister stunned the audience at the 2013 Global Security Forum in Bratislava when he said that he would be relaxed about his country becoming 'part of a greater Germany' (Mikulova 2013).

The CEE region has intensified its economic ties with Germany in political but especially in economic terms in recent years. Germany has established strong economic ties with Poland, Hungary, Slovakia, the Czech Republic and Slovakia, who have all become significant in using them as production hubs for German manufacturing, especially in the automobile sector. German investment in the region was followed by multinational companies from around the world, in particular car manufacturers. This 'externally financed growth' model has especially made the Visegrád-4 (V4) countries Poland, Hungary, Slovakia and the Czech Republic substantially dependent on the German economy (Galgoczi 2009: 624). This proved a major factor in the ability of the V4 and the rest of the CEE countries to recover quicker from the recession than some of their Western and Southern European counterparts, who did not have the benefit of being tied to the Germany economy, which managed to get through the financial crisis largely unscathed. Figure 7.4 shows the region's growing trade dependence on the German economy, which ultimately also poses the risk of severe repercussions in case of a German economic downturn. German direct investments into the Czech Republic and Hungary amounted to €23 and €16 billion respectively in 2010. The V4 countries are amongst the top 20 international trading partners for Germany. Poland was ranked as the seventh most important international trading partner for Germany in 2012 (Statistisches Bundesamt 2012).

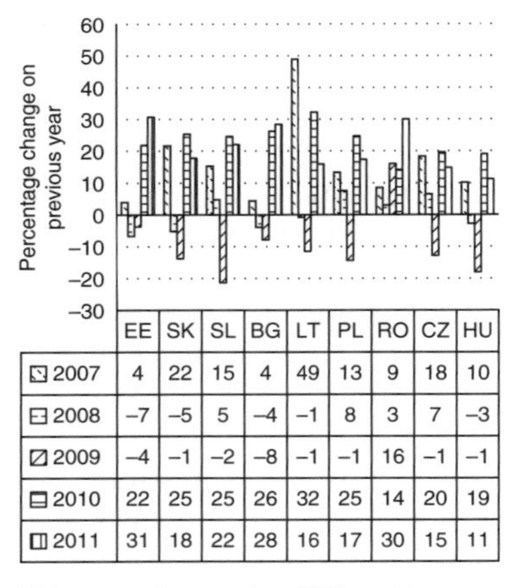

	EE	SK	SL	BG	LT	PL	RO	CZ	HU
2007	4	22	15	4	49	13	9	18	10
2008	–7	–5	5	–4	–1	8	3	7	–3
2009	–4	–1	–2	–8	–1	–1	16	–1	–1
2010	22	25	25	26	32	25	14	20	19
2011	31	18	22	28	16	17	30	15	11

(a) Imports to Germany from CEE countries

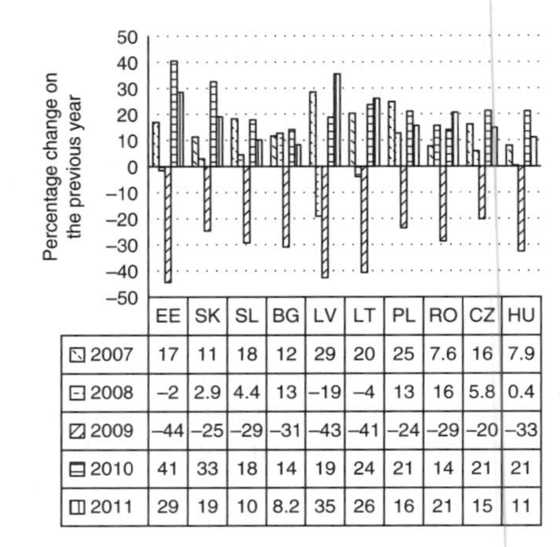

	EE	SK	SL	BG	LV	LT	PL	RO	CZ	HU
2007	17	11	18	12	29	20	25	7.6	16	7.9
2008	–2	2.9	4.4	13	–19	–4	13	16	5.8	0.4
2009	–44	–25	–29	–31	–43	–41	–24	–29	–20	–33
2010	41	33	18	14	19	24	21	14	21	21
2011	29	19	10	8.2	35	26	16	21	15	11

(b) German exports to CEE countries

Source: Statistisches Bundesamt (2013: 416).

Figure 7.4 CEE trade with Germany

All CEE countries, again with the exception of Hungary, have entered the EU in a relatively sound budgetary position and have managed to maintain this under the conditions of ongoing economic transformation and even during the impact of the global financial crisis (Figure 7.5). By 2007 all CEE countries except Hungary met the budgetary criteria of the eurozone stability and growth pact (3 per cent annual deficit limit and 60 per cent limit to structural debt). Slovenia adopted the euro in 2007 and subsequently the enlargement of the eurozone continued even under crisis conditions, with Slovakia joining in 2009 and Estonia following in 2011. This has increasingly divided the CEE group into euro insiders and outsiders. Amongst the latter the degree of enthusiasm for joining has been markedly different. Poland, Latvia and Lithuania and even Bulgaria and Romania seem to have a clear ambition to join while the Czech Republic and Hungary have remained lukewarm.

Poland has openly linked membership of the euro with its ambition to join the group of the leading member states. Foreign Minister Sikorski recently emphasised that the increasing isolation of the UK in the EU would offer Poland 'the chance of becoming part of the hard core of European decision-makers', provided that it would be able to adopt the euro in the near future (Sikorski 2013). This ambition suffered a severe setback when the Polish government had to abandon the original target date of euro adoption by 2012 as a result of the effects of the financial

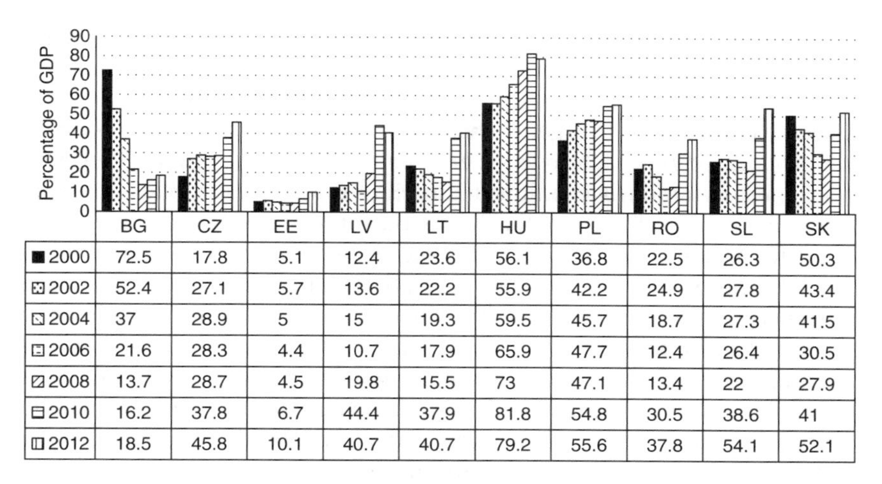

	BG	CZ	EE	LV	LT	HU	PL	RO	SL	SK
2000	72.5	17.8	5.1	12.4	23.6	56.1	36.8	22.5	26.3	50.3
2002	52.4	27.1	5.7	13.6	22.2	55.9	42.2	24.9	27.8	43.4
2004	37	28.9	5	15	19.3	59.5	45.7	18.7	27.3	41.5
2006	21.6	28.3	4.4	10.7	17.9	65.9	47.7	12.4	26.4	30.5
2008	13.7	28.7	4.5	19.8	15.5	73	47.1	13.4	22	27.9
2010	16.2	37.8	6.7	44.4	37.9	81.8	54.8	30.5	38.6	41
2012	18.5	45.8	10.1	40.7	40.7	79.2	55.6	37.8	54.1	52.1

Source: Eurostat (2013e).

Figure 7.5 General government gross debt CEE countries

crisis. The Polish government was forced to expand borrowing to 7.4 per cent in 2009 and 7.9 per cent in 2010 and still broke the 3 per cent annual borrowing limit in 2011. Poland's structural deficit has also increased to over 50 per cent as a result of the crisis. The Tusk government has therefore postponed euro entry and refrained from setting a new target date. Public scepticism towards the euro in Poland has increased sharply since the onset of the sovereign debt crisis. This caused the government to announce that it is likely to hold a public referendum on the issue before a final decision is made (Sobczak 2013). The situation is similar amongst the other euro outsiders. Latvia and Lithuania have both managed to keep their structural debt below 50 per cent and also reduced their annual borrowing levels below 3 per cent in 2012. Latvia's sound budgetary position allowed it to become the first country in the Euro Plus Pact (EPP) group to join the eurozone in January 2014. Lithuania's ambition is less obvious. The country's parliament has decided to implement an expert group which should prepare Lithuania's adoption of the euro in 2015. An official application to join is however still outstanding. Bulgaria and Romania are both in a good budgetary position to join the euro in the foreseeable future but face opposition from the existing eurozone members towards entry. This is because of the high levels of severe poverty in the two countries, where over 30 per cent of the population are considered to be extremely poor (European Commission 2013b: 3).

Although membership of the euro is generally still considered to be economically beneficial, governments across the CEE countries have become less enthusiastic about entry into the eurozone under the conditions of a sovereign debt crisis. These sentiments are most prominent in the Czech Republic and Hungary. The Czech Republic has in effect adopted a wait-and-see approach towards euro entry. The former Czech President Václav Klaus famously positioned himself as the most outspoken domestic opponent of Czech euro entry. Klaus put pressure on the former Prime Minister Něcas to opt out of the intergovernmental Fiscal Compact (Král 2013: 8). The Czech Republic hence positioned itself next to the UK at the periphery of the Single Market. The Czech Republic would currently be in a good position to join the euro with the level of annual borrowing having been reduced below 3 per cent since 2012 and the level of structural debt remaining below 50 per cent. The future position of the Czech Republic towards the EU policy framework and euro adoption will to a large extent depend on the political direction the new Czech centre-left government administration under the leadership of Social Democrat Bohuslav Sobotka adopts over the coming years. Under Sobotka a more pragmatic Czech stance in the EU is likely and swifter eurozone entry remains a possibility. The new Czech government nevertheless still face the obstacle of convincing a predominantly hostile Czech public of eurozone entry. Currently 79 per cent of Czechs are opposed to their country joining the euro (European Commission 2013c).

Hungary is in a completely different position and continues to be preoccupied with what essentially has been a very difficult transition process. Hungary has struggled to shed a culture of fiscal mismanagement which can be traced all the way back to the Communist era. The Hungarian economic liberalisation process after the fall of Communism was swift. This led to the expectation that it would have the potential to become a role model economy amongst the CEE countries in terms of economic performance. However its particular national model of becoming a 'dependent competitive state' ended up being trapped in a downwards spiral of rising debt, increasing unemployment and strong dependence on FDI, particularly from Germany and an underdeveloped domestic sector (Pogátsa 2009: 609). In spite of sluggish growth successive Hungarian governments failed to pursue a strategy of budget consolidation. The financial crisis pushed Hungary from an already difficult budgetary position into further budgetary austerity.

Ultimately it became impossible to finance the large amount of external public debt the country had accumulated prior to the crisis without external support. Hungary hence received a total €14.2 billion external financial assistance from the EU and the IMF. In 2011 Hungary requested further precautionary assistance from the EU/IMF which has so far not been granted. A major reason is the ongoing dispute between the EU and the Orbán government on domestic policy changes in Hungary. The European Commission has criticised the government for the tax levy it imposed on foreign companies, which risks to deter foreign investors. The Commission has also criticised the major constitutional changes Orbán's government implemented in Hungary, which risk undermining judicial scrutinity and democratic accountability in the country. Hungary under Orbán has given the impression that it is becoming a country who wants to go it alone in Europe. This make it less likely that Hungary will be able to count on external financial support from the EU in the future and that the current eurozone members would support Hungarian euro membership

The country continues to have severe problems with structural debt but the government has now adopted a strategy of consolidating debt without further external support. The Orbán government has embarked on a strict and unpopular programme of fiscal austerity. Prime Minister Orbán justifies the programme as essential to avoid Hungary from being governed externally by the IMF and the EU. This is part of a new Euroscepticism which the Orbán government is not afraid to demonstrate in public. It goes as far as to compare the influence of the EU with that of the Soviet Union during the Cold War. In the words of Orbán during his 2013 'State of the Nation' address:

> We are building a country in which people don't work for the profit of foreigners. A country in which we will not be told how to live our lives, what can be in our Constitution and when we can increase wages, by bankers and foreign bureaucrats. A country in which no-one can force the interests of others upon the Hungarian people (Orbán 2013).

The Hungarian government seems to have very little concern about the political effects such an attitude will have on its position within the EU. The gross level of public debt has slightly fallen from over 80 per cent in 2011 and currently stands in the high 70s. As growth in the country remains sluggish and unemployment is rising, the likelihood that the Hungarian government will depend on external financial support in the near future cannot be ruled out. A particular structural problem of the Hungarian economy is the high level of youth unemployment which currently approaches 30 per cent. It is estimated that since Hungary joined the EU in 2004, approximately 85,000 Hungarians have emigrated to work in other EU countries (Komiljovics 2012).

Unemployment continues to remain a major problem in the CEE region and has been aggravated further in many member states by the financial crisis. Bulgaria, Estonia, Latvia, Hungary, Poland and Slovakia have

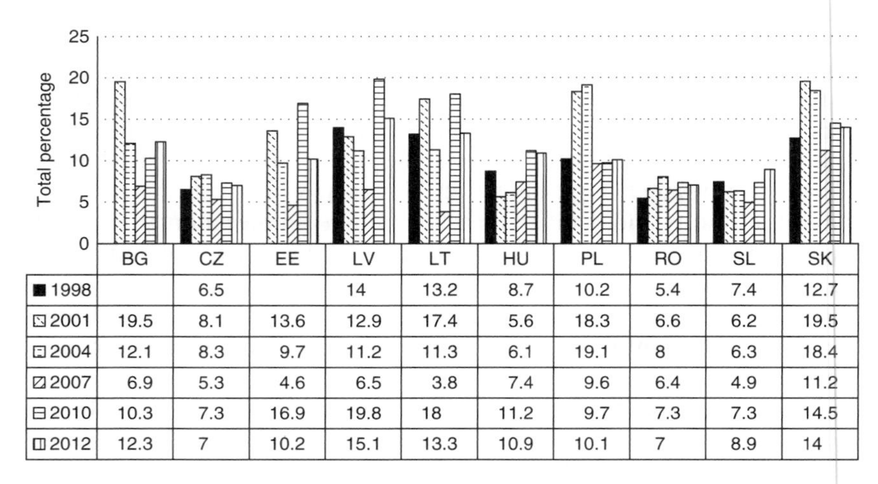

	BG	CZ	EE	LV	LT	HU	PL	RO	SL	SK
1998		6.5		14	13.2	8.7	10.2	5.4	7.4	12.7
2001	19.5	8.1	13.6	12.9	17.4	5.6	18.3	6.6	6.2	19.5
2004	12.1	8.3	9.7	11.2	11.3	6.1	19.1	8	6.3	18.4
2007	6.9	5.3	4.6	6.5	3.8	7.4	9.6	6.4	4.9	11.2
2010	10.3	7.3	16.9	19.8	18	11.2	9.7	7.3	7.3	14.5
2012	12.3	7	10.2	15.1	13.3	10.9	10.1	7	8.9	14

Source: Eurostat (2013f).

Figure 7.6 Unemployment rate in the CEE countries

returned to double digit unemployment rates and it is likely that the Czech Republic, Romania and Slovenia could follow suit (Figure 7.6).

Besides Hungary, Slovenia is the country which currently causes the EU, and most of all the eurozone, the most grounds for concern. Slovenia has deteriorated from former star performer amongst the CEE countries towards the position of a crisis economy. The country was severely hit by the financial crisis which exposed fundamental weaknesses in its banking system. Slovenia plunged into a deep recession in 2009 and only recovered briefly with 0.7 per cent GDP growth in 2011. Since 2012 it fell back into recession and the outlook for a recovery is bleak. Current Commission forecasts estimate that the recession will deepen further in 2013 and not recover substantially in 2014. Slovenia has not yet requested external financial assistance but is closely monitored by the Commission as a potential candidate for support under the European Stability Mechanism (ESM) due to the extent of public funds that had to be used for the recapitalisation of the country's banking system (European Commission 2013d: 3–4).

The other two CEE members in the eurozone have emerged from the financial crisis in a much better position. Estonia managed to achieve a very strong recovery of its growth. In 2010 growth picked up substantially and then climbed to 7.6 per cent in 2011, just to fall back to 1.7 per cent in 2012. For 2013 and 2014 growth is forecast to remain between 3–3.5 per cent. Slovakia returned to above 4 per cent GDP growth in 2010. In 2011 growth stood at 3.3 per cent and declined to 1.1 per cent in 2012

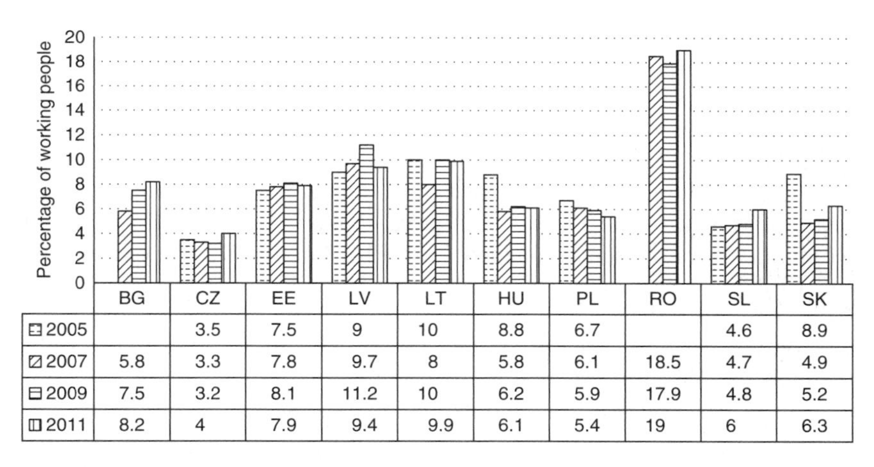

	BG	CZ	EE	LV	LT	HU	PL	RO	SL	SK
2005		3.5	7.5	9	10	8.8	6.7		4.6	8.9
2007	5.8	3.3	7.8	9.7	8	5.8	6.1	18.5	4.7	4.9
2009	7.5	3.2	8.1	11.2	10	6.2	5.9	17.9	4.8	5.2
2011	8.2	4	7.9	9.4	9.9	6.1	5.4	19	6	6.3

Source: Eurostat (2013g).

Figure 7.7 In-work at-risk-of-poverty rate in the CEE member states

with the forecast for 2013 and 2014 between 2.7 and 3.6 per cent. With the exception of its unemployment rate, Slovakia has shown an overall very good performance as a member of the eurozone. The country also shares a bottom position with Estonia in the CEE group when it comes to the overall levels of poverty. The overall level of what is considered as severe material deprivation remains high in a number of CEE countries. In 2010 over 30 per cent of the population in Bulgaria and Romania were considered to be extremely poor, followed by 27 per cent in Latvia, 21 per cent in Hungary, 20 per cent in Lithuania, 15 per cent in Poland and between 9 and 12 per cent in Slovakia and Estonia. Only the Czech Republic and Slovenia have substantially lower levels of severely deprived people (European Commission 2013b).

None of the CEE member states have managed to reach the Europe 2020 employment target of 75 per cent. A big concern for the CEE countries remains their poverty levels and the high levels of 'working poor'. Figure 7.7 illustrates that Romania has the highest rate of people who are in work but nevertheless considered to be at the risk of poverty. It is followed by Poland, Lithuania and Latvia who are also both above the EU-27 level, with between 9 and 11 per cent of those in work at the risk of poverty. Bulgaria, Estonia, Slovakia, Hungary and the Czech Republic have lower levels, with the Czech Republic at the bottom with 4 per cent. The overall level of what is considered as severe material deprivation yet remains high in a number of CEE countries.

It is obvious that under the conditions of the financial crisis and the eurozone sovereign debt crisis the national variations in the economic models within the CEE transition group have become even more distinctive than previously have been. The division of the EU into multiple integrative cores as was outlined in Chapter 3 in this book affects the CEE group directly. The CEE-10 are represented in each of the four emerging integrative groups: Estonia, Slovakia and Slovenia are positioned at the heart of the eurozone-17 core; Bulgaria, Poland, Latvia, Lithuania and Romania are in the semi-detached Euro Plus Group; Hungary is outside the EPP but nevertheless a signatory to the EU-25 intergovernmental Fiscal Compact; the Czech Republic is currently still positioned next to the UK on the periphery of the Single Market. This division also goes right through the V4 group, which is in the process of intensifying its cooperation in EU policy areas such as defence and security. Within the V4, Slovakia as the only eurozone member is currently also the only country who is fully involved in decision-making on all levels of the Single Market. In stark contrast to what was expected at the time of their accession, it was none of the CEE countries that plunged the EU into a crisis. The financial crisis itself has however had a substantial impact on the transformation process across the region and consequently increased the level of diversity in the CEE transition group.

REFERENCES

Central Statistics Office Poland (2009) *Demographic Yearbook of Poland*. Warsaw: CSO.

Cernat, L. (2006) *Europeanization, Varieties of Capitalism and Economic Performance in Central and Eastern Europe*. Basingstoke: Palgrave Macmillan.

Deroose, S., E. Flores, G. Giudice and A. Turrini (2010) 'The Tale of the Baltics: Experience, Challenges Ahead and Main Lessons'. ECFIN Economic Brief, 10 July. Brussels: European Commission Directorate-General for Economic and Financial Affairs. Available at: http://ec.europa.eu/economy_finance/publications/economic_briefs/2010/pdf/eb10_en.pdf (accessed 18 September 2013).

European Commission (2001) 'Enlargement of the European Union: A Historic Opportunity'. Brussels: Enlargement Directorate-General. Available at: http://ec.europa.eu/enlargement/archives/pdf/press_corner/publications/corpus_en.pdf (accessed 17 September 2013).

European Commission (2005) 'Internal Market Scoreboard 14 December'. Available at: http://ec.europa.eu/internal_market/score/docs/score14bis/scoreboard14bis_en.pdf (accessed 17 September 2013).

European Commission (2012) 'Summary table of Member States' policies – Workers from Bulgaria and Romania'. Available at: http://ec.europa.eu/social/BlobServlet?docId=119&langId=en (accessed 18 September 2013).

European Commission (2013a) 'Internal Market Scoreboard 26 February'.

Available at: http://ec.europa.eu/internal_market/score/docs/score26_en.pdf (accessed 17 September 2013).
European Commission (2013b) *Europe 2020 Targets: Poverty and Social Exclusion Active Inclusion Strategies*. Brussels: EU.
European Commission (2013c) 'Standard *Eurobarometer 79* Spring'. Available at: http://ec.europa.eu/public_opinion/archives/eb/eb79/eb79_first_en.pdf (accessed 18 September 2013).
European Commission (2013d) 'Assessment of the 2013 National Reform Programme and Stability Programme for Slovenia', 29 May SWD(2013) 374 final. Available at: http://ec.europa.eu/europe2020/pdf/nd/swd2013_slovenia_en.pdf (accessed 18 September 2013).
European Union (2009) 'Memorandum of Understanding between the European Community and the Republic of Latvia'. Available at: http://ec.europaeu/economy_finance/eu_borrower/balance_of_payments/pdf/mou_bop_latvia_en.pdf (accessed 18 September 2013).
Eurostat (2013a) 'Real GDP Growth Rate – Volume'. Available at: http://epp.eurostat.ec.europa.eu/tgm/table.do?tab=table&init=1&plugin=1&language=en pcode=tec00115 (accessed 30 July 2013).
Eurostat (2013b) 'Unemployment Rate by Sex'. Available at: http://epp.eurostat.ec.europa.eu/tgm/table.do?tab=table&init=1&language=en&pcode=tsdec450&plugin=1 (accessed 30 July 2013).
Eurostat (2013c) 'Employees with a Contract of Limited Duration (Annual Average)'. Available at: http://epp.eurostat.ec.europa.eu/tgm/table.do?tab=table&init=1&language=en&pcode=tps00073&plugin=1 (accessed 30 July 2013).
Eurostat (2013d) 'Foreign Direct Investment Stocks as % of GDP'. Available at: http://epp.eurostat.ec.europa.eu/tgm/table.do?tab=table&init=1&language=en&pcode=tec00047&plugin=1 (accessed 12 September 2013).
Eurostat (2013e) 'General Government Gross Debt'. Available at: http://epp.eurostat.ec.europa.eu/tgm/table.do?tab=table&init=1&language=en&pcode=tsdde410&plugin=1 (accessed 30 July 2013).
Eurostat (2013f) 'Unemployment Rate by Sex'. Available at: http://epp.eurostat.ec.europa.eu/tgm/table.do?tab=table&init=1&language=en&pcode=tsdec450&plugin=1 (accessed 30 July 2013).
Eurostat (2013g) 'In-Work At-Risk-of-Poverty-Rate'. Available at: http://epp.eurostat.ec.europa.eu/tgm/table.do?tab=table&init=1&language=en&pcode=tesov110&plugin=1 (accessed 30 July 2013).
Funk, L. (2009) 'Labour Market Trends and Problems in the EU's Central and Eastern European Member States: Is Flexicurity the Answer?', *Journal of Contemporary European Research* 5 (4): 557–580.
Galgoczi, B. (2009) 'Boom and Bust in Central and Eastern Europe: Lessons on the Sustainability of an Externally Financed Growth Model', *Journal of Contemporary European Research* 5 (4): 614–625.
Grabbe, H. (2004) 'The Constellations of Europe: How Enlargement will Transform the EU'. London: Centre for European Reform. Available at: http://www.cer.org.uk/publications/archive/report/2004/constellations-europe-how-enlargement-will-transform-eu (accessed 17 September 2013).
Komiljovics, M. (2012) 'Impact of Migrating Young Workers'. European Working Conditions Observatory, 17 December. Brussels: Eurofound.
Král, D. (2013) 'Against all, with Britain Forever, or Just Wait and See? The Czech

Debate on the Eurozone Debt Crisis', Prague: Institute for European Policy Prague Working Paper.
Lane, D. and M. Myant (2006) *Varieties of Capitalism in Post-Communist Countries*. Basingstoke: Palgrave Macmillan.
Mikulova, K. (2013) 'Central Europe's Pivot to Germany: What does the U.S. Stand to Gain', *Huffington Post*, 1 May. Available at: http://www.huffingtonpost.com/kristina-mikulova/central-europes-pivot-to-_b_3194342.html (accessed 18 September 2013).
Myant, M. and J. Drahokoupil (2011) *Transition Economies: Political Economy in Russia, Eastern Europe and Central Asia*. Hoboken: Wiley and Sons.
Orbán, V. (2013) 'State of the Nation' Speech, 25 February 2013.
Pogátsa, Z. (2009) 'Hungary: From Star Transition Student to Backsliding Member State', *Journal of Contemporary European Research* 5 (4): 597–613.
Schröder, G. (1999) Speech at the European Parliament, Strasbourg, 14 April.
Sikorski, R. (2011) 'Poland and the Future of the European Union'. Speech delivered at the German Society for Foreign Affairs, Berlin, 28 November. Available at: http://www.mfa.gov.pl/resource/33ce6061-ec12–4da1-a14501e2995c6302:JCR (accessed 18 September 2013).
Sikorski, R. (2013) 'Address on the Goals of Polish Foreign Policy in 2013', 20 March 2013. Available at: http://www.msz.gov.pl/resource/b67d71b2–1537–4637–91d4–531b0e71c023:JCR (accessed 18 September 2013).
Sobczak, P. (2013) 'Polish PM takes Gamble by Endorsing Euro Referendum', *REUTERS* 26 March. Available at: http://www.reuters.com/article/2013/03/26/us-poland-euro-referendum-idUSBRE92P0WS20130326 (accessed 18 September 2013).
Statistisches Bundesamt (2012) 'Statistisches Jahrbuch 2012: Außenhandel'. Available at: https://www.destatis.de/DE/Publikationen/StatistischesJahrbuch/GesamtwirtschaftundUmwelt/Aussenhandel.pdf?__blob=publicationFile (accessed 17 September 2013).
Statistisches Bundesamt (2013) 'Außenhandel – Rangfolge der Handelspartner im Außenhandel der Bundesrepublik Deutschland'. Available at: https://www.destatis.de/DE/ZahlenFakten/GesamtwirtschaftUmwelt/Aussenhandel/Handelspartner/Tabellen/RangfolgeHandelspartner.pdf?__blob=publicationFile (accessed 18 September 2013).

8. The new Varieties of Capitalism and the future of the European social model

In this book I have made an attempt to offer a snapshot of the emerging changes in the economic and social fabric of the European Union (EU) at a point when the effects of the most severe crisis in its history have started to become visible. It is now almost forgotten that, before the crisis emerged, the EU concentrated to a large extent on the promotion of a common reformed European social model with the aim of positioning the Single Market distinctively in the global economy. This discussion has since been pushed to the sidelines by frantic attempts to resolve the eurozone sovereign debt crisis. The central question which the now 28 governments in the EU need to address in the near future is if the crisis has made it impossible to present the Single Market externally as more than just a sum of its parts.

Since the onset of the financial crisis the EU Commission has increasingly talked about the need to preserve the social models which exist in the member states (European Commission 2010). In contrast, the first half of the past decade since the introduction of the Lisbon Strategy in 2000, was dominated by discussions on how to unify EU member states around a common social model based on best practices in individual member states. As I outlined in Chapter 2, due to the good performance of the liberal economies in the UK and Ireland, the discussion centred predominantly on a social model which promotes the activation of people's individual potential and flexibility. 'Flexicurity', which became the core of the concept of the 'knowledge economy', a concept the Barroso Commission actively promoted, originally had its roots in the Nordic economies of Sweden, Denmark and Finland but also the Netherlands. In these countries, the activation of people through targeted labour market policies, the flexibilisation of employment models and inclusive welfare state strategies (including investment in education, training and childcare provision) has been successful in maintaining high employments and overall economic competitiveness. The application of the knowledge economy concept in the EU context yet remained limited and has turned out be predominantly a technocratic exercise of monitoring national performance against the overall EU level targets. The two versions of the Lisbon Strategy in 2000 and 2005 mentioned social cohesion as an important factor of the 'knowledge economy' the EU was supposed to create. In practice they yet failed to put forward concrete proposals on how national governments can ensure that the flexibilisation of economies, labour markets and welfare states across the EU can be combined with socially inclusive outcomes. As Antony Giddens put it: 'They lack a systematic discussion of how the innovations they propose can be reconciled with social justice' (Giddens 2006: 22). Since 2005 the Barroso Commission essentially narrowed the discussion on the European social model down to the priorities of creating growth and employment in the European economies. The principle was that 'meeting Europe's growth and jobs challenge is the key to unlocking the resources needed to meet our wider economic, social and environmental ambitions' (European Commission 2005: 7). Lisbon hence never adequately addressed the preservation of what used to be perceived as the core elements of a social model which differentiates Europe from the rest of the globe. These can be summed up as follows:

- Ensuring the role of the state as a provider of *public space* in the form of universal and non-profit public services and by sheltering citizens from unfettered market competition (Marquand 2004: 27).
- Accepting a role for the state as a mediator and supervisor of economic activity and industrial relations in order to guarantee economic and social citizenship for the individual citizen in the form of guaranteed participatory rights and welfare standards (Hutton 2002: 63; Teague 1999:12).

Both Lisbon and the new Europe 2020 Strategy fail to convincingly answer how the core of the traditional European social model can be maintained in the era of globalisation and under conditions of global and regional economic as well as fiscal instability. Europe 2020 fails to move beyond the core problem of Lisbon where national governments were overburdened with a set of policy targets. This amounted to 'an impression of "over-structure", with target-setting on a multitude of particular aspects of knowledge and innovation which are by and large outside the control of policy-makers' (Soete 2006: 209). The contradiction between the emphasis of the EU's post-crisis coordinative policy framework on fiscal prudence and the new set of overtly ambitious policy targets in the area of employment, education and training, research and development, and environmental sustainability hence remains unresolved.

The result is a persistent gap between the levels of social inclusion across EU member states and a noticeable better performance in those econo-

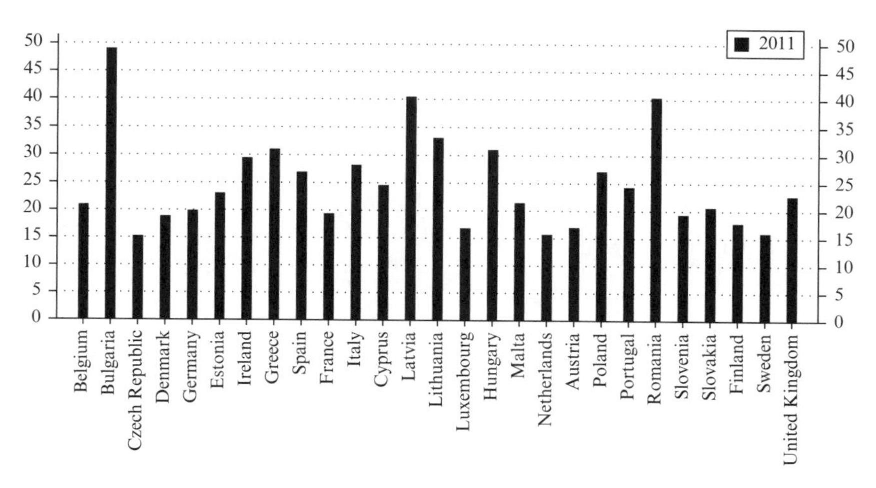

Source: Eurostat (2013a).

Figure 8.1 People at risk of poverty and social exclusion (percentage of total population)

mies with higher level of state activity. Especially the Nordic countries Denmark, Finland and Sweden but also the Netherlands have very low levels of poverty and social exclusion risk (Figure 8.1).

The Nordic countries in the EU have over a long period of time had persistently good performance rates in respect of all the Lisbon and the current Europe 2020 Strategy targets. They are the leading performers when it comes to educational attainment, research and development, social inclusion and also show no emerging budgetary crisis symptoms in spite of persistently high levels of public spending. The combined factors of economic openness, high-tech export growth, labour market activation policies, investment in education, training, research as well as development, and ultimately also universal welfare provision have been widely praised as the benefits of the Nordic model. The Nordic countries Sweden, Finland and Norway are ranked high in the World Economic Forum's latest global competitiveness index. Finland is in third place just behind Switzerland and Singapore, Sweden in sixth place just behind Germany, Norway in tenth position behind the UK and Denmark is ranked fifteenth (World Economic Forum 2013). This shows that it is possible to combine economic competitiveness with socially cohesive outcomes in a cultural setting which gives room to the state as an active facilitator of economic activity. The particular Nordic path of development has created economic models with high levels of social inclusion without enforcing collectivism or limiting

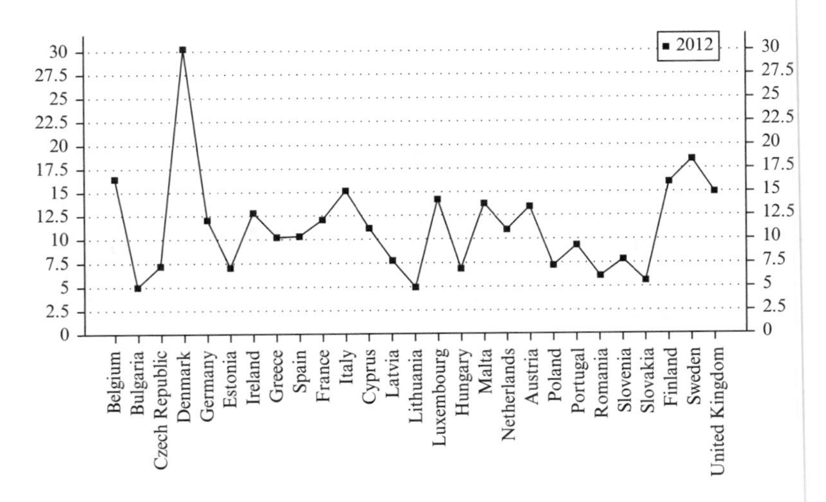

Source: Eurostat (2013b).

Figure 8.2 Current tax levels in the EU-27 (percentage of GDP)

individual self-responsibility and activism. Studies of the Nordic model, which has been widely characterised as 'Social Democratic', have emphasised that they are based on a culture where state intervention is considered as supportive of economic development. The Nordic economies hence show a high level of trust in state activity, which stands in stark contrast to the widespread scepticism of state efficiency in other parts of Europe, especially in liberal market economies. Berggren and Trägård emphasise that in Scandinavian societies the state is perceived as a 'community of law' which supports rather than hinders individual freedom:

> The central axis around which the Nordic social contract is formed is the alliance between state and individual, what we call 'statist individualism'. Hence an emphasis on individual autonomy coincides with a positive view of the state as an ally of not only weaker and more vulnerable citizens, but the citizenry at large (Berggren and Trägård 2011: 19–20).

This positive perception of the state is linked to an acceptance of the need to pay comparatively high levels of taxation and social insurance. Tax levels in Sweden, Finland and most of all in Denmark, are noticeably higher than in the rest of the EU, where it has become increasingly difficult for political parties to advocate a tax-and-spend agenda (Figure 8.2).

The Swedish example shows that, even during times of profound economic crisis, a universal welfare state culture can be more effective in stimulating economic activity and supporting recovery through providing targeted support than a minimum safety-net approach which eventually results in an increase of insecurity for the individual citizen and detrimental effects such as increasing poverty and social exclusion. The Swedish principle of supporting a lifelong learning strategy on the basis of maintaining free and universal education combined with an investment in active labour market policies, research and development to support a high-tech export industry (Kokko 2010: 22) has kept the economy and society in a good overall shape. The high levels of childcare provision and investment in public sector employment have turned out to be important factors in maintaining labour market inclusion and preventing lasting unemployment during the times of crisis. Sweden has repeatedly adjusted its welfare state without altering its fundamental principles. This occurred first during the banking crisis of the early 1990s and subsequently during the global financial crisis in recent years. Most importantly, and in contrast to the changes towards a greater decentralisation we have seen in coordinated economies such as Germany, Sweden has maintained the principle of autonomous and consensual collective bargaining in its industrial relations (Anxo 2012: 28).

The high level of trust between the social partners in the Swedish model and other Nordic economies, which allows greater autonomy from state supervision and regulation in this area, is a particular cultural feature which is closely linked to the consensual dynamics between state and individual activity. The Irish example shows nonetheless that without the existence of a deeply rooted cultural embedment of such dynamics in the society of a country it is difficult to replicate the same outcomes in other countries. This is equally the case for the cultural acceptance of high levels of public spending on the basis of substantial taxation and social insurance contributions.

It would therefore be illusionary to assume that the Nordic Social Democratic model could be replicated in economies across Europe with the same egalitarian outcomes and the same level of economic dynamism as we can find in the Scandinavian countries. The EU should nevertheless consider the principles of the Nordic social model as viable and aspirational for a reformed post-crisis social model for the whole of the EU Single Market. The Europe 2020 Strategy highlights the need for the Single Market to achieve sustainable growth, which is both smart by boosting education, training and innovation levels and ultimately also improves the levels of social cohesion. It is more than doubtful that national governments in the now 28 member states will be able to pursue this without a comprehensive strategy which goes beyond the current emphasis on fiscal austerity and the resulting rationalisation of public spending.

The financial crisis has burdened the economies of the Single European market with a new range of challenges and has been a major setback for many of them in terms of their efforts to maintain a path of solid economic and social development. The evolvement of a new complex policy framework with a multiplicity of targets and blurred responsibilities between the EU institutional and the national level risks reducing the purpose of the Single Market to that of a regulatory monitoring regime with the purpose of achieving national fiscal and macroeconomic solidity. The new wave of functionalist 'spillover' towards deeper political integration will further limit the scope of national policy-makers to determine individual responses to the particular challenges of their domestic variety of capitalism. Most distinctively this will be the case inside the eurozone, where member states are already subjected to a binding system of close fiscal supervision. The lessons from the financial crisis show that those countries who took an active role in investing public funds to counter the effects of the crisis (such as Germany who subsidised part-time work and Sweden who invested in labour-supply measures) recovered quicker than those who focused predominantly on fiscal austerity. Particularly for the countries in the eurozone who have lost control over their interest rates it will therefore be crucial to maintain a degree of fiscal autonomy to be able to 'actively address their specific national situations and promote Euro-area cohesion' (Leschke et al. 2012: 261).

Promoting a one-size-fits-all social model in a Europe with distinctively different Varieties of Capitalism (VoC) is an impossible task. Even the determination of common goals for the EU-28 Single Market which go beyond pure liberalisation measures has been a cumbersome task at the best of times. Under severe crisis conditions it has become nearly impossible. Yet the Single Market as the cornerstone of the European integration project has little prospect of survival without a vision which can fill the European demos with enthusiasm, counter the growing Eurosceptic sentiments in many member states and maintain distinctive features for the EU in the race for global economic competitiveness.

An austerity union in the eurozone loosely connected with a Single Market that operates on the basis of a list of technocratic targets would be detrimental to the ambition of the EU to thrive as the most dynamic knowledge economy in the world. The EU needs an inclusive vision to overcome the disillusionment and despair which has gripped not just large parts of the population but also the political elite in the wake of the crisis. This purpose of this vision can be developed on the basis of the Europe 2020 targets but it needs to be done by adopting best practice from member states beyond fiscal austerity. The Scandinavian model can help the EU to find its way forward and to foster a post-crisis European social model which combines 'social and environmental responsibility, flexibility and technology promotion' (Aiginger and Guger 2006: 148) with sound but flexible fiscal policies, which have to include the ability for national governments to raise revenues and increase spending to counter adverse social effects. This of course demands a drastic culture change towards greater financial solidarity and a commitment to the development of a European civil society with greater participation and transparency. The challenge is therefore enormous and it will be up to the 28 countries of the EU to extract the best from their increasingly diverse varieties of economic and social development. The future beyond the crisis is likely to be determined by the ability of the EU-28 to find a new balance between the need to streamline political coordination, achieve transnational solidarity and to preserve a viable degree of autonomy in determining the priorities of domestic policy-making.

REFERENCES

Aiginger, K. and A. Guger (2006) 'The European Socioeconomic Model', in A. Giddens, P. Diamond and R. Liddle (eds) *Global Europe, Social Europe*. Cambridge: Polity Press, pp. 124–150.

Anxo, D. (2012) 'From One Crisis to Another: the Swedish Model in Turbulent Times Revisited', in S. Lehndorff (ed.) *A Triumph of Failed Ideas: European Models of Capitalism in the Crisis*. Brussels: European Trade Union Institute, pp. 27–40.

Berggren, H. and L. Trägård (2011) 'Social Trust and Radical Individualism: The Paradox at the Heart of Nordic Capitalism', in World Economic Forum Davos, *Shared Norms for the new Reality*. Available at: http://www.globalutmaning.se/wp-content/uploads/2011/01/Davos-The-nordic-way-final.pdf (accessed 19 September 2013).

European Commission (2005) *Working Together for Growth and Jobs: A New Start for the Lisbon Strategy*. Communication to the Spring European Council, COM (2005) 24, 2 February. Brussels: EU.

European Commission (2010) *Europe 2020: A Strategy for Smart, Sustainable and Inclusive Growth*. COM (2010) 2020, 3 March. Brussels: EU.

Eurostat (2013a) 'People at Risk of Poverty or Social Exclusion'. Available at: http://epp.eurostat.ec.europa.eu/tgm/table.do?tab=table&init=1&language=en&pcode=t2020_50&plugin=1 (accessed 10 September 2013).

Eurostat (2013b) 'Current Taxes on Income, Wealth, etc. (% of GDP)'. Available at: http://epp.eurostat.ec.europa.eu/tgm/printTable.do?tab=table&plugin=1&language=en&pcode=tec00018&printPreview=true#.

Giddens, A. (2006) 'A Social Model for Europe?', in A. Giddens, P. Diamond and R. Liddle (eds) *Global Europe, Social Europe*. Cambridge: Polity Press, pp. 14–37.

Hutton, W. (2002) *The World We're In*. London: Little/Brown (Time Warner Books).

Kokko, A. (2010) 'The Swedish Model', *UNU-Wider World Institute for Development and Economics Research Paper* 2010/88. Available at: http://www.wider.unu.edu/publications/working-papers/2010/en_GB/wp2010–88/_files/84053644136415348/default/wp2010–88.pdf (accessed 19 September 2013).

Leschke, J., S. Theodoropoulou and A. Watt (2012) 'How do Economic Governance Reforms and Austerity Measures Affect Inclusive Growth as Formulated in the Europe 2020 Strategy?', in S. Lehndorff (ed.) *A Triumph of Failed Ideas: European Models of Capitalism in the Crisis*. Brussels: European Trade Union Institute, pp. 243–282.

Marquand, D. (2004) *Decline of the Public*. Cambridge: Polity Press.

Soete, L. (2006) 'A Knowledge Economy Paradigm and its Consequences', in A. Giddens, P. Diamond and R. Liddle (eds) *Global Europe, Social Europe*. Cambridge: Polity Press, pp. 193–214.

Teague, P. (1999) *Economic Citizenship in the European Union: Employment Relations in Europe*. London: Routledge.

World Economic Forum (2013) 'The Global Competitiveness Index 2013–2014 Rankings'. Available at: http://www3.weforum.org/docs/GCR2013–14/GCR_Rankings_2013–14.pdf (accessed 19 September 2013).

Index